VOICES FROM CROKE PARK

THE STORIES OF 12 GAA HEROES

Edited by **Seán Potts**

MAINSTREAM PUBLISHING

EDINBURGH AND LONDON

First published in Great Britain in 2010 by
MAINSTREAM PUBLISHING COMPANY
(EDINBURGH) LTD
7 Albany Street
Edinburgh EH1 3UG

ISBN 9781845966287

A catalogue record for this book is available
from the British Library

Typeset in Caslon and Granjon

Printed in Great Britain by
Clays Ltd, St Ives plc

Acknowledgements

Sincere thanks to all the players and writers for their generous contributions to this book, the proceeds of which will go to the GPA's Past Players Benevolent Fund. Thanks to Ray McManus and Sportsfile for supplying the photographic content and to Inpho for providing the cover picture. Thanks to the GAA for their continuing support of the Player Development Programmes, including the Benevolent Fund. The GPA thanks Opel Ireland and MD Dave Sheeran for their continued support of players. Thanks to Bill Campbell and Mainstream for supporting the project so generously. Thanks also to the production staff at Mainstream. Finally, sincere thanks to GPA Sponsorship and Marketing manager Siobhan Earley and GPA chairman Dónal Óg Cusack.

Contents

Introduction

'Any man's finest hour, his greatest fulfilment to all
he holds dear is that moment when he has worked
his heart out in a good cause and lies exhausted on
the field of battle victorious . . . Leave no regrets on
the field.'

Vincent Lombardi

Few sportsmen who have been privileged to compete at the top
level over the past 30 years have escaped the now hackneyed
words of Vince Lombardi. During my own playing days, now
unfortunately a rapidly fading memory, I was always struck by
the idea of not leaving any regrets on the field.

It is one of the great driving forces of the competitor; the will
to give all to the cause. But this unstinting desire is not without
consequence. Great athletes – our footballers and hurlers – may
aim never to leave any regrets on the field but they frequently
leave many off it.

Since the Gaelic Players Association was first formed in 1999,
we have learned a lot more about the experiences of our players
after they've retired and those same experiences have opened
our eyes to the often heavy price paid for their commitment to
their sport.

Naturally enough, players are slow to complain, most are
honoured to have made the sacrifices they did for their counties
and would do the exact same if given the choice a second time
around. But often, when you get a chance to tease out the after-

effects of an inter-county career with a player in private, you find that they wish some things could have been done differently.

Many former players have to undergo medical procedures directly resulting from poor preparation or treatment during their playing days. Others have fallen on hard times, and some cite their inability to cope, initially at least, with retirement. The lucky ones can cherish the memories and still manage 18 holes without limping back to the clubhouse.

Specifics might differ but there is no denying that the traditional idea that the 'jersey' wasn't yours, you were only passing through, was prevalent and remained effectively unchallenged until the emergence of the GPA. And that attitude, that players should be seen and not heard, is directly related to many of the problems experienced by players after the show is over, when the all-consuming excitement of taking to the field on championship Sunday has evaporated.

I've been accused in the past of trying to play up negatives, portraying our involvement in the game as a chore, but nothing could be further from the truth. I loved every second of my inter-county playing days and would give anything – including the two knees I completely banjaxed – to be still playing. I continue to laugh to myself about the brilliant times I shared with my team-mates, club and county. On the all-too-rare occasions when I meet up with former players, it isn't long before we are reminded about what an incredible experience it was to play for your county.

But while celebrating the contribution, we must not ignore reality. An inter-county career is not a pastime: it's a vocation, a wonderful vocation. It's not about giving time, it's about giving everything. We played to compete, to test ourselves, to gamble on the highs and lows of life on the edge. And too often in the past our amateur status was, at best, taken for granted and, at worst, abused. For all who prospered in the wake of their careers, there are many who fell through the cracks.

A lack of respect sometimes sullies the past players' experience; how many players can hold their hands up to say they got a good send-off from their County Board after retiring? One of the greatest players I ever knew spent nearly two decades in his county jersey and wasn't even afforded a phone call after finishing up.

Thankfully, the GAA has made huge strides in the area of player welfare in recent times and following the agreement reached with the GPA they are now supporting the implementation of one of the finest player development programmes anywhere in the world. And on behalf of the GPA, I would like to thank GAA Ard Stiúrthóir Paraic Duffy and president Christy Cooney for the commitment they have shown to players and to their welfare.

We have always argued that our players, the role models for the greatest amateur sports organisation in the world, central figures in the commercial success and continued prosperity of the GAA, are deserving of nothing less. Since the commercialisation of our games in the early 1990s, that argument has sharpened considerably with every passing year, with every extra televised game, with every new sponsorship deal, with every extra contribution made by our footballers and hurlers. That momentum brought players together in 1999 and now, 11 years later, we are putting in place a support structure we can be proud of.

The GPA fought and won a lengthy battle to have players recognised by the State through a programme of Government Funding. Politicians are quick to acknowledge the contribution of footballers and hurlers to the social and cultural fabric of the country, and indeed the economy. They never miss an opportunity to sit behind the presentation of a Cup, basking in the unique glow that surrounds the warriors who grace our arenas every summer. Government Funding gives practical expression to that acknowledgement and were the Government ever to withdraw it, the State would be discriminating against some of its greatest assets.

One of the most important components in the GPA's new welfare programme is support for the past player. Those in need, whatever their circumstances, can now lift the phone and engage with the GPA. On our Past Players Advisory Group we have put together a collection of some of the games' finest exponents to oversee and shape our policy in this area. They will ensure that that support is relevant and forthcoming.

This has always been an ambition of the GPA; that a player would not walk away from the game alone, that a formal network of support would always be there if and when they need it.

And supporting the past player is what *Voices from Croke Park* is all about. With the backing of Mainstream Publishing and MD Bill Campbell, royalties from this work will go to our Past Players Benevolent Fund. As well as supporting this important Fund, which helps former players who run into difficulties in their lives, we felt such a publication would provide us with a great opportunity to also highlight the existence of the Fund and indeed the GPA's commitment to the past player.

Voices from Croke Park is a celebration of the players' contribution to Gaelic games. It is a collection of the differing yet equally interesting perspectives of men who soldiered in the heat of battle. It is about the vicissitudes of life in a county jersey.

We decided that we'd ask 12 former players and 12 GAA writers to contribute to the project and without hesitation, those contacted, both players and writers, agreed to participate, happy to take the time from their busy schedules to support the Benevolent Fund.

I am indebted to all who contributed but also to Kerry football legend John Egan for his support in difficult circumstances. I wish John and his family the very best.

And I am sincerely grateful to Bill and Mainstream who provided this wonderful opportunity for the GPA. Also thanks to Ray McManus and Sportsfile for the player pictures, and Inpho for the use of the cover photograph.

I hope you enjoy this collection and perhaps we'll get the chance to chronicle the lives of more of the heroes of our games in the near future.

Dessie Farrell
Chief Executive Officer, Gaelic Players Association

Mikey Sheehy

Tom Humphries, *Irish Times*

> We summer boys in this four-winded spinning,
> Green of the seaweeds' iron,
> Hold up the noisy sea and drop her birds,
> Pick the world's ball of wave and froth
>
> *'I See the Boys of Summer'*, Dylan Thomas.

Mikey Sheehy, a man of autumn now, is content in this season of his life. He lives and works still in Tralee, the town where he grew up and grew famous. A townie and a homebird, he says. His summer, his prime, was such a succession of golden days that he could walk these streets with the gait of a giant if he chose to. He doesn't.

Eight All-Ireland senior medals plus an All-Ireland club medal and the memory of his tousled genius would buy him a fawning retinue of easy admirers if that was what he needed. His is one head among five in a Mount Rushmore of the game, the five Kerrymen with eight All-Ireland medals each. He is a Kerryman though and knows that modesty in a man is as vital a trait as being able to kick points. No Mount Rushmore thanks.

Football still courses through his days though. The club, the games, the faces, the memories. In a short walk of a morning he could run into Darragh Ó Sé, Seánie Walsh, Bomber Liston, Ogie Moran, any number of other men who left giant footprints in the history of the game. They'll talk football and pull each other's chains.

History? Posterity? 'Sure we had horse's fun,' says Mikey, 'horse's fun.'

Most mornings he takes a break for coffee in the company of Darragh Ó Sé who works a couple of doors up. Always the pair is joined by a small crew of expert conversationalists, men with a professorial understanding of the game of football, characters who throw their knowledge into the ring in a quiet and understated way. In Kerry there is always somebody who knows more.

This morning Marc Ó Sé has wandered in and John L. McElligott is at the table too and the lads are talking about a Champions League game from the night before. A penalty kick which almost tore a hole in that top corner of the net where the postage stamp should go.

'You have to pick your spot with them,' says Mikey admiringly, nodding his head. Mikey has always had a grá for the soccer.

There is a pause. McElligot's rapier is first out of the scabbard.

'Which spot did you pick in '82, Mikey? Martin Furlong's knee was it?'

Mikey laughs longest, surprised at himself for having given his old friend the opening. A penalty kick from a game 28 years ago! Who said something about Mount Rushmore? They'd have had him as the goat at the puck fair.

'It's a toss of a coin which people bring up more. Maybe the goal in 1978 and the only reason is that people are being nice to me as a poor old devil. Behind my back I'd say they are still talking about 1982!'

Ah. 1982 Kerry, under the lintel of history, passing through to become the game's first five-in-a-row team. The T-shirts were printed. The homecoming planned. They huffed and they puffed.

They were a point up, 12 to 11, when John Egan got dragged down, not once but twice on the edge of the Offaly square. Penalty. Fifteen minutes left. Mikey put the ball down and faced into the Canal End goal.

'Mikey Sheehy,' said Micheal O'Hehir presciently on the television commentary, 'the anxiety. The importance of this kick. Five in a row they are going for.'

From the Canal End somebody threw an orange onto the pitch. A further slight delay. Mikey standing there in the rain facing Martin Furlong in the dank grey stadium.

'I didn't kick it well. It went to his right. Not hard enough or low enough. I knew when he saved it, we were gone. We were still a point up I think but I knew it was going to end in tears.'

He was right. Kerry had lost their talent for finishing out games. They led by two points with as many minutes left. But, but, but.

For the longest time it hurt.

'When I finished playing football I was asked about memories, what do you recall most, that sort of thing. For me it was the 1982 defeat and the penalty miss. It's still the first thing that would hit my mind. Not the good days.

'It took me years to get over it. Lying in bed at night, running it through my head always. It still comes back but not in the same way. But some of the great Kerry victories, they are a blur. I can't tell you what we did after or where we went. But 1982, every moment of the week after that penalty is almost frozen in my head. What I did. What I didn't do. To this day I would find myself sitting and running through the penalty in my head.'

He laughs about it now though just as he laughs often with his great friend Paddy Cullen about the goal in the 1978 final against Dublin, Mikey chipping Paddy as the great goalie abandoned his debate with the referee and scampered back toward his goal. If Paddy could laugh at that, Mikey could come to enjoy 1982 in a way.

'In 1982 all the penalty-taking volunteers were in the dressing-room after the game. By two weeks later in the pubs they were all screaming to take it! I have a laugh about it now.'

Funny thing too. The game. The people. Perspective always comes to you, dripping slow.

'When Offaly had the twenty-fifth anniversary thing and they were out in the field in Croker they had dinner in the Old Bridge House in Tullamore later that night. They invited a few of us up. We had such a night above with them. When you look back you mellow, you accept it and you look at a county like Offaly, the size of it and what they have achieved in hurling and football. You couldn't have been beaten by a nicer bunch. We didn't win a five in a row but they took away something very special to Offaly. The way they treated us that night. So nice. Gentlemen. That's what sport is all about. It was all bigger than me missing a penalty. We were part of somebody else's history.'

Maybe it was meant to be.

Everybody has a memory like Mikey Sheehy's memory of his first big game visit to Croke Park. Few of us have such a startling context to put it all into later.

Mikey Sheehy, for whom playing in All-Irelands would become an annual event, recalls going to Croke Park when he was eight years old. It was 1962. Kerry and Dublin in the All-Ireland semi-final. His granddad, his mother's father, brought him along.

'My dad had gone off to it of course. Grandfather brought me. I remember some of the game. Dublin were on top in the first half. Mick O'Dwyer came on as a sub I think.

'Kerry took over in the second half and Kerry won. I was in the Hogan stand. I remember Mick O'Connell pointed a line ball from right in front of me. He was a genius. The presence he had, the way he carried himself. He had the collar up always, Eric Cantona must have copied it from him.

'I think John Timmons was playing for Dublin. I went to the All-Ireland final then. Kerry beat Roscommon. That was the start of it. Train journeys. We'd go up on a Saturday, stay with an aunt. My sisters used to work in Dublin later on. We'd bunk in everywhere. Throw yourself down where you could.'

History. Kerry football reeks of it and is made of it and wraps itself around it. Mick O'Connell, collar up, pointing a free directly in front of the eight-year-old eyes of a man who will equal and then surpass him. That is the essence of Kerry.

When you shake hands with Mikey Sheehy in his office in Tralee the trademark broad grin and firm grip connect you not just to one of the greatest players the game has known but to a lineage that is as glorious as anything you could make up in your head.

Stack's. The club's glory stretched back to the real birth of modern football in the epic tussles between Kerry and Kildare in the '20s and the lives of men like Joe Barrett and Jackie Ryan who won six All-Ireland medals each.

More chapters followed. Mike Doyle who had three All-Ireland medals before his 21st birthday was yet another name you conjured with. Pluggy Moriarty, Pedlar Sweeney, Gal Slattery, Bill Gorman, Rory O'Connell and Jimmy Bailey. Later the Landers brothers, Dan Ryan, Mick Healy.

The list could go on and on. Men who sprang from the tight little arteries around Rock Street to carry Kerry teams to glory and lay down the culture of Kerry football.

And after the deluge of success? Thirty years in the wilderness. Three decades of famine. They never rested though. Hard times couldn't hang around forever.

Sheehy was born and reared in St Brendan's Park, the heart of Stack's territory. The only boy among six girls (I have my purgatory done, he likes to joke) and a dad, Jim, who was a fanatic for the game. Theirs was a corner house. He could open the back door and make a field of dreams for himself. The door was the goals. He'd hop and scuff his football off the gable end. Sometimes night would fall and his mother would find him on the street, under the glow of the street lights playing soccer, pretending to be Georgie Best.

Purty Landers was a neighbour. What fuel George Best supplied to one side of the imagination the legend of Landers provided equally for the other.

Jim Sheehy never spoke about playing himself. He was from Killorglin and he had played a bit in the blue of Laune Rangers.

He had an older brother, Michael, who was handy and played for Laune too. Michael died a young man and Jim named his only son for him.

When he first came to Tralee, Jim lived in the territory of John Mitchel's, whose storied team of the '60s had won five County Championships on the trot. The Sheehys had moved to Brendan's Park by the time Mikey arrived but he was raised on tales of the Mitchel's and still has a soft spot for them.

'My dad was a lunatic for the game of football. From the time I could walk I had a football with me and I went to matches with him. That's where the love of it came from.'

He took traditional pathways, primary school in Tralee, CBS in Clounalour and then on to the Green. There was always football, always the sense of being bred for bigger things.

'I remember playing football in primary school. There was huge interest in the school. There was even hurling played. The teachers would run leagues after school. There would be a final and there would be a school band and we'd march out behind it like after the Artane Boys band.'

There was a man, Micheal Hayes, who was the link between school and club, one of those unsung servants whose work is the quiet foundation of great success.

'He was before his time,' says Mikey. 'I can remember with the Stack's when you got to 12 or 14 he would bring us on trips. Up to Dublin and other places. I think it was Good Counsel we would go to. I remember those trips, the Dublin fellas laughing at the country boys up in the city! That was part of it.'

They were lucky. There was Hayes. There was Jimmy Hobbart who had been the Irish international basketball coach and who understood space and passing and movement in a unique way and there was the late Joe Mulchinock. All devoted in their ministrations to the juvenile section of the club. And one more.

'My dad! Matches, matches, matches. I think a lot of coaching is taking the flair out of guys today. Back then as kids we played in the streets. You weren't restricted. You could do what you like.

Outside of the Primary Leagues there wasn't competitive football till you were Under-14 but you played your Street Leagues within the club.'

He tells a story. He was 15 years old and putting down his time as he often did at the pitch of the Park Soccer club in Tralee. He would later turn down offers to go to Celtic, Southampton and other spots but soccer was always a love.

Things were bad with the Stack's seniors and that day they were playing some tournament or other out in CastleIsland. A car from the Stack's pulled into near the soccer pitch to round up a few fellas to make up the numbers. Mikey was one of them.

'I know that my father came down looking for me later and there was no sign of me. It had gone late. I came in home eventually and he said, "Where were you?"

'"I was in CastleIsland."

'"And what were you doing in CastleIsland?"

'"I was playing with the Stack's Seniors."

'Well, there was murder. He was heartbroken he had missed it.'

Mikey is still too modest a man to admit it but by then he must have had a sense of his own talent. He remembers evenings when he was playing with the bigger guys in the street, usually soccer. He'd be hovering quietly around the back of the goal three or four years younger than everybody. Finally they'd ask him to fill in for somebody who'd been hauled in for the night.

'You mightn't get a kick for an hour but then you'd get a ball and do something right. They'd ask you quicker the next time.'

He developed in the Green also. He remembers one day playing Coláiste Chríost Rí up in Kilmallock. Chríost Rí were the glamour team of the time. The Tralee lads warmed up eyeing the lovely jerseys and togs and matching socks being sported down the other end of the field. Themselves, they were lucky to have put together a set of randomly shaded jerseys. Everyone had their own colour togs and socks.

'I was young enough. Playing in the corner and overawed. At

one stage I got a chance and banged it into the back of the net and I remember the good feeling of it. You never felt you were good enough but you were always hoping you were. Looking for little signs.'

And the signs were good and plentiful. There was a celebrated rivalry at the time between the Sem in Killarney and the Green in Tralee. Sheehy recalls with a grimace all these years later that the Green never came away successful, never beat them at any grade. They lost two Munster finals in a row, beaten by a point or two on both occasions. Two outstanding young fellas called Páidí Ó Sé and Pat Spillane were playing with the Sem. They were as good then as they were later on. Sheehy was just starting to blossom.

In Stack's, James Hobbart had put together a great Under-16 team. They played all the divisional teams and won the County Championship. They were beaten two years later in the minor championship but the sense of an upsurge was there.

Still it has never been in Mikey Sheehy's nature to take himself too seriously. He put in two years in the Kerry minor jersey without notable reward, and he says himself with a loud laugh that when he got in for his senior debut in 1973 and when he played Under-21 a year later he was a stone and a half to two stone overweight and going nowhere in particular. He enjoyed life, dabbling in soccer and football. He had enough talent to get by. Nobody ever pushed him for more.

His first time to wear the Kerry senior jersey was in 1973, a League game in Killarney. He was playing more soccer than football at the time although it had been a breakthrough year with Stack's. Cork had just won the All-Ireland and Mikey Sheehy plump and rounded was told to come over to Killarney.

He went on at half-time with instructions to take the frees as the regular free-taker, one M. O'Dwyer, was misfiring.

'I got a couple of points. I had no time to get nervy. We subs went out kicking at half-time when the team went in. Dinny Long who would be a great friend and a Stack's man was with

Cork that day. Anyway, I went over to dugout when the teams came back out. Andy Molyneaux, the secretary, came up to me and says, "You're in corner-forward." There was no time to get excited or nervous. The first free we got was on the 21-yard line in front of the posts. I was looking for the ball when Dwyer said, "I'll take this," put it down and tapped it over. I shrugged to the line. They shrugged back! That was Dwyer.'

Dwyer! The rogue genius would be Kerry manager within a short space of time. Dwyer knew what he wanted from Sheehy and he had the psychological equipment to get it out of him.

Traditionally in the crucifying session in Fitzgerald Stadium there was a form of apartheid between Dwyer's greyhounds and the others whom he christened the 'fatties'.

The fatties got more work and more nights in. Sheehy was always among their number but he trained under Dwyer with the same fanaticism as his comrades: long sessions on his own out on Banna Beach running the dunes.

Once, in 1981, he was in a bad car accident but walked away and headed to Kerry training a few hours later. To have missed a session was unthinkable.

His finishing and his athleticism became legendary but his time spent with James Hobbart paid off richly too. Few modern forwards have understood the possibilities of space and evasion as completely as Sheehy. When a knot of Kerrymen would move towards a ball Sheehy would be on another tangent altogether, knowing by sixth sense where the pigskin would squeeze itself free.

Stack's won a County Championship in 1973, the first of four which Sheehy would share in, but Kerry were at a low ebb. The boy who had watched Mick O' Connell kick a perfect free in Croke Park in 1962 was, in 1974, on the field playing in a Munster final when he watched the same O' Connell come on as a second half sub. He could do nothing to turn the tide against Cork.

* * *

'We were stuck. Stagnant. Training was a doddle. Two laps. Few jogs. It suited me.'

Against Meath in the quarter-final of the League that year Sheehy missed two penalties. Kerry were sinking. He isn't quite sure what happened; whether there was a bloodless coup or something more orderly, but suddenly the landscape had changed for Kerry footballers.

'The Man took over! What a man. What a change in training. The famous 28 days in a row. Dwyer came in and he knew we were in shit shape. I never trained to that level ever. He never drank. He was anti-drink. You did it his way or no way. In 1975 it was a roller coaster. Cork was the first big battle. Sligo in the semi-final. All-Ireland final and Dublin were the favourites. Ye know the rest.'

Sheehy was a lazy devil. Dwyer, a master of the carrot and stick, was nonplussed . . .

'Get out to Banna and knock a bit off your fat old arse,' he'd tell Sheehy. And he would.

Typically, after a Munster final, Dwyer would call his boys in, clearing all the hangers-on out of the dressing-room. He'd be delighted, being fresh from delivering one of his famous 'lads ye're the second best team in the country' speeches to a dejected Cork dressing-room. Eyes gleaming he'd say, 'Look we have two more games,' and he would take his boys in, 'but look, on Tuesday night I want to see the fatties.'

A big cheer from the ranks of the lithe and skinny.

'Some years it was like a concentration camp. There were about eight of us. For one week he gave the super athletes the week off. We trained five nights without them. Monday, Tuesday, Wednesday, Thursday, Friday. He killed us. When you were fit he'd be telling you, "Jesus you're in great shape." I've never seen anything like him for cajoling fellas and getting them going.'

The great cajoler's masterwork was to lead them to eight All-Irelands, their hunger, their desire to please him being as strong in the end as it was at the beginning.

Through all eight, Sheehy was constantly fending off the injuries he was prone to and putting his signature to some moments that the game will never forget.

Curling the ball over Michael Creedon's head in the Cork goal in a replayed Munster final? It would be a celebrated moment were it not for 1978 which overshadowed everything for a while.

You know the scene like a familiar tune.

Dublin cruising. Paddy Cullen comes out. Passes to Robbie Kelleher. Ref blows the whistle, evening something up from a few minutes earlier. Kelleher, being a gentleman, hands Mikey Sheehy the ball. Cullen out from goal to have a debate with the referee.

Sheehy just put the ball down and kicked it. Well he curled it into the top corner of the net as Paddy Cullen came flailing after it like a man after an elusive butterfly. Instant folklore.

'It was a rush of blood. It was very funny. In the dressing-room at half-time, Dwyer only looked at me, never said anything about it. I didn't even look at the ref. It was probably totally illegal. He had his back to me. He didn't know what I did with the ball. He didn't know what had happened. I often say to Paddy I genuinely get fed up of talking about the goal.'

Typical of the modesty of the man is that he will never decline to talk about Martin Furlong's penalty save. He won his eight All-Ireland medals, among the greatest players on the greatest team the game has seen. And when they were won he soldiered on for as long as he could.

The end came suddenly. And hard.

He stopped playing championship football in 1987 when his cruciate betrayed him. He finished with his beloved Stack's a year later as the knee refused him forgiveness for all the punishment it had taken through the years.

It's more than two decades since he ran out of a dressing-room for the last time but the void is still there.

'I still miss it. And at 56 years of age I should get sense. I miss the buzz though. I miss the lads I played with. I miss the comradeship, the challenges. I see people ask other fellas do they miss it and I hear them saying yerra no. I know deep down they do. I know on the day of a Cork–Kerry game all of us are out there, middle-aged men and every one of us would give anything to turn back the clock, to be young and involved.'

He can recall in an instant where everybody sat in the dressing-rooms in Killarney, the agony of the wire-to-wire sprints which would finish training, the superstitions and piseogs of the lads.

Small things which make up a footballer's life.

'I was involved in coaching afterwards but it could never replace playing. Once you cross the white line that is the thing you want to do. Play. I'd be mad jealous of the present-day guys to be still out there. It takes a long, long time to adjust.'

Stopping is like a little death. The boy you were grew as you had hoped, into a footballer. The game lifted you up, defined you, obsessed you, filled your life. And then there is a full stop. No more. And the great game goes on without you. You finish and tomorrow you are an ex-footballer. People are still nice. They still reminisce and draw down the names of Creedon or Cullen or Furlong for you to do some colouring on but you are yesterday's man with yesterday's stories.

'You stop and you have so much time on your hands. I was lost. I was used to going to Killarney all my adult life, out to Banna to do my own private runs. I was always looking ahead to the next match. It ended and I had to look around for some outlet to replace it all. I would still have a fierce interest in going to matches. The fanaticism is only starting to wear off me now! That's what the game left me with.'

Oddly he can see a time in his life, a bit down the road perhaps, but he can see it when he would stop going to games. His connection to those playing diminishes by the year but when he watches Kerry he still gets butterflies in his stomach as if he were still playing.

'I don't know why. The older I get the worse of a spectator I am.'

The knees are his most persistent souvenir from the golden age. He had fierce problems with his left knee from about 1981 onwards.

'A lot of people would say I was only in the corner. The guys in the trenches had it worse. I blame it from growing up playing a lot of football in the street. It wasn't the hard training. Fellas would say I was dog lazy. And later I'd play a lot of indoor soccer in Tralee. I think that has been the problem. I damaged the cruciate in early 1988, the good knee. So that finished it at that stage.'

Football is too much of a treasure in his heart for him to blame his knees on his work with the fatty crew in Killarney. Or at least not entirely.

'Possibly, we trained too hard. All the counties were doing the same thing. We had five or six PE teachers on the panel but they never stretched us. Dwyer said be on the field for 6.50 p.m. It was up to you to do your stretching. We would have trained very hard for two or three consecutive nights, that probably wasn't great for the body but I'm sure there are other guys who had it worse. Dwyer could have you running anywhere. It was hard but nobody refused it.'

Injuries?

'You'd want a doctor with you or to be in plaster to make it worth mentioning! Even then Dwyer would say, "Yerra tog out and see how it's going."'

A footballer's body. He had his right hip done four years ago and his left one needs to be done. The knees complain of course. More than their owner does.

'It's a small sacrifice, a tiny price. There is nothing serious really. You can replace hips and knees. There's a lot more trouble you could be having in your life at my age. I'm playing golf and I'm able to walk.'

And of course in the beginning there was the club and in the end there is the club.

'Stack's have been a huge part in my life. Of the eight All-

Irelands there's none I would prize more than the All-Ireland club we won together in 1977 or even winning the County Championship in 1973. Playing with guys you grew up with. There is nothing like that. Club finals hadn't the high profile they have now but it was unbelievable for us in the town.

'Were it not for the Stack's I would never have progressed. I'd still go to all the games. I coached a lot of teams with Dinny Long. Great days. There comes a time where you enjoy going to the games and you love just not being involved, just watching. I'm enjoying sitting back being a critic!'

And he grins. The circle is complete. The game will hardly ever see a record such as Mikey Sheehy's come to pass again. Yet the matches are blurry for him now. What abides are the club and the friendships.

He talks of nights out with old adversaries, getting to know men he once warred with. He recalls movingly the evening when Tim Kennelly went to the church in Listowel, the first of the gangs to die. A cold winter night and an inestimably sad one. During the service, there was a rustle from the back of the church and their greatest rivals, the Dubs walked in. Big middle-aged men in dark coats. Respect. Honour. Friendship. He weighs those things more often than he thinks about medals.

Or 1982.

Do you know of Fred Snodgrass?

He played in three consecutive World Series with the New York Giants. In the middle one in 1912, in the tenth inning of the deciding game, he dropped a routine fly ball. He went on to make a wonderful game saving catch on the next play but the Giants lost.

He had a good life afterwards. A few more years in baseball, president of a successful bank and the mayor of Oxnard in Ventura County, California.

He died on 5 April 1974 and his obituary in the *New York Times* was headlined: 'Fred Snodgrass, 86, Dead; Ball Player Muffed 1912 Fly'.

Mikey Sheehy

Mikey Sheehy, a legend and a national treasure knows in his heart that a penalty kick all those years ago will follow him around to the end of his days. And he's not spooked by it.

And though he would never admit it he knows that there is so much more said and thought about him. That kick? We will celebrate it and tease him with it because it was such a human moment in such an extraordinary life. And people will talk to him about it because of his grace and humour and perspective.

He met with triumph and disaster and he treated both imposters the same. In autumn. A man.

Tony Keady

Vincent Hogan, *Irish Independent*

Suddenly it is night in Oranmore and maybe four hours have slipped away, loose as water over a weir. We've talked the light from the day, but there is one last place to visit.

Tony Keady takes me across the yard to his workshop. This is where he loses himself to the whine of the band saw and shriek of the planer, cutting hurleys, shaping their personalities. Maybe two dozen lie already finished, curved and perfect, beside a nail-gun. On a wall, facing the door, hangs an ice-hockey stick.

He has always been drawn to the possibilities of wood because he understands that lovely, tactile thing of holding a pet hurley.

Making them is just a hobby now, an outlet for his hands. He is tickled by how they've changed, telling a little story to capture the distance travelled. What felt like Keady's first big day in hurling brought him the prize of a bicycle. It was an Under-14 tournament final in Salthill, Killimordaly against Mullagh.

The *Connacht Tribune* put up bikes for every member of the winning team and had them lined up along the Pearse Stadium sideline, glinting almost sinfully in the sun. For a 14 year old in 1976, a bicycle was a prize worth fighting for.

He remembers Killimordaly being awarded a 65 near the end, and one of the club's great, old mentors – Bill Joe Creavin – stomping onto the field with instructions. Creavin smoked a pipe and it stayed welded to his mouth as he caught Keady by the shoulders and shook the young free-taker to attention.

'I'll give you ten shillings if you put it between the posts,' said old Bill Joe, the smoke stinging like astringent in Keady's eyes.

'That day, I had a hurl with the handle cut straight across the top,' Tony remembers. 'And I had a stone on the top of the handle, taped on for a grip. Back then, they had none of the technology they have now for making lovely handles.

'You just taped something on the top to give you a grip. Anyway, I put the 65 over and we went on to win the bikes. But I never saw the ten bob from Bill Joe!'

The formal presentation never materialised either. At the final whistle, the Killimordaly team just sprinted towards the stand to claim their booty, cycling then from Pearse Stadium to the Banba Hotel for an after-match 'banquet' of sandwiches and cocktail sausages.

'It was the biggest prize ever put up for kids at the time,' says Keady, smiling fondly. 'To us, it was like nearly getting a car.'

You may not know him, but his name will register somewhere in the attic of the mind.

In 1989, the 'Keady Affair' convulsed hurling. It ran for weeks and was embroidered with so many layers of intrigue that, for a time, it was easy to believe he must have been guilty of a heinous crime. But Keady's sin was one of simple omission. He played hurling in New York without the appropriate clearance.

The details are for later, but suffice to say the story ran off the sports pages and into primetime news. Radio phone-ins and television talkshows fussed over it, as if national security was imperiled. When Galway manager, Cyril Farrell, hinted at withdrawing his team in protest from the All-Ireland semi-final against Tipperary, the old *Irish Press* upgraded the subject from the back page to a front-page lead.

'Big Match Revolt Looms' ran the headline over Martin Breheny's story on 27 July, ten days before semi-final day.

Tony Keady

It is Keady's misfortune that the extraordinary events of that autumn will maybe forever thieve a little light from the issue of his greatness as a hurler. For he was centre-back on, arguably, the finest half-back line of modern times and a man who won everything there was to win in '88, short of the Booker prize for literature.

His status in Galway particularly was maybe best captured by Joe Connolly's observation of the night when confirmation came through of his suspension for that '89 semi-final. Connolly, who was at a parish function, recalls the news hitting the assembled 'like a death'.

Time has created enough distance for Keady to be wistful in his recall of those events now. Yet there remains a latent sense of injustice too – of having been made a convenient scapegoat by the powers-that-be in Croke Park.

Some years ago, TG4 filmed an interview with him for their *Laochra Gael* series and finished by asking if there was a single line he might choose to have carved into his headstone. 'They should have let me play in '89!' responded Keady, almost involuntarily.

Sometimes, when he recalls the hurt of that time, he can't help wonder what it might have done to his father.

For even the tiniest nuance of his love for hurling was formed, in some way, by his relationship with James Keady. James died on 20 August 1985 after a virtual lifetime battling emphysema and they buried him three weeks before that year's All-Ireland final between Offaly and Galway.

That game would be just Tony's second senior Championship game in a Galway shirt. Small blessing, at least, that his father lived to see the first.

'Looking back, I never saw any sport only hurling,' he recalls now of a childhood in Attymon. Keady went to the local National School, where his closest friends would – in time – all become loyal team-mates with Killimordaly. Their evenings were enlivened by five- or six-a-side hurling matches that bubbled with natural intensity.

'There was a crowd that lived two-and-a-half miles down the road from us,' remembers Keady. 'The "Burkes in Ballyboggan" they used call themselves. We'd have a match with them every evening after school. We had two fields. The one where the bus would pick us up, we called "O'Brien's Field".

'There was a hand pump on the side of the road and we'd jump in over the pump. The minute we got off the bus, the bags would be just fired on the side of the road and in we'd go. We'd have two sticks stuck in the field and a bit of baling twine going across.

'And the hurling was hell for leather. We'd have Eamonn Burke, Eanna Ryan, Gerard Hardy, my own brother, Bernard. Loads of lads, well able to hurl. Those of us who went on to hurl for the county were always told by those who didn't, "Ye'd have made nothing if it wasn't for us!"'

James Keady was a constant, if fading, presence as his youngest son's talent became conspicuous around Galway.

Tony's form at underage with Killimordaly would earn him a wing-back spot on the county Under-16s, his career having 'really stepped up a notch' in secondary school with the Vocational in Athenry. He would win an All-Ireland Under-21 with Galway in '83 against a star-studded Tipperary team that included Nicky English in its line-up, whilst Galway – managed by Michael Bond – had future stars like Pete Finnerty, Ollie Kilkenny, Michael Coleman and 'Hopper' McGrath on board.

Keady remembers his great friend and club-mate, Eanna Ryan, coming off the bench to swing that final in Tullamore.

Every day seemed to dawn cornflower blue back then, except for that single black cloud of his father's failing health.

'I brought my father to every match,' he recalls. 'But all the years I was hurling, he was sick. When he hadn't the strength, I used to pick him up in my arms and lift him into the front seat of my car and drive to all the games. Fair play to Phelim Murphy, he knew the set-up. Any time there was a match in Athenry or Loughrea, Phelim would let me drive the car straight in.

'And my father would watch the match from the car. I used

always say to him, "I'll park right behind the goals, it's the safest place. Nothing will hit you there!"

'In the end, he was only five and a half stone when he died. He'd been sick for 17 years and was hardly able to walk. I was the last one living at home and, if I was going out anywhere, I'd always ring my mother to give her a number where she could reach me.

'My father smoked a good bit. If you pulled back the covers of the bed, you'd see Silk Cut boxes all over the place. I never took a pull of a cigarette in my life and, when he would want one lit above in the bed, I'd light a newspaper in the range and bring it up to him. Many's the time I nearly set him on fire.

'I used always to curse a calm day because I reckoned he needed wind to give him a bit of breath. By the end, he was on nebulisers every day. If I couldn't bring him to a match, I'd have to sit down with him afterwards and give him a full report. Inch by inch. Down nearly to how many were at the game.

'You'd have to give him the full rigmarole. Everything. Because he adored hurling. You might be coming in late at night and take off the shoes at the back door. His bedroom was near the kitchen and he always left the door open. The minute you tried to tip-toe past, you'd hear his voice. "What time is it?"

'He'd be wide awake, dying to hear the whole story of everything. I remember finding it hard going to matches in the end, wondering how he was at home.'

James Keady had strong allies in the desire to see his son excel at hurling. Along with Creavin, men like Tommy Hardy and Frank Burke seemed to live with an evangelist's passion for the game and, specifically, Killimordaly.

'Bill Joe, Tommy and Frank were three great men in the club,' Tony recalls. 'Whatever they had to do to better the club, they'd do it.'

One of their great days would come too late for James Keady though – Killimordaly's County Championship win in '86, defeating Turloughmore in Ballinasloe. 'We had a mighty,

mighty team,' says Tony, 'but, for a number of years, we just couldn't seem to get over the line.

'Back then, you could genuinely pick out eight to ten teams that could go on to win the County Cup in Galway. There was nothing between any of them. We were probably good enough to win two or three, but – to be honest – we were very, very satisfied to win the one. It was an absolute dream come true.

'Winning a club is something awfully special. The club is what made a man of you.'

Matches in Dublin were, largely, beyond the family's range as his father's emphysema worsened and they did not travel to the 1980 All-Ireland final to see Galway crowned hurling kingpins for the first time since 1923. Keady recalls watching the game at home, his hand clamped around a hurley for the duration.

And he remembers his mother, Maureen, sitting utterly engrossed, sporadically reminding her son how 'Some day this could be you.'

They drove in to the homecoming that Monday night and the sheer glamour of it all was intoxicating to a 16 year old. 'Being honest, it was hard to take it all in,' he remembers. 'The crowds, the Garda escort, the army. Everyone out to see the team.

'And you're wondering if you might ever be a part of something like that. 'Twas a serious feeling. All the talk back then was of the Connollys, particularly John. He was lovely to watch, his striking was always crisp and wristy, he had serious vision.

'I saw clips of him recently and it just brought home to me how I'd love to sit down some day and watch a video of him play a full match again. The funny thing is I play a lot of racquet ball and golf with him today. He keeps himself in such shape, he looks like he could still hurl this minute.

'I'd be very friendly with other lads from that team too. The likes of Sylvie [Linnane], Sean Silke, Iggy Clarke, Steve Mahon and Michael Connolly.

'But, back then, you'd have been looking on them as nearly living on another planet.'

That team was, of course, managed by Cyril Farrell. In his book, *The Right to Win*, Farrell recalls seeing Keady play a challenge for Galway's Under-21s against the county seniors in '84 and marking him down as 'one for the future'. He wrote of the player having 'good balance, was comfortable left or right and looked very, very confident'.

By the summer of '85, Keady had moved from the periphery of Farrell's thinking to a place of pivotal significance.

He would make his senior Championship debut at centre-back in that year's All-Ireland semi-final against Cork, a game weighted down with such an air of public presumption that only 8,200 spectators bothered to turn up in Croke Park. Cork were the reigning All-Ireland champions and had just retained their Munster title with relative ease. Nobody imagined Galway might be equipped to lay a trap.

The game was played in an ugly downpour, a gusting wind whipping sheets of rain into the stand, forcing the small crowd to take refuge high up in the back seats. It gave Croke Park an empty, almost echoey feel. A treacherous ambience for complacent champions.

Keady's role that day was to mark Cork's seemingly indestructible centre-forward, Tim Crowley. He remembers shaking hands beforehand and thinking momentarily, 'I'm going to get eaten and spat out here!'

Within seconds of the throw-in, Crowley scored a point, Keady having lost his footing. Already, Galway's novice centre-back was inclined to look towards the dugout. The second ball that came their way got wedged under a divot and the two of them just pulled frantically, like workmen scything at a ditch. Nothing moved but spray.

Yet Keady and Galway would settle and three second-half goals in quick succession from Brendan Lynskey, Joe Cooney and Noel Lane pitched Cork into a ten-point deficit and unexpected crisis. Typically, they rallied near the end. But it was too little too late.

Back then, Keady had just begun working in Dublin with the Bank of Ireland, and his immediate boss, Frank Kenny, was first to reach him at the final whistle. Kenny, a Glenamaddy man 'steeped in hurling', was dressed in suit, shirt and tie, an ensemble promptly destroyed as the two of them fell to the ground in a muddy embrace.

Galway's entire half-back line, Finnerty, Keady and Tony Kilkenny, would take a joint Man-of-the-Match award that evening.

'We weren't rated that high at all going in,' Keady recalls. 'They were the champions. We felt no pressure. If we won, we won. But we weren't going to lie down in the grass and go crying if we lost it. We had very level-headed fellas in that team. Great characters.

'I remember before the game, fellas were saying, "Who do they [Cork] think they are? Why should they think they're better than us?"'

By now, sadly, James Keady's life hung by a thread and, for his youngest son, that was freighted with a good deal more importance than hurling. Even the thought of playing in an All-Ireland final seemed insignificant now. Everything Tony did on a hurling field had been predicated on the knowledge of what it meant to his father.

He remembers scoring a goal in a televised All-Ireland minor semi-final against Wexford some years earlier and Athenry's Jackie O'Shea, who was over the team, running out to him, pipe in mouth, catching him by the collar and shouting 'I can see the chair coming through the television at home . . .'

So, in August of '85, his father's imminent death obscured the excitement of reaching an All-Ireland final against Offaly.

Tony explains, 'I knew he wasn't going to live too long. Every day he was still alive was a bonus. It had been going on for so long, you just didn't know when the day would dawn. So, every match I played, I could feel it as a burden on my shoulders. Wondering.

'He eventually passed away on 20 August and, to begin with, there was just no way I could get my head around hurling in the final. I had no interest in it. A lot of the players called to the house, encouraging me to go on training.

'Everyone was trying to say the right thing. You're listening to them but, deep inside, you're hurting so bad. But he was mad for hurling and I knew he'd want me to play. My mother kept saying it.

'So I went along. In the end, I even trained the evening of the funeral. I knew he was looking down over me. The problem was, when we lost that final, I was probably more upset for him than anyone.'

One year later, Cork would take revenge for their semi-final defeat, beating Galway to win the Liam McCarthy. For Keady, the defeat delivered him to an emotional crossroads. One of his brothers, Noel, ran a successful construction business in Boston and he was strongly tempted to fly over and report for work.

'I was still thinking of my father at that stage,' Tony remembers. 'A year seemed an awful long time to wait for another go at this. I was saying to myself, "I'm winning nothing at this hurling . . ." There was good money to be made in America and I was toying with the idea of going over to Noel.

'All I had won at this stage was a *Connacht Tribune* bicycle, a vocational and an All-Ireland Under-21. Who remembers them? It was nothing. You're wondering have you the time to put in another year and, maybe, get no result at the end of it again? Noel had a serious set-up over there. I was very tempted.'

He didn't go in the end, but America hadn't finished playing on his mind.

Galway's All-Ireland victories of '87 and '88 would take their colour, ultimately, from the county's relationship with Tipperary.

And, for a time, that colour was nuclear grey. The intensity of the rivalry obscured pretty much anything else happening in hurling.

From '78 to '86, Tipp won four All-Ireland Under-21 titles and Galway three. Only Cork in '82 and Kilkenny in '84 interjected to remind us that the game was being nurtured elsewhere too.

Tipp's senior breakthrough in '87, after 16 years without a Munster title, quickly propelled them deep into the national consciousness. They were easy on the eye, with the likes of English working his wristy magic in attack. And, in 'Babs' Keating, they had a charismatic manager who played the media like a master puppeteer.

No question, they became the story of that summer. Their two games with Cork were epic confrontations, the replay won only after extra time on a baking July Sunday in Killarney.

Yet Galway had won the National League with something to spare and now managed to persuade both Pete Finnerty and Gerry McInerney to return from America, where they'd been working since the previous autumn. With much talk of a 'traditional' Tipp–Kilkenny All-Ireland final on the cards (the Cats having won in Leinster), Farrell had an abundance of motivational material for his troops.

That semi-final of '87 set the template for a rivalry that consumed hurling for the remainder of the decade. Actually, Galway would play Tipp in four big games over the next two years, winning the first three. The fourth, however, would go to Tipp, a prize wrapped up in the infamy of the 'Keady affair'.

That '87 semi-final was, maybe, the purest of them as a hurling contest. The sides were level with nine minutes remaining, but Galway rallied to finish the stronger, recording a six-point win.

They then beat Kilkenny in a rain-soaked final, Noel Lane's late goal deciding a low-scoring game and sparing Farrell's men the ignominy of losing three finals in a row. This was a game the manager himself would later describe as 'very much the last chance' for a team that desperately needed to validate its class with the Liam McCarthy Cup.

It was a declining Kilkenny team they beat, Antrim having given them significant problems in the semi-final. But the Cats were stoked to high intensity by the memory of a quarter-final loss to Galway in '86, made famous by Farrell's innovative use of a two-man full forward line.

So winning a final of real ferocity separated Galway from any lingering self-doubt. 'It changed everything,' according to Keady. 'If we'd lost a third final in a row, definitely, it would have been curtains for me. I'd have been gone, absolutely. But, when we won, I remember thinking, "Jesus, we're still young enough. We could win this thing again."'

Farrell's cute man-management had been the glue that kept them together. He had a lovely, casual way of transmitting information. At meals after training, he was never to be seen sitting down to a plate of food himself. Yet, endlessly, he'd arrive at a player's shoulder, picking something off the plate whilst – all the time – monitoring individual mindsets.

'Farrell was a great man like that,' says Keady. 'He kept everyone together. And, once we won in '87, I think that job became easier. We knew, being champions, we couldn't walk away from the thing now.'

Now working in the Big Smoke, Keady needed to get back to Dublin after the homecoming, so drove his car down, pressed tight behind the team bus. Entering Ballinasloe, the cavalcade came to a standstill and people clambered onto the bonnet of a following Opel Kadett to catch glimpses of their heroes.

And there, staring as their heels sunk into the paintwork of his car, sat Galway's bemused centre-back.

He had won an All-Star for the position in '86 but was now edged out for a second award by Ger Henderson. No matter, in '88 Tony Keady would announce himself as a virtual force of nature. And Galway would frank their greatness.

Tipp won the League and successfully defended their Munster crown, yet everything about the season felt like a suspension of time before they could lock horns again with Galway. This time, upsets permitting, it would happen in the All-Ireland final.

'Tipp had a phenomenal team now,' Keady recalls. 'You

think back to that time and people wonder where were Cork or Kilkenny or Clare or Offaly? The answer is nowhere. Galway and Tipp were just dominating.'

The '88 final would be Tipp's first since '71, yet if ever a game announced the soaring maturity of Galway, it was this one. Again a late Lane goal would be crucial, Galway edging home 1–15 to 0–14 after a real white-knuckle ride of a final. Farrell described Keady's second-half display afterwards as 'as good as anything seen for years in Croke Park.'

Essentially, Galway's half-back line won the game and Keady – as its anchor – took every garland going.

He remembers, late in the game, English enquiring of the referee how much time was left and Sylvie Linnane helpfully interjecting 'One minute and a year Nicky!' Linnane had a tenacity that others drew from. With Finnerty in front of him, the right side of Galway's defence was never inviting territory for the faint-hearted.

The essence of that Galway team was an almost perfect balance of skill and manliness.

Keady chuckles at the mere mention of Linnane. 'Sylvie used have a great oul saying in the dressing-room,' he smiles. 'He'd say, "Lads, ye'll win nothing if ye haven't a few tinkers in the team." And we'd say, "Well, we're delighted to have you anyway Sylvie!"'

Galway's victory in '88 meant that, within 12 months, they had gone from the precipice of possible implosion to now embarking on a three-in-a-row mission.

Keady was named Man-of-the-Match for that final, yet never got to the post-match function to collect it. At the time, he shared a house on Phibsboro Road with Lynskey. The two had a reputation for enjoying Dublin's social scene and, if anything, they actively encouraged that reputation.

Yet Farrell trusted them implicitly. He could see from their conditioning at training that, whatever the rumours, Lynskey and Keady were not inclined to abuse his trust.

Keady recalls pounding the pavements of Drumcondra in their

socks as well as hour upon hour spent in the Phoenix Park, literally lashing sliotars at one another. 'Myself and Lynskey probably did more training than any Galway man that ever wore the jersey,' he suggests.

'Farrell knew we always did our training in Dublin.'

Immediately after that final in '88, the two of them repaired to their local, the Hut on Phibsboro Road. The owner, Bob McGowan, had promised a champagne reception if they beat Tipperary and now proved true to his word. The entire staff dressed for the occasion in maroon and white.

And, soon, evening was giving way to night, the clientele looking forward excitedly to *The Sunday Game*. At one point, Lynskey's brother stepped in to say that Farrell had phoned the house looking for them. Not only did he want the two to head straight to the Burlington Hotel, he wanted them to do so wearing the team shirt and tie.

They never did.

Keady remembers 'Next thing the programme is on, Ger Canning with the microphone. It's time to name the Man-of-the-Match. Everyone in the pub is going "ssshhhhhh . . ." And Canning says, "It's the moment we've all been waiting for. The All-Ireland final Man-of-the-Match is . . . Tony Keady."

'Everyone in the pub goes ballistic, hugging each other. There's fellas hugging me who haven't a clue who I am. And the camera starts panning the hall in the Burlington, me about seven miles away. Eventually, Ger says, "We'll have to ask Cyril Farrell to come up and accept it on Tony's behalf."

'Up goes Farrell and Canning asks him if he has any explanation as to where I might be? And Cyril says, "All I can say, Ger, is, he's such a dedicated player, he's probably out training for next year!"'

For Keady, the second homecoming would be cut short like the first. Having been coaxed from the back of the bus to address a crowd gathered in Loughrea, he then took a few steps to the back of the trailer.

'The tail of my shirt was sticking out and there was a load of my clubmates from Killimordaly at the back of the lorry,' he recalls, laughing. 'One of them, Noel Earls – a great friend of mine – jumped up and caught the back of the shirt. And didn't I fall back off the lorry, straight into their arms.

'They brought me up to Mike Carey's pub and I think I was in it for three days!'

America had never left his thoughts and, when the All-Stars went to New York the following May, Keady warmed instantly to the city.

The Championship structure of the time meant that Galway's National League victory (they beat Tipp in a thrilling final) essentially left them with three months to kill. If people were now energised at home by three-in-a-row talk, Keady's mind was resolutely in neutral.

As the All-Stars tour came to a close, he decided to stay on.

'I remember saying to myself, "What am I going home for now?"' he remembers. 'Another year of slogging for this three-in-a-row they were all talking about? To be honest, I decided I was finishing up.

'That was it. The brother was doing well in Boston, so I decided I was staying. I had a good bit won in the hurling and was happy enough. Farrell didn't travel on the trip, but I think he had an idea of what I was thinking.

'He told the lads to make sure my bags were on the bus. That way, he felt I'd have to come home. I thought Farrell knew me, but he didn't. I let off all the luggage home. After about three days, I rang Lynskey. Asked him would he hop out to the airport where there was a bag still going around on the carousel.'

Aware of Keady's intentions, Farrell would have felt that – at least – he had time to broker a solution. It was decided to leave him to enjoy the American sunshine for a while. They were confident he'd be home.

Rather than link up with his brother in Boston, Keady began working construction in New York for a Loughrea man, Martin Bruton. He adored the lifestyle, the weather, the fun, the easy informality of playing 13-a-side hurling with the local 'Laois' club.

These were training games and, as such, free of any implications for home. But Championship was soon looming and 'Laois' had expressed a desire to have Keady and two other Galway county players, Michael Helebert and Aidan Staunton, in their line-up against Tipperary.

The New York Championship had long been bulked up by the presence of visiting county players into something it should never have been. This was a source of constant irritation to Croke Park, particularly as New York was not even officially affiliated to the Association.

Calls suddenly started coming from home for Keady and, at the time, he had a rather unorthodox telephone arrangement.

'I basically had a plug socket and a phone,' he remembers. 'There was a girl in the apartment next door and we had it arranged that the wire of my phone was plugged into the back of hers. So, if anyone called, the phone rang in both apartments.

'If it was for her, I'd leave it down. And vice versa.'

The name 'Laois' was an accepted misnomer for the club now courting Keady. It was a side, predominantly, made up of Galway players and one sponsored by a native of Abbeyknockmoy, Monty Moloney.

As the phone calls raged, Keady sought assurances from Moloney that playing in their looming Championship game against 'Tipperary' would not have repercussions in Ireland. Those assurances were given persuasively.

Yet, tellingly, it was decided that Keady, Helebert and Staunton should line out under assumed names. Hence the 'Laois' centre-back was listed on the day as Bernard Keady.

He takes up the story: 'There were phone calls coming left and right. My brother, Noel, is even supposed to have come down from Boston to tell me not to play. He didn't. He rang me and just said, "Look, if you want to hurl, hurl."

'Anyway, I went down to the pitch with my gear. I'll never forget it. I was standing in a corner, only 30 or 40 yards from the dressing-rooms. The next thing, one of the doors opened and out came a blue and gold jersey. Sure 'twas like a red rag to a bull.

'I think I had my boots, togs and helmet on before I even got to the dressing-room door. That's what the sight of the Tipp jersey did to me.

'I was out on the pitch when they started calling out the teams. A ball had gone over to the wire and I went over to get it. Just on the stroke of me rising the ball, the announcer calls out "Bernard Keady". And a Tipperary fella near me says, "Tony, when did you change your name?"

'I just looked at him and replied, "You must have been out last night. You're seeing double!"'

'Laois' won the game so handily, Keady's presence suddenly looked an unnecessary conceit. 'Tipperary' immediately launched an objection and a meeting of the New York executive upheld it, docking 'Laois' the points and imposing two-game suspensions on Keady, Helebert and Staunton.

Worse, it was announced at home that the GAA's Games' Administration Committee now planned to investigate. If the players were found to have violated 'Rule 41', which governed the conditions for playing in New York, Keady faced a possible one-year suspension. And that's precisely what the GAC concluded.

Suddenly, Galway's three-in-a-row bid had hit transatlantic turbulence.

Tony recalls, 'Farrell rang me and told me it was important that I got home. The hearing [Galway appealed to the Management Committee] was coming up and he felt, if I was seen to make the effort of a personal appearance, I'd probably get off. I thought long and hard about it. Would I come home or not?

'At the end of the day, I just thought I owed it to the boys. I had a lot of good friends in that Galway squad. We'd lost two and won two All-Irelands. There were few enough teams had won three-in-a-row. Farrell's view was I'd definitely get off if I came home. He was ringing me nearly every ten minutes to make sure.

'So I decided that I would.'

Keady, thus, stood before Management in Croke Park, with Frank Burke and Joe McDonagh eloquently presenting his appeal. The experience proved utterly demoralising. He recognised the chairman of the committee, Sean Ramsbottom of Laois, but knew none of the other adjudicators.

It seemed to him their minds were already closed.

'I just felt the people judging me that night knew nothing about hurling,' he recalls. 'That's what killed me. There was no talking to these five or six people. Frank and Joe spoke brilliantly, absolutely bamboozled them with what they said.

'And I remember these fellas, sitting behind their desks, just staring into space. It was like they were saying, "When are ye going to finish, because we have our verdict made?" To me, their minds were already made up. They wanted a scapegoat. They felt they had to stop this thing of lads playing illegally in New York.

'They were going to put an end to it and they'd caught me, a high-profile player. I didn't speak at all. Just sat there. I felt all they wanted was for Joe and Frank to shut up. It's like they were brainwashed.

'Next thing, they just said, "Our verdict is that the suspension stands!" I stood up so fast that I knocked my chair over with the back of my knees. I was so annoyed with them.

'I just walked out of the room, Joe McDonagh trying to get a hold of me. "Hold on a minute, Tony, we might talk more . . ." I knew by the look of them we could talk for hours and hours and it would get us nowhere.

'Lynskey was waiting outside. I remember walking down the

stairs in Croke Park, thinking, "Why in God's name did I come home? To be suspended by five or six fellas that knew nothing about the game? Who weren't even from hurling counties?" It was absolutely heartbreaking.

'All the photographers thought we were going to come out the front door, but we slipped out the back. Luckily enough, no one said anything to me. Because you just don't know on the spur of the moment how you might react.'

The severity of the suspension appalled many, not least Galway's looming semi-final opponents, Tipperary. They sought to distance themselves from the actions of the club bearing their name in New York and would, when the opportunity arose, vote for the lifting of Keady's ban.

That opportunity came at an emergency Central Council meeting called for the Tuesday night of All-Ireland semi-final week.

This meeting was proposed by the Management Committee and interpreted as a panicked response to Farrell's threat to pull his team out of the game. Incredibly, while Tipp would vote for Keady's re-instatement through their county secretary, Tommy Barrett, it was subsequently revealed that four Connacht Central Council delegates voted against.

And, ultimately, the appeal was lost 18–20, Keady – essentially – let down by his own province.

He had trained away with the Galway team right up to that Central Council verdict, but now removed himself from the semi-final preparations. 'I kept thinking the thing would be lifted,' he recalls now. 'To be honest, up to that night, I was centre-back against Tipp.

'But now I just had to step away and let the lads get on with it. Now I was nobody. I was nothing. I was shell-shocked.'

Sean Treacy inherited the number six jersey and Keady is quick to stress that his replacement would put in a storming performance against Tipperary. Yet too much that had gone before now settled over the game like a toxic cloud. It proved mean-spirited and fractious.

Linnane got the line after an incident with English that the Tipp star subsequently admitted in his autobiography, *Beyond the Tunnel*, did not merit a sending-off. And, before the end, 'Hopper' McGrath was sent off too.

When the final whistle blew, Tipp were the victors, 1–17 to 2–11, but even Keating, the winning manager, would brand the game 'a disaster'.

There was particular fury in Galway at the performance of Wexford referee, John Denton. Farrell was subsequently suspended for 'lack of discipline', but maintains to this day that – had the normally exemplary McGrath not been harshly sidelined with ten minutes remaining – Galway would have won.

He wrote in his autobiography, 'The sending off of "Hopper" McGrath compounded our frustration. With McGrath gone, we felt that we had to beat Tipperary, the Games Administration Committee, the Central Council and the referee.'

Keady watched the game from the dugout, battling to contain his own vexation.

He recalls, 'There was a little grid over a drain in the bottom of the dugout. I had my fingers wrapped around the grid. When "Hopper" got the line, a Tipp player came over in front of us and started cheering. "Hopper" was just passing him and lashed out.

'I was absolutely boiling with anger. I walked across the pitch afterwards, fellas shouting at me. I felt like lashing out and I don't think people would have blamed me if I did. But I never lifted a finger to anyone. Just held it together.

'Whether 'twas going back to my father again, I don't know.'

Tony Keady never did go back to America.

His friendship with Lynskey eventually developed into a business partnership and, together, they would open a pub in Galway city. He hurled on with the county for four more years, but it never quite had the same dynamic after Farrell's departure.

The All-Ireland final defeat in a high-scoring contest against Cork in '90 had done little to alleviate the frustration that still lingered from the year before.

So Farrell stepped down after a heavy semi-final defeat to Tipperary in '91. He sensed an appetite for change in the county and, when Galway's Under-21s won that year's All-Ireland, it seemed logical to promote their management team, led by Jarlath Cloonan.

Keady and Cloonan never became a compatible mix. Compared to Farrell, the new manager seemed a mite inflexible in his ways and the two caromed off one another like a couple trapped in a bad marriage.

In '92, Keady was suspended from the Galway panel for a reputed breach of discipline, though the reason was never actually articulated. A one-sentence letter was left behind the counter of the bar, declaring simply: 'A chara, you have been suspended from the Galway senior hurling panel until further notice.'

The almost mechanical coldness of the language (no mention even of his Christian name) encapsulated what Keady regarded as a complete absence of empathy from the manager.

As it happened, he went to training that evening in Athenry, unaware even of the letter's existence. It was left sitting by the till and Lynskey, now retired, decided to open it.

Keady recalls, 'Lynskey sent a fella, "Spot" Forde, in to Athenry to tell me. We're playing a training match and yer man is on the line, trying to catch my attention. Eventually, Justin Campbell – who I travelled to training with – breaks a hurl, goes over to the line to get a new one and comes back out with a grin on his face.

'"Keady," he says, "I think you're suspended!"

'Going in at half-time, "Spot" hands me the letter and I nearly go baloobas. I walk straight into the shower and [a selector] Sean Kelly came in after me to talk. I asked him to leave because God knows what I would have done if he didn't.

'And I just dressed, walked down to the Shamrock bar in Athenry, ordered myself a pint and waited for Campbell. Like, in all my years hurling, I never abused the manager's trust.

'When we were in Dublin, myself and Lynskey often had a couple of pints in the Hut on a Saturday night. Go down at nine, be home at half ten. In bed, fast asleep by eleven.

'And I did nothing any different with Jarlath Cloonan to what I did with Cyril Farrell.'

In '93, Galway were back in Dublin for the All-Ireland semi-final against Tipperary. Pucking the ball around on St Stephen's Green, Cloonan put a hand on Keady's back and, essentially, told the Killimordaly man that he was surplus to requirements.

'He said to me, "We're shortlisting you today",' recalls Keady. 'Sean Treacy was standing just next to me. I hadn't a clue what he meant. For a second, I actually thought he was making me captain.

'I togged in the dressing-room and put a jacket on me going out on the pitch. Boots, socks, togs, but no jersey. "Shortlisting you!" That's how he put it. I'll never forget the words.

'And that was enough for me. I just thought this was bullshit. That's the way my Galway career ended.'

Discarded at 29.

He still looks taut and trim enough to hurl today.

And the game continues to enchant him. Keady works as caretaker in Calasanctius College, coaching all the college hurling teams. He trains Oranmore with his old Galway colleague, Gerry McInerney, and looks after Abbeyknockmoy intermediates.

Some of the best friends he ever made in hurling were members of that Tipp team with whom they raged for national primacy in the late '80s. Keady thinks especially of a benefit night held in Ballyfa for Eanna Ryan after he had been badly injured in a club game.

It took place on the night of a shocking storm, trees down all over the country. Yet the entire Tipp squad travelled by bus, a couple of chainsaws in the back in case a road needed clearing along the way.

And Bobby Ryan, Tipp's captain of '89, told the assembled that 'nothing' would have stopped them travelling that evening. Keady smiles at the memory, reflecting, 'I suppose, at centre-back, I faced three of the hardest nuts you could ever come across against that Tipp team, Declan Ryan, Donie O'Connell and Joe Hayes.

'I made some great friends with lads off that team, Bobby Ryan particularly. Eanna would have been marked by Bobby a lot. They were wonderful lads. If you go through the team they had, in every position, they were just on a par with us really.'

Today, he is married to Margaret, a Meath woman, and the couple have four children – Shannon (eight), Anthony (five) and the twins, Jake and Harry (three).

His life is full and enriched by thousands of small blessings. Sometimes, lost in the din of the workshop, he encounters moments of indescribable serenity. When the twins were born, it felt like they represented gentle correspondence from the Heavens. James Keady was a twin too.

The circle never breaks.

Peter Canavan

Brendan Crossan, *Irish News*

FINDING PETER THE GREAT

After the roundabout it's a smooth left swing into Ballygawley. Make the short climb to the top end of the village and follow the signposts for Carrickmore and Sixmilecross.

Climbing still, the narrow road bobs and weaves. As quickly as you breezed through the village, you'll find yourself deep in the bosom of mid-Tyrone.

This is Canavan Country. Glencull, Ballygawley, Garvaghey and Dunmoyle – four corners of a proud parish.

Errigal Ciaran's goalposts peek from over the western hills. The last dirt road that leads to the field tumbles from a daunting height and rises again. It's the last connecting capillary to the heartbeat of a community.

The spring nights have stretched sufficiently for mid-week football in the O'Neill County.

You'll find Peter Canavan on the far side of McCrory Park in Dunmoyle with his feet planted on the sidelines.

Tracksuited in Errigal colours, he cuts a pensive figure. Tonight, Aghyaran and Marty Penrose are setting the Errigal Ciaran manager and his team a few early puzzles.

For a brief moment, you're wondering when the Errigal manager will shake off his tracksuit, lace up his boots, wet his gumshield, race onto the field and kick the ball over the bar.

He looks fit enough for the fray. But it won't happen tonight.

Not any night. That boat sailed some time ago.

The man they call 'Peter the Great' retired from inter-county football after Tyrone's second All-Ireland triumph in 2005. He held on for another two years with his club.

Canavan's fighting weight was 11-and-a-half stone. Retirement has generously lent him an extra half stone, but it makes not the slightest difference to his slender frame.

Like most ex-players, Canavan grapples with the next chapter. In many ways, he was destined to retreat into the ether of club life after Tyrone. He might have scaled many mountain peaks in an illustrious inter-county career that yielded six All-Star awards, but he hasn't forgotten his roots.

Don't expect polished anecdotes of halcyon days. Truth be told, he's an average Joe, slightly reticent about talking up his playing days. Canavan was a foot soldier who sacrificed everything for club and county and was richly rewarded by the end of his playing career. Now in his second season in charge of Errigal seniors, he is clearly energised by the challenges of football management.

There is no grand plan in place though. He'll happily chip away with his club and enjoy the journey. Tyrone's footballing icon certainly has no enthusiasm to succeed Mickey Harte as senior county manager.

'As a youngster it was always my dream to play for Tyrone. I couldn't say that it's my dream to manage Tyrone,' he says. 'I see what it takes to manage a club team and it's fierce commitment without the same pressures of being county team manager. I think you'd want to be very much ready and wanting to do it and, at the minute, that's not the case.'

So, what are the defining differences between Canavan the player and Canavan the manager? Does he rant and rave, or is he the calm sideline general?

'I wouldn't see myself as a person who roars and shouts – definitely not. Maybe as a player I did. When players are putting in the amount of hard work they do, I think, they deserve better than somebody roaring and shouting at them.'

He declined several firm offers to manage other top clubs in Ulster. You only have to scrape the surface to understand why. Canavan bleeds Errigal. He bleeds a place called Glencull, too – and remembers how his birthplace became embroiled in the most bitter dispute in Tyrone GAA history.

Canavan sometimes refers to the time between 1981 and 1990 as the 'Lost Years' – but it was during that period he honed his skills alone on a small field in Glencull. Tyrone's most gifted footballer never kicked a ball in minor club football because of a row that broke out between the members of Glencull and St Ciaran's, Ballygawley, as Errigal Ciaran was formerly known.

In 1981, the four rural areas that made up the St Ciaran's, Ballygawley club – Glencull, Ballygawley, Garvaghey and Dunmoyle – took part in a Parish League tournament. The games were designed to help with preparations for the upcoming Tyrone County League.

'Back in the early '80s things weren't right in the club,' Canavan says. 'I suppose there were internal difficulties and the Parish League was the trigger point. Someone decided that before the start of the League, and to help training, we would have a Parish League. Bad idea! In the first game Dunmoyle were playing Glencull. There were a number of incidents in the game, but one of them resulted in two people being sent off – Mickey Harte of Glencull and an opponent from Dunmoyle, Brendan McCann.

'At the time the club wanted to suspend the players and they wanted to suspend Mickey from participating in the start of the League. It was the equivalent of, say, St Gall's having an in-house training match and one of the players getting sent off and the club suspending him for a month. It wouldn't be heard of. The club was suspending their own players over a parish league match! The out-workings of all this was that Glencull said they would go their own way because there were a number of players not getting football.

'The Glencull members weren't happy with the way they were being treated. They had good enough players and numbers to start up their own club. So various meetings were held and it was decided they would form a new club, so they applied to the County Board to be officially recognised. But, out of loyalty to the existing club, the County Board refused the application.'

Despite recommendations from the Ulster Council to recognise Glencull as a fully-fledged member club of the Association, Tyrone officialdom refused their application for nine years. During that time the County Board warned other clubs of playing friendly games against the reluctant rebels of Glencull.

When the row began, Peter Canavan was a budding ten-year-old prospect. During those years he spent endless hours kicking a football at the Holm pitch in Glencull.

'There wasn't much else to do,' he recalls. 'The fact that I wasn't being thrust into competitive situations was giving me the opportunity to practise. The development of my left foot was primarily down to that fact. I would have practised at the Holm kicking points over the bar on my own.

'There was a big grassy bank directly behind the goals, so I had my own Hill 16. If a shot went to one side of the goals in particular the ball could end up in the river. So I would kick the ball from 30 yards and chase after it before it reached the river. Without that, I might not have got the opportunity to develop the skills in the way that I did.

'Looking back, one of the benefits of the dispute was that I wasn't playing the same amount of games as others. Burn-out was never going to be a factor and I had more time to practise. If you look at what's happening now to talented Under-14 or Under-16s, they're out every other night training.

'They don't even get to train with their clubs because they're with development squads, their county teams, and if their schools are successful, they're going to be heavily involved there. I didn't have that at an early age, which meant I had a stronger appetite for the game by the time I was 18, 19 and 20 years of age. And because I didn't play as many games as a lot of other players, it probably left me more competitive.'

Glencull may have been disenfranchised from the competitive arena, but as a youngster, Canavan remembers 'the energy, excitement, and countless meetings over the split and people who were angry'.

'The energy that developed sustained Glencull for those years. There were céilis and Irish language classes in the hut, which was a mobile beside the chapel. So all aspects of the GAA didn't stop just because we weren't registered members of the Association. At the time we felt we had good reason to do what we did. A lot of people who weren't heavily involved in the St Ciaran's club all of a sudden were taking part in Gaelic Games on and off the field – and it gave the area a strong sense of identity. The only football we were getting at senior and underage level for the people of Glencull were challenge matches.

'For nine years, Glencull applied for affiliation and in the meantime played challenge matches in Derry, Fermanagh, Monaghan and other teams in Tyrone. And at one stage the County Board sent out a warning to other clubs not to play us because they would suffer the threat of suspension. I was going into school and my mates were talking about the league games they played in and they would ask what I'd done, and I'd say, "I had a challenge game against Teemore in Fermanagh . . ."

'But the split opened my eyes as to how seriously people took Gaelic Games. I got a greater understanding of how important it was to the local community and what it meant to people.'

With intransigence the order of the day, Canavan at least had schools' football to nurture his talents. At St Ciaran's, Ballygawley High School, the young teenager announced his arrival on a competitive stage under the watchful gaze of schoolteachers and coaches Mickey Harte and Robbie Hassan. An integral member of the school's Under-14 team that won county and provincial honours in 1985, Canavan also picked up a county title at Under-16 level. More podium appearances followed. After winning the All-Ireland Inter-county Vocational Schools title in 1988, he captained the side to back-to-back successes the following year.

Still, the young forward from Glencull wasn't insulated from the sharper edges of the dispute. 'I remember at the presentation night of the 1988 All-Ireland Vocational winners in Omagh, there were begrudging comments made by the then-county chairman referring to Glencull and what was going on. I ended up walking out. My exit created a good laugh among the other boys – but there was no football in Glencull for eight or nine years.

'My own brothers, who were good enough to play for Tyrone, missed out. And for people to belittle what we were doing . . . I felt we were as much Gaels as anybody else. We had a love of Gaelic as much as anybody else and we felt we didn't need to be belittled in any shape or form. I was a member of the Association, and was doing my best for my county and yet these comments were being made. We were the guests of honour that night.

'Of course, there were a lot of members of the County Board who treated us with respect and any time I was with the minors that's the way I would have been treated. There were one or two isolated incidents, though, that made you feel you weren't part of the Association; that you were a black sheep, but that soon changed.'

After nine insufferable years, Ballygawley's entire GAA community was war-weary. The first signs of a thaw in relations began to emerge. Fr Sean Hegarty arrived in the parish and initiated a peace process of sorts between the warring factions.

'Fr Sean Hegarty arrived – be it by chance or design – and wasn't in the parish too long before he made it clear that he was going to sort this dispute out. Through his knowledge and love of Gaelic games, he had a good appreciation of just how seriously people took football. He got talking to both sides of the dispute and he told us the Ballygawley people were missing us badly and he told the Ballygawley people that we were ready to come back, neither of which was the truth.'

However, Fr Hegarty's caressing diplomacy helped soften opinions on either side of the fence. Canavan's precocious talent also accelerated an accommodation, for it would be sheer folly that Tyrone deprive itself of the county's most exciting prospect in generations. At least that was the thinking of former county minor manager Francis Martin.

'Francie was adamant that, as a Tyrone man, I should be playing for the Tyrone minors and he didn't care what the dispute was about. He was manager and he wanted the best 15 players in Tyrone to be playing for the Tyrone minors.'

With the dispute still to reach the end game in 1988, Canavan was representing his county at minor level. Loopholes were found and Canavan became a registered player of Killyclogher Hurling Club. He made his Ulster Minor Football Championship debut against Antrim in Omagh at half-forward.

'I never actually played hurling for Killyclogher; I played a bit of hurling for Dungannon. But I'd signed for Killyclogher, which meant I was a legitimate member of the Association. While I didn't miss out on playing county minor football, my older brothers – Pascal and Steven – did. There were other players at the time who were good enough to play for Tyrone minors before me and they didn't because they weren't a member of a club. Tyrone played in an All-Ireland final in 1986 and I should have had a brother on that team. That's a high price to pay.

'There are people who refer to those times as the "Lost Years" because everybody suffered, everybody was a loser. It may be considered as the Lost Years in terms of a lack of competitive football, but if it hadn't been for that period the club may not have progressed in the way that it did whenever we united.

'If the dispute had not arisen in the club, the same lethargic, easy-come-easy-go attitude might have prevailed. When the club was re-named Errigal Ciaran [in 1990], you had people working hard to make the club successful. We were a focused and determined outfit. Every aspect of club life was taken more seriously and had a big bearing on why the club was successful. Within a few years we'd won our first county title in over 60 years in 1993 and we went on to become the first Tyrone club to win an Ulster title that same year. From that day, the club hasn't looked back.'

Errigal Ciaran's day of emancipation arrived on 29 August 1993. The club defeated champions, Moortown, 0–11 to 0–10 in a memorable county final in Edendork.

'I remember Moortown were very confident beforehand. We got the feeling they underestimated Errigal after winning it the previous year and probably felt they were a stronger team. I remember the game fairly well. We played well in patches, but Moortown came back into it near the end and had a number of chances from free-kicks to draw level, but we managed to hang on. We got scores when we needed them. Paudge Quinn came on late in the game for us and gave the team a boost. It was a day for defenders – and our defence won out.'

Canavan was involved in an epic struggle with Moortown's Chris Lawn.

The *Irish News* described their duel:

> In times of doubt and indecision, when they had to look to their effervescent captain Peter Canavan, they were not disappointed. Canavan's sheer class and genius shone brightly despite Chris Lawn's commendable man-marking job, and the two points he swung over were out of the top drawer.

Canavan recalls, 'Chris would tell you he came out on top and I would like to think I came out on top! I got a few scores from play but we probably broke even. Mickey McGirr was full-back in that team. You'd Colin McCann, whose family is steeped in the club. Cathal McAnenly was goalkeeper, who went on to captain and manage Errigal and is now involved in coaching the Tyrone minors. Ciaran McCrory, who now has three sons playing for Errigal, played centre half-back for what seemed like 25 years and would be considered a legend here in Errigal. He was a rock-solid defender. You had the Quinn brothers – Leo, Hugh, Paudge and "Tiffy" – who were all strong characters and very central to our success. You had a young Eoin Gormley, who was maybe 17 or 18 at the time, and had a big year for us in '93. Eamonn McCaffrey, who played with me in various Tyrone teams, scored five points against Moortown, and of course my own brothers – Barry, Pascal and Steven – were involved that year.

'I will never forget that game. The scenes of joy I witnessed in '93 by so many people in the parish were unreal. Seeing men partying to the early hours of the morning, men intoxicated with sheer joy, Mickey Harte among them; men who were much older than I was and who had given far more to the club than I did, had waited a lifetime for this. They'd worked so hard and they were there to witness it in Edendork. Some of them have since departed. I'll never forget the scenes after the final whistle and what those men did for the club. They died happy men as a result of us winning a county title.

'At that time there were two men who never stopped talking about the club and how the game should be played – and they were my father [Sean] and Barney Horisk.'

In 2006, veteran club member Barney Horisk suffered a massive heart attack in the stands, and later died, after a row broke out on the field between arch-rivals Errigal Ciaran and Carrickmore. 'Barney was always on the periphery, helping out and giving advice when it was needed and when it wasn't needed,' Canavan fondly recalls. 'He pushed and encouraged young lads to do their best and any time there was training up in Dunmoyle and things needed done, Barney was always the man you would have turned to get it done. He was just a light-hearted character and anybody of any age could go and have the craic with him.'

The loss of his father on Independence Day 2003 left an indelible mark on Canavan. Sean Canavan saw Errigal reach the summit in '93, but never got to see his son Peter lift the Sam Maguire ten years later. Peter's father died after a short illness in hospital. He was 73.

'It was natural that you wanted to please your father no matter what you were doing. Nothing pleased him more though than watching his sons do well on a football pitch and doing well for the club. The only time he'd get sentimental was when there was a drop of John Powers on the job. He talked much more freely and openly. He would be ready to tell you things that you didn't want to hear and I think looking back you can see where a lot of parents are going wrong by mollycoddling their sons and daughters and telling them what they want to hear.

'My father spoke when he had to speak. I mightn't have appreciated some of it at the time but looking back it was solid and sound advice. The most important thing I learned from him was to be grounded and there was no better man to do that if he thought you needed to be brought down to earth, whether it was some aspect of your play or the way in which you were dealing with success. There were other nights he would have told you openly how proud he was of us.

'He was reliving his youth through the things that his sons were doing in Clones or in Omagh, just as he'd done down at the Holm. He loved nothing more than reminiscing and telling stories about what men had done on the pitch and how they looked out for one another. I enjoyed listening to stories about how he was able to mark Frankie Donnelly of Carrickmore – a legend in Tyrone – when nobody else was fit to mark him.

'Wee small things like that, I'd remember . . . They were great memories to have, but unfortunately he wasn't there to see us lift the All-Ireland and that is a big regret. He died that summer, 4 July 2003.'

While Canavan was dealing with the personal trauma of losing his father, football provided the best possible release. Tyrone had threatened big things for a number of years leading up to '03. Mickey Harte had taken over the senior management and carefully stitched together two generations of Tyrone footballers and turned them into All-Ireland champions.

'I really enjoyed my football in 2003 up until I got injured against Kerry in the All-Ireland semi-final because the football we were playing was great. If you look back at 2002 when we won the National League the football we played was fast, fluid and brilliant. And you had the young boys coming through – Kevin Hughes, Brian McGuigan, Ryan McMenamin – who were flying. We were tapping into this new-found energy. You knew then we had some great footballers coming through and I was fitting in with these boys, really enjoying it and getting plenty of ball. With Mickey coming in there was a freshness, and training wasn't as severe as previous years in terms of the physical nature. It left us fresher, the football was enjoyable and the team was flying.

'While it was difficult dealing with my father's death, to play along with those boys was a great release. In my later years, when I was aware I was getting older and wasn't as fast, I was using the players around more than ever. In a lot of cases I was finishing off the spade work done by other men. It was a case of knowing when to run, and through experience I was still able to get on the end of a bit of ball.

'Mickey Harte's philosophy was pretty straightforward and clear. He would tell me, "Stay close to the goals; you're better close to the goals." Ninety-nine per cent of the games I played under Mickey, that's where I played. I wasn't the biggest full-forward or corner-forward, so I needed the right ball played in – and people like Brian McGuigan could put it on a plate. I'd a good relationship with Owen Mulligan on the field, too. He was a very unselfish player and while he was one to grab the headlines, he was never out seeking the glory for himself. He's a great team player, works hard off the ball and knows when to give it.

'Even back to the early days with Tyrone when Plunkett Donaghy was in midfield, I remember that before I came on the scene Donaghy was criticised for his use of possession at times. But the first couple of years I played with him a lot of my scores came from passes Plunkett Donaghy put into me. That was strange for someone who I'd never played with before. He was able to read my runs and put good balls in.

'The Tyrone management might've done more in '95 to hold

on to Plunkett Donaghy because if we had had him coming on in the last ten minutes against Dublin [All-Ireland final], he would have had a massive effect. In the early '90s, he was maybe not covering the same amount of ground but he came on at different times to help us win important games. I'd like to have seen him staying on.'

If losing to Dublin in '95 was a devastating blow to a county's brittle psyche, '96 was arguably worse. Meath were a muscular, battle-hardened crew – and much too streetwise for the Red Hands in the All-Ireland semi-final that summer. Almost an entire generation of Tyrone footballers was lost on the field that day.

'The game was probably more cynical back in the '80s and early '90s than it is now,' Canavan says. 'When you talk now of taking somebody out of the game you put two players on him. You don't take them around the neck or break their ankles. You use tactics rather than physical force. The irony about the Meath game was that there were three poor tackles. Somebody landed on [Brian] Dooher. "Dinky" [Ciaran McBride] got a head injury and I got hit late. Two men had to get stitched and I should have gone off. I tore ligaments in my ankle. We played Derry earlier that year and there were late tackles going in and hard shoulders.

'I remember Brian McGilligan shoulder-charged me – very similar to the John McDermott challenge – after I'd kicked the ball over the bar. I bounced up and got away. It didn't take a thing out of me. John McDermott does the same thing and he wrecks me. It was just everything about that game. Everything that Meath did, they put a Tyrone man down – and it looked bad from our perspective that we couldn't stand up to the physical aspect of that game. Bad enough as the physical scars were, it took us a long time to get over the mental scars. We never recovered. The Meath defeat took four or five years out of that Tyrone team. It was effectively the end for a lot of players.'

After '96, Canavan remained the county's totemic leader,

but success came dripping slowly. It wasn't until Mickey Harte arrived in '03 that the hopes and dreams of the O'Neill County were realised. Neither did it matter to Canavan, who'd soldiered through many bad days in the red and white jersey, that sections of the GAA media criticised Tyrone's new style of play that became euphemistically known as 'blanket defence'.

'There was a certain amount of sympathy for Tyrone in '96, but when Meath won the All-Ireland they weren't talking about poor Tyrone,' he says. 'I think that form of football under Mickey developed out of a respect for the likes of Kerry – that if you gave them time on the ball, they'd hurt you. Every Kerry player was so confident on the ball such was their level of skill throughout the team. You just couldn't give them time, hence the ferocious work rate that ensued in the '03 All-Ireland semi-final. It was out of admiration for them that led us to defend and tackle like that. But in 2005, with an All-Ireland medal in your pocket, you're a different team. If anybody wants to see a good game of football you'll see it in that '05 final.

'We wouldn't have been fit to do what we did in '05 without '03. We nearly did it in '03 because we were brilliant in the first 20 minutes against Kerry. People seem to forget that. We maybe didn't have the confidence in ourselves to go on and beat them by 15 points. We retreated somewhat. But two years later, we felt we could score against Kerry every time we attacked.'

Five years on and with two Celtic Crosses, four Anglo-Celts and six All-Star awards to his name, Canavan can afford to be phlegmatic about that rugby-like tackle on the 'Gooch' Cooper in the dying embers of the '05 final. Again, sections of the GAA media raced to condemn Tyrone's football and cited Canavan's crude tackle on Cooper that stopped him becoming involved in Kerry's final assault.

'I've been pulled down enough by Kerry men during my career,' he says. 'If I was as fast as "Gooch", or a few years younger, I would have run beside him to prevent him from getting the return. He was too fast. If the roles had been reversed the "Gooch" would have done the same. I would have been as frustrated as him in that situation because you're losing an All-Ireland final by a couple of points, time's up and somebody pulls you down. It was a professional foul. There was one person that you didn't want to see on the ball near the goal, so it didn't take a pile of figuring out as to why it was done.'

The lessons of Meath '96 had been wholeheartedly absorbed. Integral to Tyrone scaling the highest peaks during the latter stages of Canavan's career was Mickey Harte. The two had shared the same changing-room space when Canavan was a prodigious 13-year-old talent. Nobody knows Harte better than his former pupil.

'As a player and as a manager, Mickey was ultra-competitive and a very sore loser. Now, he's ultra-competitive and a very sore loser – but he disguises it better! His fine-tuning the week before a match was his biggest strength. You looked forward to the week before a game because you knew there'd be great intensity about him and he'd pick up on a few points to hone in on and hammer home. Mickey made sure you were in the right frame of mind. In the team meeting on the morning of a match he would have left you in no doubt that this was going to be our day. That was the biggest strength that I found in Mickey. It was the same with the club before an important match; he'd a knack of saying the right things.

'The intensity of our training was spot on and pitched just right ahead of big games. It gave you a great sense of confidence to see everybody flying in training, and the drills fast and furious. It was obvious that boys were eager and in the right frame of mind. Mickey's style was never to go around players individually; maybe the odd time he would. Generally, though, he doesn't do that. He'll not be on the phone to you every two or three weeks.

'I remember in later years Mickey got a psychologist on board to try and help out, but nobody was going to come in that was a better speaker than him. The players wanted to listen to Mickey. They didn't want anybody else coming in.'

Canavan pondered retirement after Tyrone's maiden All-

Ireland triumph in 2003. After the bitter experiences of '95 and '96, he could walk away having reached the Holy Grail. But the tragic death of Cormac McAnallen on 2 March 2004 was a key factor in him prolonging his inter-county career.

'Cormac's death had a bearing on me going another year. I was tempted at that time to hang them up, but there was a sense of unfinished business with the team. I felt we were still good enough to do something.'

After a tumultuous encore in '05 and aged 34, Canavan was relieved to be stepping away from the inter-county scene.

'Whilst playing was great and I was getting a great buzz out of it, it was frustrating the amount of time I was having to put into it. I felt I was never off the treatment table. From that point of view, it was a relief that it was coming to an end. I'd a great sense of satisfaction going out on such a high note [against Kerry]. Regardless of how I'd done, I'd made up my mind even before I went back to Tyrone that year. I knew that it was my last year. While there was a sense of relief, part of me was devastated to be finished with the club two years later. I could have played on with Errigal, but I knew I wouldn't be able to contribute. That was very hard to take. When you're bigger and stronger you can hang on and play longer. But when your strengths have been speed, agility and mobility, when they're not there, it's harder.

'I'd asthma which made things difficult for me as well. It just became less enjoyable. My last competitive game was a County Championship quarter-final replay in 2007 when Donaghmore beat us. That was it for me after that.'

Three years on, Canavan suffers occasionally from championship pangs when Errigal Ciaran or Tyrone are playing, and still has fond recollections of some old foes. In his pomp, the highly decorated forward enjoyed the enduring rivalry Tyrone shared with Armagh and the various jousts with Derry in the mid-'90s.

'When I came into the Tyrone set-up, the Tyrone–Armagh

rivalry was fierce. They killed each other on several occasions. One of the first-ever games I played against Armagh was in Castleblayney under lights in '89, a tournament game. A bad row broke out and there were three men not involved in the row – myself, Leo McGeary, a corner-back and a cousin of mine, and Benny Tierney of Armagh. We looked at each other and thought we should be in the middle of it because they were tearing lumps out of each other.

'So me and Tierney started sham-fighting. Tierney came over to me then and said, "Come, on Canavan, I'll take you on now." He was bouncing around the place. The Armagh supporters saw this and started shouting, "Go on, Tierney, take the head off the wee bastard!" That rivalry was bitter. Then in the mid-'90s it was Tyrone and Derry. There were a few incidents in games against Derry during that period. The rivalry then was unbearable. We'd a number of players from the Loughshore on the team and there was no love lost. We'd Paul Devlin, Fay Devlin, Chris Lawn and Stephen Lawn. And towards the latter part of the '90s we were going so poorly that we didn't have any rivalries. And then from 2002 onwards it was Armagh and Tyrone again. But, at county level, I could say I didn't fall out with anybody. And I was involved in some ferocious battles during those years, none more so than with Derry's Kieran McKeever. For the first two or three years when I was coming out of successful Under-21 teams, cock-a-hoop with myself and ready to make a big impact on the senior stage, Kieran McKeever put that notion right out of me.

'In '91 to '92, I'd captained Tyrone to All-Irelands at Under-21 level. In '91 we'd beaten Kerry in an Under-21 All-Ireland final and I scored 2–4 or 2–5 and I was ready to win a senior Championship. We were playing Derry. I was taken off with 20 minutes to go. That was Kieran McKeever making a statement, and for me to realise he was no Under-21 player, and that this certainly wasn't Under-21 football. That was a hard way to learn. McKeever was strong, physical and could read a game. He was ahead of me at that stage, so it took a bit of learning to get the better of him.

'We always shook hands after the match. He wasn't one for talking during games. Likewise, Sean Marty Lockhart and Enda McNulty. There was never any bad talk or slagging going on. They never did anything to rag me. It was obviously effective for them because they were hard men to get the better of. But McKeever was, without doubt, the best and the toughest corner-back I played against. He was different. There were men who would have marked me and they didn't care what the score was as long as they stopped me from scoring. McKeever was a team player; he could read the game and would cover for other defenders. He was willing to go forward and support the attack too. I would have great admiration for him.'

These days Canavan carries the extra half stone in weight and memories of his playing days quite lightly. Playing a bit of handball down at Holy Trinity College, Cookstown, where he teaches PE, would be the extent of his sporting activity. In the school's handball alley, he takes great pride in beating colleague and ex-Antrim player John McKeever who is 'about ten years my junior. I'm not a fitness freak. I wouldn't be into going to a gym, not at all. I wouldn't be one for looking myself in the mirror.'

Now 39, he ran the Dublin marathon in 2008, but never much liked the grind of road running.

'There was a sense of achievement when completing it, but to hobble around the streets of Dublin didn't give me the same buzz as winning a Championship match.'

Peter Canavan is a not a particularly nostalgic man – but there are some things, little things, he misses about his playing days. Married to Finola with four children, Canavan was never one to feed off the adulation that often stalks gifted sportspeople.

Nor does he yearn for the flash photography and the All-Star bashes at CityWest. The years of '93, '03 and '05 were the best of times, but the trappings of success never really mattered.

The words of his late father, 'Always stay grounded,' echo still.

'The GAA has given me memories that will keep me going

for the rest of my life. You would like somebody to go back over all the things and the craic that I've had with various teams and the different characters within those teams.'

You get the feeling Canavan would gladly trade some podium appearances of his career to relive the car journeys to training and sometimes matches with Mickey Moynagh and the boys. It's those little things – the wind-ups, the banter, the yarns and the unspoken camaraderie in Moynagh's car that ferried the same bundle of people to training twice weekly for what seemed like forever. Happiness, they say, is the path you travel. Years later, that's what counts. That's what Canavan misses.

'You could write a book on the episodes with the famous Mickey Moynagh, the Tyrone kit man. It was always pantomime with Moynagh and the boys in the car – Paul "The Hog" Donnelly, Pascal, me, Ciaran McBride and Eamonn McCaffrey. The craic was 90. You were barely fit to train for laughter getting out of Moynagh's car . . .'

Nobody noticed the blinding low sun slip behind the rolling hills in the distance. And now an evening chill has taken a firm grip of the place. Errigal claimed the scalp of Aghyaran tonight. In the fading light stands the Errigal Ciaran manager.

Forever the GAA foot soldier from Glencull who lived the dream a thousand times over in a place called the Holm.

This is Canavan Country. Where a reluctant legend was born. He keeps moving forward. Rarely looks back.

In this life when one journey ends, another begins. You haven't lost him. He's just further on up the road.

DJ Carey

Garry Doyle, *News of the World*

At some point in the last century, gossip replaced the potato as the staple diet of the Irish people. No one knows precisely when the transformation occurred but DJ Carey is certainly aware of the consequences.

As the face of Championship summers for 15 years, hurling turned him from small-town hero into national treasure. So much so that today, five years after the final bell tolled on his career, he remains one of the most recognisable men in Ireland.

That much is clear on a dark Friday evening at the K Club. Wearing an open-necked shirt and navy suit, his path through the clubhouse is blocked by several people who stop and request his time. Politely he gives it and in those brief seconds when he communicates with strangers, you catch a glimpse through the window of his personality. Possessing natural warmth, he effortlessly engages in small-talk about the state of the nation, the weather and Kilkenny's prospects for five-in-a-row. Then, recognising he is due into a meeting, he quietly but firmly moves on.

Minutes later, DJ Carey sits with a cup of tea in one hand and a biscuit in the other. Now 40, he has a distinguished look, his hair is slightly thinner than when we last saw him play and that face of summer is mainly relaxed now. Yet when upsetting reminders are introduced, tension returns to the surface.

It is a little over 12 years since Carey's first retirement. Then 27, he was plagued by the incessant rumours circulating Kilkenny, most of which concentrated on the health of his business and the dynamic within the Cats' dressing-room. 'People will say they are unaffected by that sort of stuff but I don't believe them,' says Carey, 'because when you are in the middle of it, it can be awful upsetting.

'I have learned how to ignore it, learned that people simply have obscure opinions and start rumours very often to deflect attention away from their own troubles. Yet I'd be lying if I said those things didn't hurt because all I ever did was play my game on a Sunday, get in my car and go home. I didn't go into any nightclubs or pubs, deliberately avoided situations where I could be quoted or misquoted.

'Yet still things were said and written – that I was fighting with Kevin Fennelly [then Kilkenny's manager] and fighting with everyone in the Kilkenny squad. The truth is I didn't have any fall-outs with anyone. All these perceptions, that I was a trouble-maker, that my business was about to fold, that I owed money all over the place, that I was angry my brother wasn't on the team, were just relentless. And, after a while, I began to question why it was happening to me. I wasn't paid for playing the game. I was doing my best. But no one was paying me. And yes, I was under pressure in work. I hadn't the security of a staff job. I was working for myself and it was very difficult continuing on. Any time I didn't play well, I heard my business was going to fold. Eventually you reach a point where you say enough is enough.'

So, in March 1998, Carey delivered the biggest bombshell to the hurling world in decades. At 27, the age players supposedly peak, he was saying goodbye.

A nation was stunned. For here was the man the Gods had conspired to turn into the perfect hurler. With a combination of technical excellence, tactical authority and terrorising speed, Carey created an air of wondrous possibility beyond the scope of any other player in Ireland.

Yet the Gods can be cruel masters. Though a double All-Ireland winner early in his career, Carey's true prime coincided with a time of Kilkenny recession. Relegated to the supporting cast by Wexford, Offaly, Clare and Limerick, they were desperately seeking to reclaim centre stage. 'Each year we weren't winning All-Irelands, it always seemed to be around me. Then in 1998, we were struggling in the National League and I was getting stick for Kilkenny's form and I thought I'd go. It was as simple as that.'

Yet it was actually much more complicated than that. What DJ Carey didn't appreciate was the level of affection he held. People who simply loved the game loved DJ for the way he played it. So they wrote and begged him to reconsider. Six thousand letters arrived within a couple of days, 20,000 more in the six weeks it took for him to change his mind and go back. Yet that redemptive show of support couldn't fail to derail the mischief-makers from applying fresh hurt.

'At some point, I looked at what was happening and asked, "What's this all about?" I was able to identify who the people were who started these rumours. I knew them. They were from the same county as me, from not too far away from where I grew up. The more I looked at them and the things they were saying, the more I realised they were jealous. That's a sad thing and it is an Irish thing. People find it very hard to give credit where it was due.'

All that, though, seems to have changed.

'Maybe because I'm away from it, I very rarely hear anything bad or silly in terms of rumour about the Kilkenny team now. That's a good thing because it can be disruptive – that sort of talk. And it didn't just happen to me. I remember Eddie Keher getting an awful roasting – and he was retired from the game maybe 20 years.'

The whole point of this story is to not just illustrate the poisonous nature of a section of Irish society but to also remind ourselves that Carey, Keher and today's generation of inter-county players are amateurs, pointlessly suffering the side-effects of mastering the sport they love.

So in this context of personal pain, Carey spent the summer and autumn of 1999 surveying the inter-county horizon, seeing injustice and unfairness everywhere. And when that winter, the GPA formed, a marriage between the pair became inevitable. Though not a founding father of the Association – 'I wasn't there on day one but by day two I was' – Carey quickly rose through its ranks to become President.

Carey said, 'The reality is the GPA was badly needed. Badly. I remember when I started my inter-county career, in 1988, and how bad conditions were then. Now we would have been one of the top teams in the country but the rules within the GAA were very funny. Players weren't properly insured. That had nothing to do with our County Board as such – because the Kilkenny secretary, Ted Carroll, was a lovely guy and he would sit down after his dinner and his day's work each evening to do another day's work for the sake of Kilkenny hurling.

'So I've no axe to grind with anyone. But the reality was that I remember being out of work with a hurling injury for six weeks in the early '90s and not getting a penny because of the lack of proper insurance and the fact no one got an application I sent in for reimbursement. I nearly got sued by the Health Board for a lack of payments when I was in hospital getting X-rays. All these things should have been paid back then. Guys who were injured were told to go and sign on the dole rather than get a payment. And that was wrong.

'The GAA were taking in millions and millions and millions. Yet we, as players, weren't allowed to endorse anything or else we could be suspended. But yet we were expected, as a duty, to travel around the country and present medals. So, on the one hand, it was fine for us to be ambassadors but not for us to endorse. Newspaper articles and television interviews were part of our requirements too and again we got nothing for that.

'In terms of gear, up to an All-Ireland semi-final, you bought your own. And in Kilkenny, we were ahead of the game because I remember travelling to non-hurling counties and learning how money, which was meant to be designated for hurlers, would end up in the footballers' pool. So much was wrong. The GPA was born out of absolute necessity.'

And its birth happened to coincide with Carey's rebirth. For, by 1999, he was back in love with hurling. That year was his first sharing a dressing-room with Henry Shefflin and Brian Cody and in their company he'd go on to win three more All-Irelands.

Along the way, Carey and the men who helped rehabilitate him captured the nation's imagination. Cody, the coach who had suffered snide remarks from Kilkenny supporters during his playing career, rewrote the manual on how the game should be played. Shefflin too had overcome his own personal traumas, having suffered rejection as a teenager. And then there was Carey, surely the most rapturously acclaimed player of his generation. Together they would dominate the following decade.

Well, kind of together, for, by 2005, the three Musketeers had become two. It all seemed to happen so quickly, this passing of the baton from Carey to Shefflin. One minute, Carey was there on his own. Then this young gun came along. And then Carey was gone.

Hard to believe then they shared six years together on the circuit, Carey, inevitably, as the senior partner in the coalition for the first couple of years, before Shefflin flexed his muscles and took control.

That the relationship worked so well is because Carey put so much time into it.

'I remember arriving up to training the first night,' Shefflin once said. 'DJ would have been my hero, and all that, but he kind of has this way about him that makes you relax in his company. From the very start, he made me feel good about myself.'

Yet if Carey was good for Shefflin then so too was Henry for DJ – their love affair blossoming with Cody as chaperon.

'There's no doubt Henry took the pressure off DJ,' says Eddie Brennan, who joined the panel in November 1999. 'I mean, while it would be unfair to say DJ carried the Kilkenny side of the '90s on his own, by the same token he was head and shoulders above the rest. He was our banker to pull a result out for us. He was the free-taker, the go-to man, the guy other teams knew they had to stop. Think back to the 1997 All-Ireland semi-final between Clare and Kilkenny. Clare knew if they handled DJ, they'd win. And they did. But by 1999, Henry was there to share the free-taking duties, leaving DJ to think more about his own game. Plus, Charlie Carter was at the peak of his powers then too. All that would have taken a hell of lot of heat off DJ.'

And all of a sudden, Carey smoothly moved back into top gear, winning a second Hurler of the Year title in 2000, scoring nine goals in eight Championship games during Shefflin's first two seasons, the hottest streak of his career. 'In many ways, they'd be similar characters,' Brennan says. 'There'd be no ego there with either of them. Both would be fierce grounded and would talk to any new lad coming into a panel. Like, I remember when I joined, DJ would have been like a God to me. He'd been the player I'd have gone to see and here I was sitting in a dressing-room with him.

'That sort of thing can intimidate you. So what did DJ do? He came across and spoke to me and because he is quietly spoken, because he's just an ordinary buck like the rest of us, the fan-worship thing goes. He showed that to Henry and clearly had enormous respect for him. Think about it. Here was the best player of his generation letting a new guy take the frees right from the word go on his Championship debut. That tells you DJ is the ultimate team player. If a pass was to be made, he'd make it. He wouldn't have cared if it was Henry or him scoring. There'd be no debate or fighting over who should take the frees, no sulking that this new star had arrived onto the scene. DJ's no prima donna. And even if he was, Brian wouldn't have tolerated it. He'd have no divas in the dressing-room.'

Instead, he had two of the best players in Kilkenny's history forming two-thirds of his full-forward line, a combination which was enough to bring the Cats All-Ireland glory in 2000 but not a year later.

By now, it was clear there was a malfunction in their system. To start with, Shefflin hated playing corner-forward. He didn't score from play in the Leinster final and in the All-Ireland semi against Galway, Gregory Kennedy 'horsed him out of it'. DJ was still the man.

But the next year, arguably, saw the changing of the guard. Traumatised by the Galway defeat, Cody restructured the spine of his side, relocating Shefflin to centre-forward, where in the All-Ireland final, he put manners on Seánie McMahon. That day, he and Carey contributed three-quarters of Kilkenny's scores, Shefflin getting 1–7, Carey 1–6, and in terms of statistical evidence alone, you could argue they were equals.

But others thought differently. One was Johnny Pilkington, the Offaly midfielder, who felt holding Shefflin was now the key to stopping Kilkenny. 'He was the supplier and finisher mixed into one,' Pilkington said. 'Up until then, we'd have thought DJ was the one to look out for. But by that year we felt Henry had overtaken him.'

And Brennan is inclined to agree, saying, 'By 2002, Henry had really taken over as a leader of the team. He was the centre-forward, the one who went toe-to-toe with Seánie McMahon and David Kennedy, and outplayed them. DJ was still DJ but Henry was voted Hurler of the Year.'

And from here on in, the dynamic of the Kilkenny team changed. Carey would play three more years, win a fifth All-Ireland and remodel his game the way Ian Rush did in his twilight years at Liverpool. Yet he wasn't the same man. In his last two All-Ireland finals he failed to score and for all the talk he never did it on the big day. Before then, it is worth pointing out Carey scored 4–32 in his nine finals, 3–12 from play. His other goal, a penalty in the 1992 decider, proved hugely significant.

Yet so too was an incident in the 2004 All-Ireland final when Shefflin walked up to his side in the first half of a game Kilkenny would ultimately lose, to demand the right to take a 70-yard free. Carey, having missed a couple of shots prior to then from similar distances, handed over the sliotar, symbolically acknowledging his time was up.

The years since have confirmed Shefflin's status as the better player, the higher scorer, the winner of more All-Irelands. Is Carey bothered?

'Not in the least,' he says. 'I have no regrets from my career. I had a great time. I won five All-Irelands. And OK I sometimes wish I was born later so that I could have been around for this Kilkenny era but I suppose in my day, I got more kudos for playing at a time when Kilkenny were perceived to be not as strong. So you have to give Henry his due because in my eyes, he is the best player I have ever seen. I cannot talk about Christy Ring or Eddie Keher because I didn't see them play. My view of the hurling world only dates from 1980. And in that time, Henry's all-round ability, strength, skill, athleticism, nerve and dedication makes him superior to any other player.'

Even DJ.

If Shefflin was an important navigator in the final years of Carey's journey then Cody's role was arguably even more significant.

As a player, he had contributed vitally to Kilkenny's winning All-Ireland teams of 1975, 1982 and 1983, yet despite the excellence of this personal record, Cody walked into management feeling desperately unfulfilled. And it was this hunger, coupled with an appreciation of the way the game had changed dramatically in the '90s, which laid the foundation for a decade of unprecedented success.

Memorably, they lost the 1999 All-Ireland final, outmanoeuvred by a Cork side whose work rate exceeded theirs on a rainswept September Sunday, and in the following years, Cody jettisoned the idea of picking players on their past reputation, focusing instead on men who would sacrifice their ego for the sake of the team.

Into this context, Carey, the self-proclaimed individual, whose slalom run through a forest of Wexford defenders and subsequent goal in the 1991 hurling Championship signalled his arrival as a phenomenon, adjusted accordingly.

Brennan said, 'DJ might say he was the ultimate individual but to me he was the ultimate team player. Not just in terms of the way he spoke to the panel or the way he conducted himself but also in the way he played. He could be very unselfish. He played so the team would win, not so that he would look good.'

Besides which, Cody was intolerant of selfishness. And in Carey he found a like-minded individual. Carey said, 'Very few people have more respect for Brian than myself. I saw how he handled things. There was no favouritism. There was no nonsense. You never heard what Brian Cody said about you. He spoke straight to your face. Managers get respect out of the honesty they show and Brian is one of the most honest men I've met. Plus he has a high intellect and a huge passion for the sport.

'I played under him for six years and in that time he missed half a training session which was the night his mother died. Otherwise he was always there. He led this revival from the top. Sure he could be very strict. At the end of the day, you come late for training once – and that is it – unless there is a proper reason. But he can also be very fair and that is why there are two or three changes on every team that plays – even up to an All-Ireland final because if someone comes into form then he will be picked. That's his system. He earns respect because of the respect he delivers.'

It was respect which brought DJ Carey with his two sons to Cillin Hill, just outside Kilkenny city on a Monday evening at the end of September last year. A couple of weeks had passed since Kilkenny's seventh All-Ireland of the noughties and nearly 1,300 people queued to get their copy of Cody's autobiography signed by the author.

Carey, with his two children, arrived just after 7 p.m., waiting just over an hour to get Cody's autograph. He wasn't the only ex-player to do so. Noel Skehan, Joe Hennessy and Christy

Heffernan were also in the line as were two of the current crop, Shefflin and PJ Ryan.

Yet nearly everyone who saw DJ smiled or winked or nodded their head upon recognising him.

'How are you?' they asked. 'Had you not have retired, you'd have nine All-Irelands by now.'

'No, I wouldn't,' he replied. 'I wouldn't have got near the team.'

Others talked about that goal against Wexford in '91, some about the impetuous flick which deceived Davy Fitzgerald in the opening minutes of the 2002 All-Ireland, others about the day he single-handedly brought Kilkenny back from the dead to defeat Galway in the 1997 All-Ireland quarter-final.

And on it went, Carey, one of the most loved players the game has known, queuing along with other Kilkenny supporters, humbly acknowledging that, for all his gifts on the park, he didn't deserve special merit for it.

'Why shouldn't I have queued?' he asks. 'Who am I to jump ahead of other people? My neighbour was going up to get his book signed. Opponents of mine stood in the line. They are the very same as me. They may not have been given the talent I was given and I was lucky enough to have it. But why should I be getting ahead of those people? Those people pay their €25, €30 or €50 to get into a match. I am no better than them.'

And that is largely why DJ Carey and so many of our leading GAA players have retained such respect and affection within this country. At a time of huge uncertainty and anger, the core values of GAA players, their love of the game not the dollar, has reminded a troubled society that sport can provide an escape from grim reality.

'The GAA should hold onto its traditions,' Carey says. 'That means staying amateur. I have never looked at the sustainability of professionalism but I would be dead against it because the day a professional aspect comes into our sport is the day we lose the local parish involvement.

'You then enter into the elite player element and eventually you will find that whoever can pay the most money will produce the best teams. But let's not hide away from facts here, either. The most important people within the GAA are the players, whether it is Under-6s or seniors. We are in an era where we are competing with soccer and rugby and the GAA needs to look after players and nurture them. That means taking care of the Tommy Walshs and the Henrys because they are the men who attract 50,000 people to Thurles or Croke Park. They are the ones I go to see. Let's not forget about their importance.'

No one has ever forgotten DJ Carey. Though retired five years he remains a constant draw by everyone from charities to Corporate Ireland, which, in a sense, is remarkable, given how, in the meantime, Kilkenny have put together the longest winning streak in hurling history. So by rights, his stock should have fallen. Instead it has held its value. And unless you grew up Irish, it might be difficult to fully appreciate the beauty and significance of the DJ Carey story.

As a sports-mad nation, we need our heroes. More than that, we need them to have a humility too. A peacock like Cristiano Ronaldo would never do. So that was why Carey became so loved. On the park, he had this magical capacity to enthral. But off it he didn't look like a famous sportsman. Instead he looked like any other bloke from any other town, refusing to court publicity, retaining his dignity when news reporters asked about the break-up of his marriage, silently turning down offers to work as a pundit on *The Sunday Game*.

When he'd appear at prize-giving ceremonies at GAA clubs, he'd refuse to take a penny. 'When you saw the look on kids' faces it was worth it,' he said. His charity interests stemmed from a need to 'do something good'. 'Every hurler,' he said, 'should have an interest beyond the game.'

And you have to appreciate the context of his time, too. The 1990s and 2000s were the era of the Premier League. Television was changing sport forever, and hurling, people feared, would get hit in the crossfire. In this context, Carey carried with him more than the dreams of a single man.

The GAA needed his mercurial genius to enlighten non-believers and convince them to flock back to the fold. Let's not dismiss the notion they needed the Clare and Wexford fairytales too or indeed the modern warfare provided by Guinness' marketing machine.

But Carey, unwittingly, was an important cog in the machine. A Celtic Tiger was pumping more money into Irish society than ever before and consumers wanted things to spend it on. Hurling became a show and every show needs a poster boy. Carey, instantly recognisable across the land, had what boxing promoters call 'crossover appeal'.

His charisma was part of that. Yet so too was his vulnerability, the fact he had retired so young and then come back, that he was later hounded by the press, that he resisted attempts by the showbiz set to get him and his partner, Sarah Newman, to join the It crowd.

So instead of becoming hurling's answer to Posh and Becks, DJ and Sarah avoided publicity like the plague: 'I'm a very private person and try to keep it that way,' said Carey.

Besides he had responsibilities, to the two sons from his marriage, whom he dotes on, and also to his business, DJ Carey Enterprises, which makes and distributes cleaning detergents and which, like so many other firms, has known better times than the last two years.

'There was never a Celtic Tiger in my business,' DJ Carey says. 'I had a small business which grew generically as opposed to going very big, very quickly. I've been running it 16 years now, and I'll not lie, it's hard work, right now. I employ 30 people and I'm keeping the head down and getting on with it. I've no other choice, do I?'

The choices he does have relate to his time. Family comes first on his list of priorities, then work, which sees him travel

70,000 miles a year, then his charities and the GAA. If there is an issue to be spoken about, he is prepared to do so, famously tackling then Finance Minister, Charlie McCreevy, in 2002 about plans to scrap an initiative which would have given tax breaks to GAA figures.

'Huge revenues are being generated year in and year out and when we look for a break we don't get it. It continues to be a kick in the teeth – whether it's from Croke Park or the Government,' said Carey at the time.

And then four years later, the fire went out. He was 35 and getting tired.

'Tired of all the travelling from Dublin, where I was then living, to Kilkenny three or four times a week. I was aware that when I came onto the panel I was one of the fittest players there. Now there were 21 year olds passing me by. I was ready to let it all go.'

Still, just as it is often said that every politician's career ends in failure, it also has to be recognised that you don't see happy endings in sport. Even the rare occasions that throw up a perfect goodbye, like Peter Canavan's in 2005 or Darragh Ó Sé's four years later, cannot disguise the sense of grief every inter-county man suffers as he comes to terms with a permanent parting from it all.

That was why in March 2010 as Carey, by now as comfortable within his own skin as any man could be, was able to openly acknowledge how retirement has left him with an open wound.

'I was born to hurl,' Carey poignantly says. 'I always felt it was my profession, just something I wasn't paid for. For me, the ultimate adrenaline rush came on Championship days, when I got the ball on the end of my stick and ran. In those brief seconds of perfection, I got this buzz. I can't describe it now. All I know is that I've never got it from anything else. Not from golf, not from work. Instead a big void is there now. I hurt and long for the routine which defined my life for 18 years. I go to Championship matches, enjoy the spectacle, marvel at the brilliance of the individuals playing and still have a sense of involvement from my seat in the stand. Yet sitting there brings its frustration too because you know you cannot do a damned thing to affect the outcome.

'But look,' he reasons. 'I have no regrets. I had a great career. I enjoyed it. It's gone now. This is Henry's time. And in a few years time it will be someone else's time. Mine has gone.'

Yet it is far from forgotten, a point illustrated by my exit from the K Club that miserable Friday night when your correspondent came across a quartet of Scottish golfers who were holidaying in Ireland for the week and required a lift back to their hotel.

Asking me if I'd been out on the course, I replied, no, I had arranged to meet a hurler.

'A what?' one of my passengers asked.

'A hurler,' his friend said. 'It's an Irish shinty player. You know the game? It's the one that lad DJ Carey plays.'

Gone but never forgotten.

Liam McHale

Frank Roche, *Evening Herald*

Liam McHale always stood out from the GAA crowd and not just because he towered over most of them. He had the giant physique that you demanded of your ball-winning midfielder, and he could soar with the best of them too, but McHale never conformed to inter-county stereotype: the local hero who proudly declares he would die for the jersey.

Part of the 'problem' is that he devoted large chunks of time to another sport. And he was good at it too. Good enough to play basketball for Ireland. Good enough to claim national titles and visit nationwide curiosity upon small-town Ballina, even while simultaneously excelling as a county footballer. Perhaps the biggest sacrilege of all, though, is that he never shied away from speaking his mind. He was an open book, and he always admitted that basketball was his first love.

This 'dual' persona helps to explain why a minority of long-suffering Mayo Gaels didn't trust McHale. Never mind if he committed two full decades to the county cause: firstly as one of Mayo's most enduring and important players of the modern era, and later as an Under-21 and then senior selector. His critics, it seemed, were always waiting for him to fail.

'They didn't believe that I cared,' he says, looking back. 'It probably was a mistake, I could have kept it to myself, but I always said that basketball was my number one game. So a lot of people that wouldn't have known me would say, "Well, how can he commit to Mayo and be as determined as, say, Colm McManamon or James Nallen? It's not even his number one game." But, like Ronan McGarrity, once the bug bit, it became equally as important. And after losing the first All-Ireland in '89, I wanted to have a season like that again and I wanted to try and win an All-Ireland.'

Most of the criticism was like water off a duck's back. He recalls playing in New York, when he came off the bench and kicked the ball 'a mile wide' to be greeted by a loud cheer. The local media made a big deal of it; McHale himself just laughed it off. Or there was the time the *Western People* carried the views of a Ballyhaunis man who declared his intention never to watch Mayo again so long as McHale was playing. Some of his family were aghast that this insult be printed by their home town paper; Liam didn't know the man from Adam, didn't know where he was coming from and just thought the whole thing bizarre.

On the odd occasion, though, the barbs hurt. As the 1989 Connacht final against Roscommon loomed, his father Tony was close to death. For two and a half years he had battled serious illness – first a stroke and then cancer in each lung. He had already lasted six months longer than expected, but then he took a very bad turn and the family feared that he wouldn't make it to the Sunday.

McHale played and the final finished in disappointing stalemate. He didn't even wait to shower in Castlebar, with a friend ready to drive him straight back to the family home. 'I had the car waiting for me outside,' he recalls, 'and I was walking through the town with a pair of shorts and a T-shirt, and I got a bit of abuse: "You're no good, McHale!" And they'd Mayo jerseys on. That wasn't nice, especially in the circumstances.' He got back to Ballina in time, and the entire family was there when Tony passed away about an hour later.

The question of whether he'd play in the replay, a week later, was never an issue. His father would have been 'very disappointed if I didn't play, so there was no talk about it or no big family meetings. I missed training Tuesday night; I was at training

Thursday night. All the boys were walking around on eggshells. They didn't know what to say to me.'

Fortunes swung back and forth in the Hyde Park replay. McHale knows of diehard Mayo fans who took off 'effing and blinding' after Roscommon struck for a late goal, convinced they had lost . . . only to discover, back in the hotel, that their team had forced extra time and gone on to win it. McHale was man of the match and – looking back on his long career – rates it as possibly his finest game in green and red.

His worst hour in green and red lasted barely seven minutes. The 1996 All-Ireland final replay will go down in infamy as the day of the big mill in Croke Park; the day Pat McEnaney sent off Liam McHale and Colm Coyle from a cast of dozens.

McHale had been the best player on the park in the original stalemate. He was their midfield colossus, their talisman. The veteran wing-back Coyle, notwithstanding his improbable late equaliser in the drawn game, had a far less central role in the Royal scheme of things. Some 14 years after that manic event, the Mayo man's sense of grievance hasn't dimmed. No, he doesn't lie awake at night thinking about what might have been . . . but neither would he care to share a placatory pint with McEnaney.

'Ah, it was hugely disappointing. But the thing that killed me was that they sent me and Colm Coyle off. If they'd sent a [Meath] midfielder off, we probably would have won the game,' he maintains.

This is no slight on Coyle's ability, rather a basic recognition of the more profound tactical readjustments forced upon 14-man Mayo. Ray Dempsey, their goalscorer in the drawn final, was first to be sacrificed as manager John Maughan opted for the more athletic PJ Loftus in his new attacking configuration of five forwards. This was the era when just three subs were allowed. 'If it was five subs, it wouldn't have been as big a deal,' says the banished midfielder.

He doesn't shy away from his own involvement in the mêlée

– it's there to see on the video. At the subsequent disciplinary hearing in Croke Park, he agreed with the GAC that his entrance was 'dramatic' in that he jumped over a Meathman lying on the ground – but only because he was trying to reach a team-mate who was clearly in trouble.

Despite the ugliness of the fighting and the numbers involved, he still believes that no one had to go – that Pat McEnaney could have brought the two captains together instead and made it abundantly clear that the next person stepping out of line was off.

'When there are 20 guys in a mêlée, and you get sent off, you're very unfortunate,' he maintains. 'And then it's easier for Colm [Coyle] . . . Colm won an All-Ireland medal. In December they had a presentation and he went up and got his medal or whatever. We didn't.'

McHale's personal disappointment is even more understandable in the context of a career reborn that season. The promise of 1989 had long since dissipated and morale was low in the years preceding '96. 'The same laughter and enthusiasm in the dressing-room hadn't been there for a long time,' he explains.

Now hovering around the 30 mark, he didn't play a single match for Mayo during Anthony Egan's 12 months in charge. The new management had set their stall out by demanding his full commitment for the 1994–95 National League. But McHale had always juggled both sports in the winter . . . something would have to give, and it wasn't going to be basketball. So he said, 'That's it now, that's me finished.' In his own mind, he was now a retired inter-county footballer and finally said yes to Brian McStay, his brother-in-law, who had been cajoling and pestering for several years about coming out to play summer football in Boston.

'After the league campaign, Anthony [Egan] rang me and asked, "Are you right to come back in, are you ready?" And I said, "I thought I was gone . . . I can't possibly. I'm going to America, I made a commitment."'

And that was that. McHale helped the Mayo club in Boston

win the Massachusetts title. In his absence, Mayo crashed out to Galway in the Connacht final. He wasn't long home when John Maughan came on the far end of a telephone line stretching all the way to Cyprus, where the former army officer was then on UN peacekeeping duty. His old team-mate, who had already earned his managerial spurs with Clare, was taking over as Mayo boss. He wanted to know was McHale in good shape and, moreover, was he interested in coming back.

Maughan knew there was a clutch of talented players coming on track, guys like James Nallen, John Casey, Maurice Sheridan and David Brady who had all played in one or more All-Ireland Under-21 finals. McHale knew it too and readily signed up – albeit with Maughan's imprimatur to juggle both sports during the league. He would generally miss Tuesday ('the harder night!') but train on Thursday. He might be playing SuperLeague basketball in Waterford on Saturday night, with a car waiting to whisk him away for National League football in Fermanagh on the Sunday afternoon.

Mayo were learning the winning habit through a series of low-scoring dogfights in places like Scotstown and Gorey. Long before toppling Galway in the Connacht final, long before scalping Kerry in an All-Ireland semi-final, the veteran midfielder knew they were heading in the right direction. In fact, he recalls, 'I remember thinking we had gone too well. We had played about six challenge matches and we were blowing teams apart; the younger lads were absolutely flying.'

On the pitch, he never felt they were going to lose the Kerry game. They approached the final with confidence too, even though fully expecting a very physical encounter against Meath opponents who had played on the edge, but also brilliantly, against Tyrone.

'A lot of people, even in Mayo, felt that we weren't going to match them physically in the build-up to the final. And we were going, "What?" You know, we were huge. Maybe it was said that Mayo weren't tough, they're soft – and we didn't feel that way. We were determined to prove to the country that we weren't going to be pushed around, and I think we did that in the first game. But it got a little bit out of hand – there were words spoken upstairs [in the players' lounge] afterwards when Jack Boothman was making a speech.'

Of course, it would never have gone to a replay if various Mayo defenders and John Madden hadn't conspired to let Coyle's speculative punt hop over the crossbar for that late equaliser. For the most part, McHale believes goalkeepers should guard their line and did not view Madden as the most culpable party. Rather, he was left to ponder: 'Why didn't Pat Holmes come out and catch it? Why didn't Kevin Cahill come out and say, "My ball", catch it and kick it into the Hogan Stand . . . and we'd be All-Ireland champions. I don't believe in luck. That ball should never have bounced there like that.'

The subsequent verbal sparring upstairs left McHale convinced that the replay was going to be a 'dynamite' affair. Maughan also anticipated a row and warned the players to make sure no one was sent off – that if trouble should erupt, they should stick up for their team-mates, make their presence known, but shouldn't throw thumps.

'In the two weeks it was building all the time, through the media. And I had got a good few letters at home, to say that I wouldn't be finishing the game – I'd either be sent off or carried off,' McHale relates. Some 20 anonymous letters were thrown in the fire. His mother was going crazy with worry.

Those maternal fears were well founded. McHale himself, while sensing that something was brewing, never anticipated the epic scale of the eruption. He denies running 40 yards to join the mêlée, and doesn't court any long-lost popularity in Meath when he claims, 'There were four of them around me, like that. And it looked like they were organised and they knew exactly what they were doing . . . and us being naïve, we just went in to show a little bit of strength in numbers.'

After the dust had settled, Mayo rose heroically to the

challenge of playing without their midfield colossus. Initially backed by a big wind, they led most of the way only to be left beaten and bereft by Brendan Reilly's 70th-minute point. 'Probably just didn't believe in ourselves enough,' McHale concludes, citing poor shooting attempts and wrongs options taken in the pressurised dying minutes.

The All-Stars function came as an awkward sequel to the affair. The two midfield berths were filled by the 'Mayo One' and his Royal sparring partner, John McDermott – hardly a scene conducive to loquacious small talk. At the banquet, McHale shared a table with Graham Geraghty.

'When the function was over, we were over in that corner drinking beer and the [Meath] boys were over in this corner. I remember, Joe Rabbitte [the Galway hurler] was with us and none of us knew who he was – because he had the helmet on him all the time. And about three or four pints later, Kenneth Mortimer says, "Who the f*** are you?" And he started laughing, "I'm Joe Rabbitte!" Oh Jesus! We all shook his hand. It was a good night . . . a bit tense early on.'

For 13 years, the championship paths of Meath and Mayo didn't cross. Then they met at the quarter-final stage in 2009 and, inevitably, McHale was prevailed upon by RTÉ to revisit the haunted house of '96.

Marty Morrissey had invited him and Geraghty to talk before the game. Colm O'Rourke was apparently 'giving me a hard time' in the studio, and Morrissey asked McHale if he wanted to respond.

'It's easy for Colm, he's won a couple of All-Irelands, he played on a great team . . . it's easy for him to say let it go. I could let it go if I had a couple of All-Irelands maybe, but not when you work so hard for so many years to try and win something and it's taken away from you like that. I could be 110 years of age before I die and I still feel that I was sent off in the wrong, and nobody can ever change my mind.'

Sport has always been at the epicentre of Liam McHale's

life and continues to be so, over a decade since he last donned the green and red. We meet in his home town of Ballina on a Thursday afternoon in January 2010: that evening McHale will travel to Ennis for a training session with the Clare footballers, in his new brief as Micheál McDermott's team coach. The following day, he will make the even longer trek to Cork where the Ballina basketball team – now under the moniker Team Loftus Recycling – face a National Cup semi-final against Blue Demons on the Saturday. McHale has spent his entire adult life shooting hoops with Ballina and now he's their player-coach (although he doesn't bring himself on in the 70–58 defeat to Demons).

'I was squatting yesterday,' he reveals, 'I was doing dead lifts. I'm nearly 45 years of age; I shouldn't be doing that, my back is sore. I went playing basketball after that. I probably won't get a chance – because of you! – to train today, but I would have liked to.'

This self-confessed sports fanatic has just been asked which game – after all these years, all the highs and lows – holds the greater affection. 'Ah, basketball,' he confirms. 'But I really love football.'

'I prefer the basketball because it's more technical, it's more of a thinking man's game,' he expands. 'And I know people will probably cut me down for that, but that's the way I look at it. Athletic ability, strength and size are not enough in basketball; you need more.'

He was hooked from a young age, following the lead of his older brothers Seán and Anthony. He would practise by himself on the outdoor United Courts in town, for hours at a time, morning and afternoon; then there might be an impromptu game in the evening.

'I was very small,' he says, surprisingly. 'It was an advantage to be small when you're trying to be a basketball player because I would have been a ball handler on the team up until Under-16. Then all of a sudden I grew, so you're 6 feet 5 inches and you've ball handling skills – which is just luck really.'

He had scholarship offers from the States – Drexel University in Philadelphia showed the greatest interest – but by then he was 'glad to be out of school' and had no great desire to return, while football was also taking hold.

McHale went on to become one of the biggest personalities of Irish basketball's golden age, winning two National Cups (in 1991 and '96) along with one National League title (in '92). This was the era of the glamorous American imports and Ballina had one of the most exotic in Deora Marsh, yet McHale could mix it with the best of them. He would have played many more times for Ireland but for his football commitments and a growing disillusionment with the international set-up, crystallised by one training camp in Dublin when a four-hour session was followed by a team talk where diet was discussed – 'and then we were given those big silver pound coins to go to McDonald's and get a burger and chips.' Even back then, some two decades ago, the Mayo players were being given protein drinks and menus after training and everything had become 'very professional'.

Instead, McHale's basketball career would become a story of home-town heroics. The core of that storied Ballina team comprised the three McHales – Liam, Anthony and Seán – along with Liam's brother-in-law Paul McStay and the remarkable Marsh, an Ohio native who took Ballina to his heart (it's still his home) and who in turn was embraced by the people of north Mayo. 'His timing was amazing. He was so quick that you could fake him and he'd jump, and he'd be down and up and block you again,' McHale enthuses. 'Then again that improved me so much because he was marking me every night in training, so one of the best defensive players in Europe at the time was covering me every Monday, Wednesday and Friday.'

Back in their 1990s pomp, Ballina played all their home fixtures at Killala Community Centre. The atmosphere was akin to an extra man for the home team, and McHale recalls one period where they went two years unbeaten there. Eventually, the club would be shunted into Division One because the facilities were no longer deemed SuperLeague standard . . . they can now boast a plusher home gym in Ballina itself but maybe some of that old Killala magic has been lost in the ether.

'For opponents, it was a horrible place to play,' says McHale. One of the rims slanted down. Behind one of the baskets, opposing players faced an unusual distraction taking free throws – the sight of a dummy turkey being waved just above the rim. 'We used to have buses coming from Ballyhaunis and Castlerea, Claremorris, Castlebar. We had a mad fan base at that stage; why wouldn't you when you've the likes of Deora Marsh playing? That guy was capable of getting seven or eight dunks in a game, and nine or ten blocked shots. He was absolutely electrifying.'

The family ties involved ensured a close-knit dressing-room, but sometimes it was too close and McHale remembers some 'awful rows'. Their journey to the summit was a tale of gradual, painstaking progression – punctuated by the odd controversy, such as the 1990 Top Four final. With only seconds remaining, McHale brought his own points tally to 34 with what appeared to be the winning basket against the host club, St Vincent's. The buzzer sounded, the court was invaded by ecstatic Ballina supporters . . . but the game was not quite finished and when calm was restored, St Vincent's launched one final attack.

McHale recalls their giant Canadian, Danny Meagher, zigzagging down the court: 'He gets to me and I just grabbed him. The game was over – I was looking at the clock. Four big zeroes up. I gave him a little bit of a hug; that was it. We were all jumping around thinking it was over.'

Instead the referee blew for a foul – McHale's fifth – and Meagher converted the second of his free throws to force extra time. Except . . . a furious Ballina stormed into the dressing-room and refused various pleas to play on. Afterwards, they would pore through the video tape, armed with stopwatches, and McHale remains adamant that time was up. Officialdom wasn't so forgiving and lumbered the club with a record Ir£2,000 fine.

Looking back, McHale reckons the whole controversy imbued them with a siege mentality and made Ballina stronger. Their drive to win a national title was now an obsession, and came to pass the following year when they beat the dominant force in Irish basketball, Neptune, in their own Cork gym.

The return trip north was the closest McHale has come to an All-Ireland homecoming that wasn't shrouded in melancholy. 'We were taken aback when we got to Gort, which would be the first stop in Connacht – and there was a bonfire,' he recalls. 'There were maybe 500 people out; they brought out pints on trays for us. And we were there like, "Jesus, what's going on here?" We were heading home in cars; we didn't even have a bus.'

More bonfires and more liquid nourishment ensued before reaching Ballina, where a massive crowd had gathered in the Market Square. The bishop was on stage with a host of other dignitaries. By now, the players were all 'half in the bag' prompting their perennial father figure, Seán McHale, to go around warning them all to 'behave yourself now, don't be cursing, keep your act together'.

Liam McHale can only visualise the epic scale of the homecoming if Mayo had ended their All-Ireland hex during his own playing career. He played in the senior finals of 1989, '96 and '97, each one ending in heartbreak. Later, as a selector in 2004, he would endure the same hollow feeling. He hated the idea of standing on a stage, looking down on familiar faces, when all he wanted to do was hide in a corner of Mick Byrne's pub. 'I just felt that when we lost, no matter how hard we tried or how well we played, in a losing effort we didn't deserve ten thousand people coming into Castlebar waving their flags,' he concludes.

Coming in the slipstream of his trilogy of Mayo trauma, the 1999 All-Ireland club final and its homecoming aftermath were every bit as tortuous. Having raced into an early five-point lead, Ballina Stephenites kicked wide upon wide and duly conspired to kick away a game that was theirs for the taking. The consequences were painfully inevitable, as John McEntee's late dagger-to-the-heart sealed a 0–9 to 0–8 victory for Crossmaglen.

The Armagh champions had claimed their first All-Ireland just two years earlier: they wanted to win with style, whereas Ballina, chasing their maiden title, weren't remotely bothered by the aesthetics. The atmosphere at the post-match reception in Croke Park was 'surreal' and more akin to a 'bloody morgue', says McHale, who recalls talking to Jim McConville and being struck by how Crossmaglen were 'disgusted with themselves', as if embarrassed to have won this way. 'We were dead and they were worse,' he concludes.

The cumulative effect of these All-Ireland tribulations could have the effect of leaving you scarred forever, yet McHale insists he has been able to get on with life after playing. He owes this to his successful basketball career, allowing him to believe he's a winner, not a loser. He recalls Peter Ford once asking him how the Ballina club could win national titles from such a limited playing base. The reply was short and to the point: 'It's easier to get five guys on the same page than fifteen.'

He finds it difficult to compare victorious dressing-rooms – football versus basketball – for the simple reason that he never won a national title with Mayo. To win Connacht finals and All-Ireland semi-finals was 'beautiful' but it was still only a stepping stone to future glories, never to be experienced.

So was it a case of malign destiny shaping all this Mayo misfortune? Did he actually deserve an All-Ireland? 'Ah no, I don't think we did,' he reasons. 'We never got blown away, we were always competitive, but we just couldn't get the job done. When you look back, it's very easy to say, "Ah, we were unlucky, the ball bounced over the bar, and I hit the post and then James Horan hit the post [in 1996]." They're opportunities that we failed to execute, and to me that's just as simple as that. You can't be saying it was luck all the time.'

Other self-inflicted wounds didn't help, and McHale is still animated by the memory of some unnamed team-mates allowing parochial club rivalries to cloud the greater county cause. 'I would always have felt that I was consistent – that I played at a certain level and kept it there for a long, long time – and I'm proud of that. I know there are fellas I played with that have to have regrets, and I honestly don't,' he relates.

'If I saw a man open, I gave it to him . . . he might have kicked the legs off me in a club match two weeks before that. Fellas have stood on me – county players – and I'd play with them the following week because I could see the big picture. The Munster and Leinster [rugby] boys have to put up with that, and some of our fellas couldn't do that.

'I've been in situations where I was wide open, bearing down on goal, and the ball never came – and your man would look straight at me. I'd be there like, "How could you not see me? You looked at me, our eyeballs met!" And I didn't get the ball, and I could have scored a goal, and we lost by a point. And they make you sick to your stomach.'

He cites a more benign reason to help explain why Mayo lost to Cork in 1989, the county's first All-Ireland senior final since the salad days of '51. 'We made a decision not to foul,' he states. 'We were afraid of Larry Tompkins, and in hindsight that was a mistake. Now it wasn't John O'Mahony's decision or the selectors – the whole group talked about this. Obviously I didn't have much to say about it, but the older fellas would. And that was reinforced by that wonder kick he took, as good a free kick as you've ever seen in Croke Park: it was a sideline ball and he opened the club face and bent it over the bar like Maurice Fitzgerald. I remember looking at this: "Oh God, what's he after doing there?" Basically we had aggressive backs and a very aggressive midfield. And we weren't aggressive, we kind of stood back and everybody enjoyed the game, one of the best finals seen in years . . . but the problem was we lost.'

For all that, McHale reckons Cork were rattled after Anthony Finnerty's second-half goal and, if Mayo had taken their chances then, the memory of losing back-to-back finals would have come back and 'haunted' Billy Morgan's men. His other abiding memory of that final is the physical buffeting. McHale was the rising star who had performed heroics in both the Connacht final replay against Roscommon and the All-Ireland semi-final against Tyrone. And then he ran into Shea Fahy.

'I could have gone into the final a little bit less known,' he admits. 'I took an awful lot of hits in the first 20 minutes of that game. I remember Barry Coffey got me with a big hit in the chest. Niall Cahalane got me. And Teddy [McCarthy] and Shea weren't sparing me either . . . I took a lot of abuse that day; they were very physical and strong around the middle of the field. I remember saying afterwards that you'll see a different Liam McHale next year; you'll see a bigger, stronger Liam McHale.'

The only trouble was that, as McHale got stronger, many of his colleagues grew older. 'They were getting up to 27 or 28, a lot of mileage on the clock. We only got a two-year shot at it,' he suggests.

John O'Mahony's controversial exit in '91 prefaced the arrival of a Mayo-based All-Ireland winner from Dublin, Brian McDonald. His short-lived reign bottomed out with an 'awful lifeless' semi-final performance against Donegal but only gained notoriety in the aftermath. Player revolutions were not the done thing back in 1992, when the Mayo squad released a lengthy statement seeking the removal of their manager and regaling us with various reasons why, including the infamous tale of footballers being asked to push cars around a car park, all because a pitch hadn't been booked for training.

Immersed in his basketball commitments, McHale wasn't around for the car park affair or the incident where a couple of players got shin splints after a road-running session. He also enjoyed a pretty good relationship with the manager from his own formative days as a young Mayo senior: McDonald, then a selector with Liam O'Neill, would bring McHale for private lunchtime tuition to improve his kicking.

Looking back, he says you can't blame players who had become accustomed to the professional regimes of O'Neill and O'Mahony – even though he advised his colleagues against signing a petition. But when all the boys signed it, he did too . . . and then his picture ended up in the paper with the accompanying tag line 'McHale wants change'.

If the McDonald era is recalled for its black comedy, the Jack O'Shea years were dark without the humour. What can you say about an All-Ireland semi-final that finishes Cork 5–15, Mayo 0–10? 'I suppose that's what happens when you're not well prepared,' says McHale, citing the fact that two players never showed up for the team meeting in the hotel beforehand – and still started the game. Their team-mates presumed that disciplinary action would follow but, when no changes were made, 'obviously the arse just completely fell out of it'.

Jacko was a playing legend but a rookie boss; McHale recalls him as a good coach and a 'lovely fella' who fatally didn't act when something needed to be done. When morale isn't right, he surmises, collapse is just a 'kick of a ball away' and Mayo went from chasing a six-point deficit with 20 minutes left to losing by 20.

'You shouldn't be beaten like that in an All-Ireland semi-final. There are four teams left, you're supposed to be the best from your province, and I thought it was embarrassing that we just downed tools like that,' says McHale who – unable to face home – got the boat to Anglesea the next morning, went to Manchester, and ended up at the Notting Hill Carnival in London.

The next year, Mayo lost a Connacht final to Leitrim – a case of history masking the poverty of the losers' performance. The following year, with Anthony Egan in charge, McHale didn't even play.

After John Maughan's arrival, and the madness of that Meath replay, Mayo picked themselves off the ground and made it all the way back to the All-Ireland final in '97. 'But it was kind of a struggle,' McHale admits. 'There was wear and tear on us, physically and emotionally. Sligo should have beaten us in that Connacht final – and you know, the year before we would have beaten Sligo by ten points if we had felt like it.'

They were still confident approaching the final against Kerry, whom they had scalped in the previous year's semi-final. He didn't realise that Mayo would be so flat in the first half; or that Maurice Fitzgerald, for all his undoubted talent, would be so 'aggressive and determined and good as he was' that day.

The following year, the long wait ended and Sam Maguire finally crossed the Shannon. To Galway. And the next year, 1999, Liam McHale made his last appearance for Mayo as a late substitute in an All-Ireland semi-final against Cork. He had torn a quad muscle in early summer and spent the rest of it playing catch-up. He cut down on his work hours because he wanted to double-up on training. And ten days before the Cork game, the 'B team' played the 'As' in a trial match and 'hammered them off the pitch'. McHale, Noel Connelly and Pat Fallon were all pushing for recalls but Ciaran McDonald was the only player promoted.

Mayo's elder statesman had now turned 34 but felt in 'great shape', having worked so hard for what he deemed his last shot at the summit. 'The team was winning, we'd beaten Galway in Tuam, and then it was a big decision for a management team – do you go back with the boys that have served you well for the last four or five years, and drop the young lads that have come in and done well? Or are you going to sit tight? And they decided to sit tight, which in my opinion was a mistake.'

McHale came on for the last 13 minutes but felt he should have got more. Fionán Murray's late goal sealed a 2–12 to 0–12 victory for Cork.

That short cameo would prove his Mayo swansong. Pat Holmes had taken over the reins of management from Maughan, and – 'like the fool I am' – McHale said he'd give it one more year. Then at one training session that winter, he was called into a meeting with the new boss and selector Micheál Collins. Holmes laid it on the line: if he didn't give up the basketball, they didn't believe he could continue doing both.

'And that was definitely it then! Pat and myself would be great mates, still very good mates . . . he wanted me full-time, and it was a fair point. He said, "You're 34, coming 35, you probably can't do it."' McHale thought otherwise but immediately knew there was no decision to make. He couldn't give up on the basketball – and just to prove the point, he is still playing it ten years later.

Liam McHale did a lot more than shoot hoops in the noughties. He became a selector with the Mayo Under-21s and was handed his first real coaching role by Kevin McStay.

They reached the 2001 All-Ireland final, losing to a 'really good Tyrone team', but his three years with the Under-21s whet the appetite and he duly became a senior selector for the second coming of John Maughan. Again, they were good enough to reach an All-Ireland. Again, it would all end in tears. Only this time, the 2004 showdown with Kerry left no room for lamentations about missed chances, mêlées or balls bouncing over crossbars. 'When John took over nobody expected us to do anything,' McHale recalls. 'In 2004, when we got to the All-Ireland final, we went to New York and a lot of people were saying New York would beat us. We prepared differently than you normally would for New York; we prepared like we were playing Galway or Roscommon.'

They met with non-existent resistance, yet the clinical manner of that 3–28 to 1–8 turkey shoot infused the team with confidence. 'It was like '96, the players developed as we went on,' says McHale. But having reclaimed Connacht and peaked for the All-Ireland quarter-final against holders Tyrone, they required two fraught attempts to struggle past Fermanagh.

'Deep down, John, George [Golden] and myself knew that the Kerry game was going to be a big ask – that we needed a couple of goals to win it,' he recounts. They worked on this at training, over and over, practising three-on-two and two-on-one scenarios. And then, hey presto, Alan Dillon popped up for an early goal.

Dillon was 20–1 with the bookies to be first goalscorer. McHale had watched him waltz around their 'keepers in training and knew he was onto a good thing. Before leaving for Dublin he told his wife Sinead – sister of Kevin and Paul McStay – to slap down €50 on the Ballintubber man.

Suffice to say, his exuberant celebration of that early goal was as good as it got for McHale that day. Mayo were crushed by eight points and then came the double whammy afterwards, when Sinead admitted that she'd forgotten to place the bet. Another All-Ireland down the plug hole, washed down with €1,000. More seriously, he maintains that Mayo weren't 'nearly good enough' to beat Kerry in 2004, even a Kerry team without Seamus Moynihan or Darragh Ó Sé in its starting line-up.

The following year, when battle resumed at the quarter-final stage, Kerry had Moynihan and Ó Sé back and yet only prevailed by a goal as Mayo rallied with the last five points. From a tactical perspective, McHale felt they had played Kerry much better and that the team was making progress. But, he adds, 'There was awful pressure on us then, because everybody wanted John O'Mahony.'

Certain off-field 'distractions' clearly bothered the Mayo management in 2005. By then, O'Mahony was at the zenith of his media career. Early that summer he had named an alternative Mayo team in his *Western People* column – 'We were very disappointed with that,' McHale recalls. O'Mahony was also co-hosting the weekly 'Sports Talkshop' show on *Midwest Radio* and again, McHale maintains, 'They seemed to have an agenda against our particular management.'

By the end of the 2005 campaign, Maughan had had enough. 'He wanted support from the County Board and it wasn't really coming. And he said to us if he didn't get it, he was going to pull.' And so it came to pass, heralding the long-awaited return of O'Mahony. McHale had some 'big rows' with Maughan over the years, but never ones that lingered. He still has great respect for the Crossmolina man and maintains he was a better coach and manager by the time of his second Mayo tenure.

On the subject of his relationship with O'Mahony, he says, 'Ah, I wouldn't see him much but it would be fine. He brought me into football [with the Mayo Under-21s]. I'd meet him at the odd function every now and then, but we wouldn't be in touch that much.'

A year after Maughan's resignation, Mayo found themselves back in another All-Ireland final following their roller-coaster win over Dublin. He recalls being up in Dublin for the All-Ireland weekend, surrounded by excited family and friends, being asked the obvious question. 'And I said we're not.' He had gone through the match-ups and reckoned it would take a miracle for Mickey Moran's team to beat Kerry. He was chided for his pessimism but even McHale didn't envisage the calamity to come. Yet he doesn't blame that generation of Mayo players. 'I really believe that in America, with the psyche they have in sport, that team would have been classified as overachievers – and would have got a pat on the back,' he concludes.

As we speak, it is 59 years and counting since Sam Maguire last took up residence in the county. McHale fears it could be another 20 before the famine ends. He agrees that the legacy of failure, this perennial monkey on Mayo backs, will never go away until they finally win one. Yet he then rhymes off the more basic impediments blocking the path to All-Ireland deliverance. Starting with a dearth of clinical forwards: they can produce the occasional Alan Dillon but not enough of his ilk. Why so? Because the coaching at underage level – club, county, as well as schools – simply isn't good enough. To underline his point, he estimates that 50 per cent of players called up by the Mayo Under-21s are not 'fundamentally solid'.

'We are always striving to get the best manager and the best coaches with the senior team – but it's too late. These fellas are

24, 25; it's hard to break them down and start all over again,' he declares.

'We need the Kevin McStays and the John Maughans and the John O'Mahonys coaching or overseeing the Under-10s; showing up for these elite camps and having a look around and making sure that the coaches are doing it right. So that when they're 18 or 19 and coming into the senior panel, they can kick with both feet; they can pass with both hands; they understand how to get open; they understand the timing of a pass; they understand all the aspects of the game. Like the Kerry boys or the Tyrone boys.'

He clings to the belief that if Mayo get the coaching structures right, they will start producing their own Declan O'Sullivans and Peter Canavans and Colm Coopers – and then they will win. 'But until that is done, it won't happen,' he stresses. 'With the back door now, you just can't fluke an All-Ireland. Somebody is always going to get you. So, to answer your question, I think we'll win an All-Ireland but we won't win it for another 20 years . . .'

Liam McHale had been a retired club footballer for two years by the time Ballina finally reached the All-Ireland summit, in 2005. 'Sinead had my heart broken – "go back training, go back training" – after they won the Connacht title,' he recalls. 'I would have loved to have been part of it, but at the same time . . . to go back and put you on for the last five minutes and a big bald head on you! No, that wouldn't be for me at all!'

He later managed the Stephenites for two years, at a time when two-thirds of the All-Ireland team had either retired or emigrated, taking on a batch of youngsters and 'coaching the living daylights out of them'. From there, his next stop has been Clare. He concedes that coaching, as opposed to management, is his forté . . . and yet his ultimate ambition is to manage Mayo, even though he can see the obvious contradiction in this personal desire and his own prediction of 20 more barren years.

'I have learned an awful lot over the years from the likes of John [Maughan] and Kevin [McStay] and people like that. I'd like to give it a shot,' he says. 'I do believe that I tried very hard to win an All-Ireland as an individual with the team, but the next thing you can do is maybe win an All-Ireland [as a manager]. It would be very special if we could do it some day and be part of it. When you're 20 years at it as a player and as a coach . . . that's a lot of time going up and down to Castlebar. I just can't let it go that easy.'

Michael Duignan

Brian Jaffray

A tiny wooden cross marks the final resting place of Edel Duignan. She was just 41 years of age when she lost her battle with cancer in the autumn of 2009.

Perched on the decorative pebbles is a terracotta vase, newly filled with fresh flowers. The scent of 12 red roses permeates the early summer air.

Durrow cemetery is on the Offaly side of the county boundary with Westmeath, half way between Kilbeggan and Tullamore. It is less than a mile from the house Edel shared with her husband Michael, the two times All-Ireland medal winner with Offaly, and their two sons, Seán, aged twelve, and nine-year-old Brian.

On a hillside, the graveyard is adjacent to the church. It's totally exposed to the elements. There are no trees or shelter. It's bleak, terribly so.

Michael, Seán and Brian stand together by the grave. Seán has just made his Confirmation. Today, as a family, they come to share a special day with their late mother. A day of celebration. A day of reflection.

They tell her what a great day it has been already and about the party planned back in the house. About how all the neighbours, who have been so good to them since Edel died, have promised to call in. About the giant bouncy castle in the back garden. Above all, they tell her how much they still love her, how much they miss her. They miss her terribly.

The card Seán and Brian placed on Edel's grave for Mother's Day is still there.

The pink envelope, battered by weeks of hail, sleet and snow, protects the card from the elements. The card is simple; the message is heartbreaking.

> This comes with warmest thoughts to bring a special wish your way.
> For lots of love and happiness to fill your Mother's Day.
> Have a lovely day,
> Love Seán and Brian.

Beside the vase a miniature crib stands alone. Inside the crib, protected by plastic, is a card:

> Happy Christmas. Love Michael, Seán and Brian xxx

The grieving widower pulls his two sons closer. He tells them how proud their mother was of them and how they will celebrate Seán's special day in a way only Edel wanted.

Today is not a day for tears.

Standing just two inches over six feet, Michael Duignan is a no-nonsense type of guy. He is opinionated, controversial and straight to the point. What you see and hear is what you get. Above all he's a passionate GAA man.

It's just over a year ago that the Duignan family's life came crashing down all around them when Edel died at St James's Hospital in Dublin.

Michael and Edel's paths first crossed in Dublin in 1990.

She was an O'Connell from Kilminchy, Portlaoise, he was from Banagher. They were both employed by the AIB [Allied Irish Banks]. Edel initially embarked on a nursing career at Peamount Hospital in Dublin but the world of finance called and she left nursing after a year.

The back end of 1989 had been a horrific few months for Duignan. Weeks after he was the losing captain in the All-Ireland

Under-21 final against Tipperary he was diagnosed with a rare, life-threatening skin disorder called Stevens-Johnson syndrome.

Over a nine-day period he lost three-and–a-half stone. Doctors feared for his life. 'This thing developed very quickly over a couple of days. Medication failed to cure it and for a couple of hours it was touch and go. The thing that saved me was that I was so fit.'

Duignan was on sick leave for four months and when he did return he started a new chapter of his life and his career at the Rathfarnham branch of the AIB. 'Edel had just been transferred from the Cabra branch and we just got on very well from the start.'

She worked in numerous branches throughout the city before she became Human Resources Manager. Based in Finglas, her brief covered a dozen branches in the Dublin region. Five years after they first met they married.

Three years later Seán was born and, in October 2000, the Duignan family was complete with the arrival of Brian. Within 12 months their lives changed forever.

Edel Duignan's stock in the Bank was on the rise. At 34 she was one of the youngest executives in the AIB Group. Living in a beautiful house in Naas and married to an All-Ireland champion and with two doting children aged four and two, life could not get any better. Then in September 2001 everything changed utterly when she was diagnosed with breast cancer.

She had a mastectomy. A year of chemotherapy and radiotherapy followed. Against this backdrop Edel showed her true character. 'She never complained about the hand that life had dealt her, she never complained during her long and intensive treatment. She was without doubt the bravest and most courageous person I have met,' Michael remembers.

Together, and with the children in mind, both Michael and Edel took stock of their lives and moved from Naas to the midlands. They purchased Edel's 'dream house' in Durrow, three miles outside Tullamore.

'Edel had a very senior job in AIB at the time of the first diagnosis and we said, "Look, there's more to life." We were both working and very busy in our own lives. I had just gone out on my own. As both of us were country folk we had always wanted to bring the lads up in the country.

'We loved Naas and had many happy years there but with Edel's cancer we said, "We'll move back down to Offaly," nearer to her family and nearer to my family. We came down here and loved it from day one. We had great years even when she was sick. The lads settled in very well.'

After her family, her home was Edel's pride and joy. Michael's burgeoning auctioneering business was at full tilt, struggling to keep up with the voracious Celtic Tiger. Edel returned to work on reduced hours. It was all good and very positive.

Their house is surrounded by green fields, an oasis of tranquillity and the perfect location for recuperation. It was here Edel found a new enthusiasm for life. She took up art, photography and, enthused by her recovery, she became involved with 'Dóchas', a cancer support group in Tullamore.

Tragically, however, her joy was fleeting. A routine visit to hospital in Dublin in 2006 revealed secondary cancer, shattering the lives of the young couple once more. As a family, the Duignans were on borrowed time.

'I knew that when the secondary cancer came back Edel was not going to get better. She was told she had six to twelve months to live. She ended getting three and bit years. Edel was an incredible fighter,' explains Michael.

'The weekly chemotherapy took its toll on Edel but she never complained. She never complained at all during that difficult time. She just adored the two boys. They were her reason for living and putting in the brave fight she did.'

Seán and Brian were aware that their mother was sick but they were protected from the gravity of the situation. Conscious of her situation, Edel selflessly ensured that an especially strong relationship was forged between Michael and the two boys.

When they all adjourned to watch television together, she would sit on a separate chair and let the lads cuddle into their dad on the sofa.

'I never noticed but what she was doing was creating a bond between me, Seán and Brian. She had deliberately done that. She had pushed them towards me.

'Then about six months before she died, she said, "I want them back". She knew her time with them was limited and she wanted them as close to her as possible until she died.'

Edel lived the last few months of her life to the full. The summer of 2009 holds only fond memories. Despite her illness and chemotherapy, Edel ran the mini-marathon in Dublin and celebrated with family and friends with a few drinks in famous Dublin watering hole Doheny and Nesbitts.

'She ran the mini-marathon for Dóchas. On the Friday she had chemo and was back in Dublin running with all her friends on the Monday. She was thrilled she finished the race but did she suffer when she returned from Dublin. She probably put down the worst night I ever saw anybody in pain with after she came home,' remembers Michael.

The recession and the decline in the property market came as a blessing in disguise for Michael. He was able to spend more time at home with his sons, but more importantly, he was able to enjoy Edel's company more than ever.

The month of August was spent in the west of Ireland. Three weeks in a mobile home in Connemara and a week in Clare turned out to be the happiest four weeks the Duignan family had ever spent together.

'We were in a mobile home right on the beach in Ballyconeeley. It was such a wonderful few weeks. We then headed for a week to Clare to meet up with some of Edel's family. She even got her nose pierced. In all my time I'd never seen Edel so happy.'

They came back to Durrow on the Saturday evening. The kids started school on the Monday and by the following Sunday, All-Ireland Sunday, Edel was admitted to St James's Hospital in Dublin. Her death notice was in the national papers a week later.

'For years you're preparing for Edel's death but in the end it came very suddenly. I always knew Edel was going to die but when it happens it's very difficult. It was still so very sudden the way it happened.'

High up in the Hogan Stand, Michael sat beside RTÉ broadcaster Ger Canning, co-commentating on the All-Ireland final between Kilkenny and Tipperary. His mind was on the action below but his heart was across the city in Dublin 8. His work commitments completed, Duignan made his way from Croke Park.

Monday afternoon and the signs were encouraging. 'We spent the afternoon sitting outside under the trees drinking white coffee. Edel was in good form and all chat about the match.' Tuesday there was a little deterioration and Wednesday a lot more.

'It really dawned on me Wednesday evening that things were bad when the doctor called me aside and said Edel had pneumonia.' The medics tried five different antibiotics to get a handle on it but to no avail.

'They were kind of preparing me for the inevitable. By Thursday and Friday we knew things were not going well. You're kind of waiting for it to happen but still nothing can prepare you for the end. It was really so sudden, we were just back from the best family holiday we ever had.'

Surrounded by her husband and family Edel Duignan died at 2 a.m. on 15 September 2009.

Family, friends, neighbours and the GAA community rallied together in the Duignans' hour of need. 'The support shown to myself, Seán and Brian by people will never be forgotten. It was unbelievable.'

Edel's funeral was the biggest ever seen in Offaly. People came from all over the country and many from abroad. The funeral was centred on the Duignan house according to her dying wish.

'Home was everything to her and I said to the lads when she

died that their mother would want people to be here in the house to celebrate her life and to give her a fitting send-off.'

Makeshift car parks were erected in the fields adjacent to the house. Members of the Ballinamere/Durrow GAA club erected floodlights and directed traffic. People came to support Michael and his sons but they also came to celebrate Edel. Thousands and thousands of mourners streamed through the house in the days leading up to the funeral. GAA stars past and present from all over the country came to lend their support.

'At the wake the likes of Henry Shefflin, Eoin Kelly, Nicky English and Niall Quinn brought the two boys out the back and had a puck around with them. To this day both Brian and Seán talk about it. That's friendship, that's support and that's the GAA for you.

'Edel's death is a massive loss. It's a huge loss to both Seán and Brian. They were incredible and they gave me the strength to get through it all. They had to mature very quickly. They are after seeing a lot but you have to remember that they are still only young lads. I sometimes forget that Brian is only nine and you have to think of him as a little child.

'We have a good relationship, they are good craic and good characters but I find the easiest way to come to terms with the grief is to include Edel in our conversations. I'd often say, "What would your mother say or what would your mother do?" And more often than not they will always take their mother's side.'

There have been good days and bad days but as a family Christmas was the hardest time since the funeral. 'Christmas Eve was the worst day I've had since Edel died. She was huge into the house and huge into Christmas and occasions. She had a diary and had everyone's birthday written down. I don't think I sent a card in my life. She was an unbelievable organiser. She was the complete opposite to me in nearly every way.

'She loved Christmas more than any other time in the year. The boys wanted the house decorated just as if Edel was here. We did up the place. We put up two trees, a real one in the conservatory and an artificial one in the front. The place was lovely but the atmosphere was obviously different.

'On Christmas Eve, both here and in Naas we always had drinks for the neighbours. This year the neighbours ensured that tradition remained and they all came over to be with us. It was grand but then they all went home and then the lads went to bed. That was a hard time. That particular night was really tough.'

Life is cruel and life goes on and for the Duignan family they have had to adjust to life without a wife and a mother. 'We think of Edel all the time but you'd be trying to hope you're not blocking it out but you've to get on with life. On the one hand you're trying to put a shape on the future and remember Edel with great affection every day on the other. It's not easy. There are different stages. I've no experience of it and I think everyone has to go through it themselves.'

On the pitch Duignan enjoyed an illustrious career playing both hurling and football with his local club St Rynagh's and with Offaly from the 1980s to the early 2000s.

Just a puck of a sliotar from Michael Duignan's home at Cuba Avenue in Banagher, Co. Offaly was the famous St Rynagh's pitch. It was his field of dreams. And it was there on that hallowed turf deep in the heart of Offaly, that Michael's love of hurling took root, was nurtured and blossomed.

Rynagh's were the undisputed kings of Offaly hurling during his formative years. Of the four senior Offaly All-Ireland hurling triumphs, three were captained by men from St Rynagh's.

'St Rynagh's has always produced a particular type of player. You will hear hurling people in Offaly say, "Offaly won't be back until Rynagh's are back." And it's hard to argue with that.'

Names of greats and legends trip from his tongue. 'Damien Martin, Padraig Horan, Aidan Fogarty, Hubert Rigney and Martin Hanamy. They were all unflinching men and were some of the toughest hurlers in the history of the game. They mightn't

Mayo footballer Liam McHale, pictured above during the 1997 championship, always stood out from the GAA crowd, and not just because he towered over most of them.
(© Matt Browne, SPORTSFILE)

Bernard Flynn in action during the 1994 league final against Armagh, where, typically, he scored two goals. It was Flynn's last season in a Meath jersey. A year later, he was told he would end up a cripple if he played on.
(© Ray McManus, SPORTSFILE)

Legendary Cork hurler and footballer Jimmy Barry-Murphy in action for the Rebels during the 1983 championship. His doubled goal against Galway in that year's semi-final is considered the greatest ever scored. (© Ray McManus, SPORTSFILE)

Michael Duignan, now one of hurling's top analysts, pictured in action for Offaly during the 1998 championship, when he won his second All-Ireland senior medal and an All-Star.
(© Ray McManus, SPORTSFILE)

9 August 1992 witnessed one of the great individual displays when Down's Gerard McGrattan, pictured above during the 1998 Ulster championship, starred against Cork in the All-Ireland semi-final. (© Damien Eagers, SPORTSFILE)

Tony Keady playing for Galway in 1990, a year after the 'Keady Affair' had convulsed hurling. (© Ray McManus, SPORTSFILE)

Cork hurler Eamonn O'Donoghue in action against Tipperary's
Paddy Williams in Semple Stadium during the 1980 Munster championship.
(© Ray McManus, SPORTSFILE)

'I was born to hurl. It was my
profession, just something
I wasn't paid for,' admits iconic
Kilkenny hurler DJ Carey,
pictured above in 2001.
(© Ray McManus, SPORTSFILE

Sam's for the Hills: Anthony Molloy lifts the Sam Maguire after captaining his side to All-Ireland glory in 1992. Molloy believed it was his destiny to lead Donegal up the steps of the Hogan Stand.
(© Ray McManus, SPORTSFILE)

Peter Canavan gathers his thoughts before lifting the Sam Maguire for Tyrone for the first time in the county's history after the 2003 final victory over Armagh.
(© Brendan Moran, SPORTSFILE)

Kerry legend Mikey Sheehy in action against Tyrone during his last All-Ireland final, in 1986. Mikey, one of the greatest forwards of all time, collected his eighth All-Ireland medal that day. (© Ray McManus, SPORTSFILE)

When Ciarán Whelan retired after 14 years in a Dublin jersey, he was acknowledged as one of the finest footballers of the modern era. Tributes pointed to his 'high fielding, acceleration on the ball, power in possession and ability to kick accurately off either foot when travelling at full pace'. (© Oliver McVeigh, SPORTSFILE)

have been all flair and style but they were all great men and great leaders.'

Michael won his first of four county medals with the Banagher club in 1987 and also collected a Leinster title with his club-mates in the 1993–94 season. On the national stage, he first came to prominence as a member of the Offaly minor hurling squad in the mid-1980s. He won Leinster and All-Ireland honours at minor level in 1986, the same year as he made his senior inter-county debut.

Three Leinster senior titles followed in 1988, 1989 and 1990. However, on each occasion Offaly came up short in the All-Ireland semi-final. Michael was a member of the Offaly team that won the county's one and only League title in 1991. However, a deltoid ligament injury continued to cause problems. For two hard years he played through the pain barrier for club and county. 'They were the peak years of my career but the injury just wouldn't go away. It was an unbelievably frustrating time. The ankle gave me serious bother. You begin to doubt yourself and managers begin to doubt you and lose trust in you. It was a horrible time.'

Former Limerick player Eamonn Cregan guided Offaly to All-Ireland glory in 1994 and while Duignan saw action from the bench – coming on for Daithí Regan – the victory left him with an empty feeling. He was far from happy with the manager after Cregan had failed to pick him for the final against Limerick, particularly after he had made a huge impact as a sub in the semi-final against Galway. As far as Duignan was concerned, he had done enough to cement his place.

'Ten minutes into the Leinster final against Wexford my ankle snapped. I could feel the blood flowing into my ankle. The pain was unreal but I played the entire game. I was unable to train for the semi-final but thought I did really well when I came in the second half and was confident that I would make the team for the final. And I have to admit I was shell-shocked when Cregan told me I wasn't playing. In fairness to him he came to me beforehand to tell me his reasoning. He wanted to use me as an "impact" sub. I wasn't happy. I sat in the car park with Martin Hanamy across the road from O'Connor Park in Tullamore with all sorts of emotions going through my head.

'Martin was a friend, clubman and team captain. I was thick; I told him I wasn't going to go to the final. I was like a baby, which is not my style. To his credit Martin listened to my rant. It took him a while but he calmed me down and he encouraged me to join the rest of the lads for a meal after training. I was hurt but I got on with it.'

He is frank and forthright about his relationship with Cregan: 'I would have had a difficult relationship with Eamonn Cregan from all that went on with my injuries. I was frustrated with him and he, I felt, was frustrated with me. He brought me on with 15 minutes to go. I scored a point but I can honestly say that was the turning point in my career. That afternoon I decided to sort my injury out once and for all.'

Four years later and injury free, Duignan realised his dream and played a starring role in Offaly's All-Ireland success over Kilkenny – scoring his side's first and last points. And he finished off the year in style, winning his first All-Star.

The success of that infamous 'sheep in a heap' team has gone down in Offaly legend and GAA folklore. They were the first team to successfully come through the 'back door'; their epic three-match saga with Clare and referee Jimmy Cooney's faux pas where he blew full-time early will always be mentioned when great hurling games are talked about.

And then there was Babs Keating's outburst against his own team after the Offaly side he managed had been beaten in the Leinster final. 'People say Kilkenny hammered us in the Leinster final. They got two late goals from frees but it just didn't happen for us on the day. We hurled alright but it was one of those flat days when nothing happened for us.'

Minutes after the game, Keating let loose. He tore into Offaly. He compared the team to 'sheep running round in a heap'. The players were outraged. 'I think the natural inclination of Babs is, "Well, they're bet [*sic*] now and it's not my fault, it's someone else's fault." If he said what he felt to us in the dressing-room we might have been able to take it. It blew up and went from there. And that was the last time Babs was ever involved with Offaly.

'But Babs couldn't help putting the boot in at every opportunity and in his column in the *Sunday Times* he kept having a go saying that from 8–15, "Offaly didn't have it." He just wouldn't give up.'

The Offaly County Board wasted no time in finding a replacement for Keating. Three days after the Tipp man's tirade, Galway school teacher Michael Bond took charge of the Offaly team.

'We'd never heard of him. I remember Joe Dooley saying that he heard from someone in Galway that Bond had trained rugby in New South Wales. After the session he told us he was a school principal in Loughrea, he had 550 pupils; it was a great school and brilliantly run. He then told us we were great hurlers and that we were the best team in Ireland. Straight away he was blowing us up and we couldn't wait to get back playing hurling. We had ten weeks with him and we trained fifty-two times in the seventy days we were together.

'It was all back-to-basics stuff. In fairness to Babs our physical condition was fantastic. Babs brought in Johnny Murray, an army trainer who lived in Leixlip. Physically we were in tremendous condition but in hindsight we needed sharpening up. When Bond came he could see that and concentrated much more on ball work and drills. And combined with the stamina we had built up, it brought us to a peak. He also brought great man-management, enthusiasm and confidence back to the panel.

'After the Babs debacle a lot of the lads were totally deflated and if you run lads down and constantly criticise then you're not going to get much out of them. Players need reassuring, need mollycoddling and at times need a bollocking. Bond told us we had plenty of ability, plenty of talent and told us to go out and express ourselves in the way he knew we could.'

His formula worked and Offaly were crowned All-Ireland champions in the autumn of 1998.

The morning after the day before, and Michael Duignan wakes up in his room in the Burlington Hotel. The Liam McCarthy Cup is perched on the table beside the television. Duignan takes in the enormity of the occasion. 'That feeling and that sensation that Monday morning will live with me forever. At last all those years and hours and hours of training were worth it. It just did not get any better than that.'

Two years later, the Cats got their revenge and that 2000 defeat to Kilkenny was Duignan's last time as a player in Croke Park; the following year he announced his retirement from inter-county hurling. 'I was travelling from Listowel to Birr for training when I got this blow out. The car went across the road and I was lucky not to have been killed. It was a miserable winter night and I made my way to Limerick and booked into Ryan's Hotel on the Ennis Road. My body was shaking. I reflected on what happened and rang Edel and said I was packing it in. Seán was only a young lad and Brian was just a few months old. I'd had 15 great years playing hurling and now was the time for the family. Michael Bond left the door open but there was no turning back.'

Retirement was a hard reality. No more training, no more matches. The dressing-room banter with the lads gone forever. Edel's support and understanding provided a reassuring base. 'Inter-county players have to be selfish and I was no different. Club and county meant everything to me. It's all about you. It wasn't easy for her, especially in the early years. Training three nights a week and then games at weekends. Edel never complained. She was particularly strong after I retired.

'Here I was after 15 years of hurling and now with nothing to occupy my time and now I wanted to let my hair down. That was more of it and, for her, there was never a big deal. You hear stories from lads getting hassle from their wives or girlfriends but I can honestly say Edel was so supportive of me. She was also great friends with the lads on the team. She had their trust. She had a terrific mindset. All of her friends would say Edel was fierce loyal, discreet and honest. I don't think I ever heard her say a bad word about anybody. Whereas a lot of us are very quick to make up our minds when we meet someone, Edel would give everyone a chance, she took everyone on their merit.'

The void left by Edel's passing has been filled by Michael's love for all things associated with Gaelic games. Recognised as the country's top hurling analyst he has just finished another season of hurling championship punditry for RTÉ.

Duignan loves the media work and is no stranger to controversy. He has landed himself in hot water many times with his comments and criticisms. His direct style has won him as many detractors as fans.

'I call it as I see it and sometimes I get myself in hot water. I've been accused of being pro Kilkenny. Bullshit. The fact is they've won seven of the last ten All-Irelands with one of the greatest teams of all time. I can't help that. It's a fact. Supporters from other counties mightn't like it but Kilkenny have the medals to prove it. I've great respect for everyone who hurls at county level. Like anything in life you might like some lads more than others due to their style of play but you try not to personalise anything. And as I say to people, "It's only my opinion," they don't have to like it or agree with it.

'I always try not to be over-critical of individual players but many of the modern players are immature and childish when it comes to criticism. They are not able to take it, and go into a sulk if you say anything about what they've done on the field. I'll be the first to admit that I was no angel on the pitch but I was also prepared to take whatever criticism or punishment that came my way.

'I'll always fight my corner when they approach me and a lot of them do. I've no problem with that. If I see a dirty play or cynical tactics I call it. I always come to games with a clean slate. I prepare nothing and never come with an agenda. I am always conscious of the fact that these guys are amateur and you don't want to slate anyone. But at the same time you have a duty to the GAA and to the thousands of people who are attending and watching the match at home. It's my duty to make the call and it would be remiss of me if I failed to bring something to the attention of the viewer who had just seen the incident themselves.

'There is too much "cute-hoorism" in some sections of the media and here I'm including past managers and players alike. There's no point going on television and radio panels if you're not prepared to call it straight.'

The treatment of referees by the Croke Park authorities is also another bugbear of Duignan's. The game he loves has evolved since he was winning All-Ireland medals in the '80s and '90s and he has great empathy for the men in black whose job it is to keep a handle on hurling today. And the mere mention of referee assessors gets him visibly animated.

'You have these referee assessors sitting up in the stand who are making a mess of the game. He's up there ticking boxes and will call the referee to book over some technical nonsense or some other bullshit. What people want in hurling is the bad stroke and cynical play punished. A lot of referees now, because they are been assessed, are looking for the lad who takes four and half steps. All technical crap. Hurling is such a fast and spontaneous game you need to ref it the same. You can't have a lad blatantly fouling or acting the eejit. You need to deal with the foul play and deal with it early and let the lads know you're in charge. There's no consistency. You don't know from one ball to the other if there's going to be a free.'

During his playing career and laterally as a GAA pundit he has seen many great players but, for Duignan, Kilkenny's Henry Shefflin stands head and shoulders above all. 'For what he has done and won and what he's continuing to do on the hurling field you would have to put Shefflin on top of the pile. I just can't see how there could have been a better hurler than him. And while there are some outstanding modern day hurlers only Joe Canning has the potential to challenge Shefflin's greatness.

'Looking back at my time I can categorically say that the '90s as an era will stay as the greatest decade of all. The Offaly team of the '90s, even though we only won two All-Irelands, was a very special team. The '90s was a very competitive era. You had Cork, Tipp, Kilkenny, Offaly, Wexford and Clare winning All-Irelands and then you had Waterford and Limerick with brilliant teams in the '90s who didn't make the breakthrough. They were so unlucky to have been around when so many teams were at their peak of their power. In Offaly we had Brian Whelahan, all the Dooleys, Johnny Pilkington, Kevin Kinahan, Kevin Martin, John Troy, Hubie Rigney and Martin Hanamy. We'll never see the likes of those players again in Offaly.

'You look at DJ Carey, what a talent. Joe Cooney, another unbelievable hurler. Willie O'Connor, all the Clare lads, the Lohans, Seánie McMahon, Jamesie O'Connor while Tipp were blessed with Pat Fox and Nicky English. It was a special time for hurling.'

Today, if not playing or training with his local club Ballinamere, Duignan is traversing the roads of west Offaly and east Galway on the way to Portumna where he was appointed trainer to the Galway champions in 2010. Hurling, whether it's underage, junior, intermediate or senior, is his passion but he is worried about the game's future. The decline in the standard of hurling in the perceived stronger counties is of most concern.

'The hurling championship is now between five or six counties but has it ever been any different? It used to be three. Most of the history of the GAA it was Kilkenny, Cork and Tipp. Some might see this as progress and people are talking about hurling in the weaker counties.

'However, I think we have to be really concerned about the other so-called stronger counties. Offaly, Wexford, Clare and Limerick are traditional hurling counties but they are under severe pressure. The standards in these counties both at club and inter-county level are dropping. Alarmingly so. As I see it one of the big contributory factors for the decline is the All-Ireland championship. It has taken over. For the last number of years in most counties in Ireland they might play a match before the county starts and they might not play again until August. This situation is absolutely crazy.

'The standard of the club game throughout the country has dropped dramatically. It's now turning into a social game. When I played club hurling it was serious stuff and when you went back from the county the players were preparing for that. You might have been away with Offaly for a few months but the lads back at the club in Banagher weren't sitting on their arses doing sweet feck all when we were away. There was no welcome on the mat when you came back into the dressing-room from your efforts on the inter-county scene.

'Apart from a few clubs throughout the country some of the modern club hurlers couldn't care less. They'll use any excuse now not to play – weddings, christenings, stags, hens, any auld kiss-me-arse excuse and they are gone for the weekend and as a result players are not developing up through the ranks. Years ago many counties might find a lad in the club championship who was a late developer. It's not happening any more. Now if a lad doesn't make it through the county minor route, he will, more than likely, never make it as an inter-county player. The intensity in most of the club matches is not there anymore.'

The solution? Let's start with the All-Ireland championship itself. 'It's not an easy solution but the championship needs to be condensed. Starting in May and not finishing until the middle of September is just crazy. That's four months of the prime time of the year. Bigger counties are able to play their club championships through the summer but most other counties put everything on hold until the inter-county team is out of the All-Ireland. I know it's not easy but more club matches must be played during the summer.

'Players going into the county set-up should be the finished article. They should need some fine-tuning and they're ready for step up to inter-county. In many counties now it's taking two or three years. In one way a lot's been done but you have to think some of it is misplaced. It's not easy solution. We're talking about promoting hurling in Leitrim and Donegal but we want to be very careful not to take our eye off the bigger picture.

'A lot of the coaching is misplaced. Some of the modern coaching is taking some of the natural ability out of the game. When we were kids we did bit of ground hurling and played matches and developed as you went along. You can't argue that the modern players are not fit. They are incredibly fit and expertly toned but for many of them their basic hurling skills are not great.

'I'm talking about counties that have won All-Irelands in the last 15 or 20 years. Wexford are going very poorly, Clare and Limerick were up there. Even look at Cork, these bunch of lads have been on the go a long time but there doesn't seem to be much coming through. If you take three or four of them out of it, who are going to be going in the next year or two, you'll wonder where they will be.

'The easy option it is to blame the County Board that they haven't the proper structures in place. There's a lot of stuff going on. There's development squads, there's coaching in every club but you have to ask what are they actually doing.

'What sort of coaching are they doing? What I find if I go to an underage match the minute the game starts there is someone shouting at the kids, "Raise it, pull this way, and pull that way." That's no good. Sure how are they going to learn? How are they going to develop leadership? How are they going to develop decision-making if you don't let them.

'Kids must be allowed to find their own level. Let them go for a ball and give them three options, rise it, pull on it or get it and pass it. They have to develop this themselves and the only way they can do that is create an atmosphere where they are not under severe pressure to express themselves. They have to be allowed to find their own level. I would be the first to say there is no miracle solution to the problem. Hurling is a simple game but you have to master the basic skills. You have to stay at it, but if a young lad comes to 12 years of age and he doesn't enjoy it or is being forced to play, he'll be gone. You'll lose him forever.

'I think lot of the coaching is misdirected. It's not real; it's cones and power points. It's not a situation you're going to be in during a match. I'd prefer to see the coaching through the matches. Yes, you do drills for speed work, skills and ball work but really, players should be doing that on their own anyway.

'Should every county in Ireland be playing hurling and given the opportunity to play hurling? The fair answer is they should be but is there any point? The answer is probably there isn't. But you'd be shot for saying it.'

At one stage he was all for every county being given the equal opportunity to play hurling and football. After his retirement he took charge of the Meath senior hurling team in 2001. During his time there the Royal County managed a dramatic Leinster championship victory over Laois. They even put it up to Offaly but Duignan's brief love affair with Meath hurling ended when the County Board refused to accede to his request to postpone some football championship matches just 24 hours before the hurlers were due to play Antrim in a crucial National Hurling League clash.

'I hold my hand up now and admit that it's nearly impossible to be successful in hurling and football in the modern day. OK, Cork have a huge population and Dublin and Galway are huge counties and Offaly has the tradition in that they can keep both codes going but look at Kilkenny.

'They are never going to be a football team so they don't waste their resources. Tyrone are the same. Of course you must acknowledge that there are genuine hurling people in these counties that love the game but resources are finite. The warning signs are there.'

* * *

The bouncy castle is long gone; the boys have grown out of their confirmation clothes. The first anniversary Mass held only painful memories. Seán has started secondary school in Coláiste Choilm in Tullamore; Brian is now in fourth class.

The little wooden cross up in Durrow cemetery has been replaced with a beautiful marble headstone. The evenings are closing in; Christmas is not too far away.

Michael Duignan is sitting at the kitchen table helping Seán with his maths. Brian is outside pucking the ball against the side wall. A wooden plaque erected by Edel to display all the medals Michael won, but most importantly that the kids won, hangs in the kitchen.

Under it is a handmade card made by Seán and Brian's classmates in Durrow National School. They gave it to them the day their mother died. On yellow background there are four initials. All in caps, they spell out the name of their late mother.

E: extraordinary person.
D: delightful artist.
E: elegant lady.
L: loving mother .

In the hallway there's a family photograph, taken at Durrow Church on the occasion of Brian's first Holy Communion. A statue of Our Lady is beside.

Two candles flicker to signal a breeze is coming from the front door.

Every night when they are home together, the Duignans light a candle in memory of a loving wife and a doting mother. Edel is buried just a mile away. She will never be forgotten. Time moves on but her memory remains.

Michael Duignan's best days on the field are behind him but, at 42, the greatest challenge of his life is still before him.

Bernard Flynn

Kieran Shannon, *Sunday Tribune*

Bernard Flynn saw every hour that Tuesday night, just like he had the night before. As the pain shot through his every fibre, forcing him to grit his teeth and grab the monkey pole above his bed in Mount Carmel Hospital, he reminded himself: 'I'm one of the lucky ones.'

He thought of Jimmy Stynes, who he befriended on the Compromise Rules tour Down Under in 1990 and who for ten years would visit him and Madeline in Mullingar every Christmas, staying over in their house for days. Now Jimmy, one of the world's great gentlemen and specimen, was fighting cancer and a brain tumour at only 43; how Jimmy would love to only have a hip operation, followed by a knee replacement, to put up with.

Flynn's mind also raced back to the funeral of his close friend, Edel Duignan, wife of Michael, who the big C claimed at just 41 years of age a few months earlier; how Edel suffered and how she would love to trade places with him now. He spared a thought for Eamonn Coleman, who he'd often have some tea and a laugh with over lunch when the soul of Derry football used to work on the sites of Mullingar, and for John Kerins and Mike McCarthy from Cork, who denied him an All-Ireland and who he denied All-Irelands before they all realised too late it was only just a game.

Other thoughts would flash through his mind, briefly

tormenting him. Why didn't he get this operation done a few years ago? Was business really that thriving that he'd keep putting it off and instead take up to ten tablets just to play a round of golf? Was his business really struggling that much, with the value of all his properties falling through the floor, that he couldn't afford to take a few months out for fear it would completely sink?

Why did he take all those injections to the hip to play in and win all those Leinster and All-Ireland finals? Or that jab to the ankle playing for Ireland Down Under in 1990; was winning the series and being its leading scorer worth it now? What on earth possessed him to come back after '92 when doctors said he wouldn't walk again after his knee was made shit or after he was the victim of a hatchet tackle playing for the club? Was hobbling back to win another three counties with the Shamrocks really worth it . . . ?

Then he thought of Edel again. And of Gráinne Keigue, another friend that was taken away far too soon. And of his wife Madeline and his three kids. 'I'm one of the lucky ones.'

The week before he went in for the operation Dessie Farrell called. 'Have you insurance?' Thankfully, Flynn was able to answer in the affirmative. Way back in the day playing for Meath when the injuries were starting to mount up, Gerry McEntee strongly advised him to take out and keep up his health insurance; he'd need it. As he grimaced at the ceiling, Flynn thought of all those old warriors from the quiet fields and killing fields of the '80s and '90s who needed it but didn't have it – or the inter-county medals to show for their battle wounds either. He had the medals, the All-Stars, the plaudits – and the health insurance for the hip operation. A lot of poor bastards out there hadn't.

He thought of some sad bastards as well, for at least in his eyes that's what they are. He'd just read the paper to learn there were counties objecting to Croke Park's decision a few days earlier to finally recognise the GPA and the player welfare schemes Dessie and the boys intend to roll out. Dessie had visited him in hospital. No past or present officer of the Meath County Board had. Nobody from 'Of One Belief' called in either. 'There'll be more like me,' thought Flynn, 'and Dessie and Christy Cooney are trying to do something for them. Then those self-righteous boys object to it. Pathetic.'

The third night after the operation Flynn managed to get some sleep, and after waking up at 5.45 the following morning, he again reminded himself of how lucky he was to be alive. His surgeon, Dr Kieran O'Rourke, brother of his old friend Colm, had told him the harder he worked at the start of his rehab, the better it would be for him. So did Seánie Walsh, his old room-mate from the GAA legends golf tours whom he had shared a few pints with the previous Saturday night after they'd been at the Ireland–South Africa rugby game in Croke Park. Seánie had his hip replaced a good few years earlier and was now in mighty form. So once he awoke that Thursday morning in November 2009, Flynn did some programmed exercises in his bed before somehow manoeuvring his way off the bed and completing 20 laps of the corridor on his crutches.

We often think of him merely as a member of one of the greatest full-forward lines ever, just one partner in the firm that was Flynn, Stafford and O'Rourke, but never as a great player in his own right. Keener observers tend to view him as exactly that.

The night before Flynn went in for that hip operation, Martin McHugh, who went through the same torture himself 18 months earlier, sent Flynn a lengthy and touching text message. It was prompted primarily out of empathy but out of a great deal of admiration too. In 1990 he was on a Donegal team that played Flynn's Meath in an All-Ireland semi-final. In the same game Flynn cracked his chestbone yet stayed on to score 2–2, the difference between the teams. He was a lethal finisher, able to kick goals and points off both feet. He was sharp, he was smart and, boy, was he brave. McHugh's measure of a player is how much he stands out for his club and in his eyes the fact Flynn was able to move to Mullingar and win four county titles on the trot for the local Shamrocks club was one of the great individual achievements of any forward of modern times.

Ned Moore, the former Westmeath footballer, soldiered with Flynn throughout all those campaigns. He knows how the general public tend to view Flynn – the tanned pretty boy on *The Sunday Game* with the gelled hair, Meath's answer to Cork's Tony Davis, and on the field a bit of a shaper too. 'Nothing was further from the truth,' says Moore. 'He had the biggest heart I know. He had to withstand more hardship than any player but never shirked a battle. Football was a different game in those days. There was a lot of cynical fouling, cheap, dirty hits, yet he was never intimidated.

'After we won the county in '92, we were playing down in Aughrim in the Leinster club championship. Bernard had scored something like 1–4 when just after half-time I saw him in a heap on the ground at the far end of the pitch. I still remember visiting him in Navan Hospital the following week. The ligaments had snapped to such a state they found them halfway down his shin and halfway up his thigh. The knee cap had been smashed in umpteen places. The doctors said he wouldn't walk again. Six months later he was back playing. He was only hobbling about the place and still players couldn't mark him.'

Flynn was no angel himself; he'll accept that. Indeed he could be downright saucy. He recalls the 1991 Leinster final against Laois when he was being marked by Tommy Smyth, a team-mate and brother-in-law of Flynn's best man and business partner, Mick Dempsey. Only two days before the game the three of them had lunch together, as they routinely would. When that Saturday came all cordiality, all civility, was suspended.

'Leo Turley got this great point under the Hogan Stand into the Hill 16 goal to put them two up early on. Tommy did this little jig and said in my face, "We have ye now, youse hoors ya!" I wasn't getting the ball so I slipped out to centre-forward, got this ball, dished off to Jinxy [David Beggy] and he got the goal that changed the match. I ran back in, went straight up to Tommy's face and said, "You're not f***in' laughing now, you hoor ya!" Bang! He thumped me and got put off. The rumour was I spat in his face. I didn't. But I was right up in his face.'

He remembers another Leinster final, against his old friends the Dubs and getting a few clips out the field from the likes of Tommy Carr and their new half-back Keith Barr. With his blood boiling Flynn couldn't resist referring to the rookie's skin condition and indulging in some tasteless verbals. Flynn at the time was a sales rep for Tennent's and for months later he'd walk into pubs around Dublin and be dressed down by publicans, telling him, 'That's an awful thing you called young Barr.' These days Carr and Flynn coach the same primary school team together while he has raised over €1m for charity with Barr a fixture at all those gigs, yet still Flynn winces at the memory of his antics that day.

Every now and then he'll also twist at night thinking of his first game back from that horrific injury down in Aughrim. It was a challenge match against Clare, there was a big crowd there to see his return, and when his marker started with the digs and the verbals, Flynn turned round and split the young fella's nose and mouth. He can still see the kid's blood and the stretcher carrying him off.

That's how it was back then, though; that's how football moulded him. He was a product of football's killing fields, a member of the old great Meath team.

He recalls one night in Páirc Tailteann in the lead-up to the four-game saga against the Dubs in '91. 'We'd had a team meeting a few nights earlier. Boys had agreed that training had gone slack. Mick Lyons said we'd gone too soft. So this night we were training and I sidestepped Mick when he gave me this feckin' awful dirty belt. We exchanged words and I said to myself, "If that happens again, I'm going to pull." Anyway, Mick did it again and I turned around and hit him as hard as I could. Next thing, all I could see was blood. I spent the rest of that training session looking around, left, right and centre. I genuinely had a fear that I was going to wake up in hospital.

'I kept out of Mick's way for the rest of the training session. He never said a word, just let the blood flow down his nose. But I remember going into the dressing-room after and there was hardly a word spoken. I was thinking to myself, "You're fighting for your life here." I went into the showers and it was like something from *Midnight Express* with the steam rising and everything. I positioned myself so that if anyone came in, I could see them. Next thing, Mick walks in, and I swear to God, I clenched my fist and said to myself, "If he pulls, I'll pull first."

'What does Mick Lyons do? He put his arm around me. "That's the sort of stuff we f***in' need!" After me splitting him! I said, "Mick, I didn't mean to split you but it's just you hit me . . ." He said, "Don't worry about it. It's only blood." With that I undid my fist, finished my shower and when I walked out all I could see was Mick showering away, all blood and shampoo.'

That was Mick Lyons. That was Meath. That was football back in those days. Flake hard, no hard feelings.

That philosophy could even extend to the opposition. When Flynn thinks back to his playing days, the memories and friendships shared with opponents are treasured as much as those with team-mates.

He tells the one about himself and Dave Synnott. On weekdays Dave worked alongside Flynn as a sales rep with Tennent's. On Saturdays he and his wife Marie would often go for dinner with Flynn and Madeline. Then on Sundays he played for Dublin.

The week before the 1988 Leinster final, their sales manager in Tennent's had this great idea. After the game on the Sunday their customers and clients and a whole range of big shots would be able to meet and greet both Dave and Bernard in Meagher's in Ballybough.

'We were the two guests of honour. After a Leinster final! After a f***ing Leinster final! Listen to this; this is a true story. Madeline and Marie go to the game together, watch the game together up in the stand. And who's marking me that day, only Dave. Two mates marking each other but it's Dublin and Meath and the two of us feckin' hate each other. Now, Dave was a brilliant wing-back – very good on the ball, speedy – but Dublin were short a few corner-backs so they put Dave on me. It was like putting Paul Curran on Mickey Linden in '94; I couldn't understand it, but that was Dublin back then; they did a lot of things we could never figure out. Dave had marked me for a bit in that year's League final as well and I'd got a few scores, so his dander was up and he hit me the dirtiest belt in the feckin' yoke.

'That wasn't his style and I said it to him but then he did it again so I threw back the dirtiest elbow into his face, as hard as I could. And what happened, and it was totally unfair, but as he's punching me back, blood streaming out of his nose, the ref turns around, catches him hitting me and he's sent off.

'We go on to win the game but up in the stand Madeline is crying along with Marie. After the game the two of them show up in Meagher's along with all the publicans and the crowd but no sign of Bernard and Dave. Then I show up. One thing about Meath in Seán Boylan's time, it was sacrilege to miss a team meal or team meeting, but that evening I said, "To hell with the Meath set-up; I better square things up with Dave." So my boss in Tennent's is wondering where the hell I've been, Boylan is wondering where the hell I am, the two women are giving me the daggers while Dave is clearly pissed off because there's no sign of him. And for hours there's no sign of him. Then he shows up and he's in a desperate state. The clients and all the big heads from work are all long gone; the only reason he's there is because Marie is still there, and at first he's very cool, thick as a double ditch with me, understandably so.

'Then he comes over, puts his arm around me, we shake hands and make up. The four of us are the last people to leave the pub; close the place. The next day is a bank holiday Monday, I'm doing promotional work for Tennent's in a pub called Gibney's and who comes in on his day off unannounced to give me a handout? Dave Synnott. The day after losing the Leinster final! After being sent off in a Leinster final! After me having split him!'

They still hear from each other. Dave now lives in Wexford where he's good friends with Liam Dunne. A while back Flynn learned Dunne had been a huge admirer of Boylan's first great Meath team so Flynn posted him down an old Meath jersey, a gift which Dunne reciprocated by presenting him with a signed hurley of his. Just last year Dunne and Synnott were back in Dunne's house after a few pints when they called Flynn up for a chat. An hour later they were still yapping away, just like that night in Maher's all those years ago.

He always knew they had something special in Seán Boylan but how special, only after the operation he knew.

Flynn is a big admirer of Mickey Harte and long ago spotted the similarities between the Tyrone maestro and the one from Dunboyne, but he shook his head when he read that extract from Harte's book about Cavanagh's inability to start against Cork in the 2009 All-Ireland semi-final. 'Cavanagh nearly single-handedly won Tyrone the [2008] All-Ireland. Boylan wouldn't dream of criticising one of his players in public like that.'

He had a way of seeing right through his players and handling it accordingly. 'I remember coming into training the Tuesday night after we'd won either a league or Leinster,' says Flynn, 'and Boylan knew I had not seen bed. He called me to the side, pulled me out of training and said in front of the team that I had an injury. Then he turned to me, "Go home, get some rest and never come into training like that again." I never did either out of respect for the way he handled that.'

They would clash though, and occasionally Flynn would feel he'd been treated unfairly. 'There would have been times,' says Flynn, 'when I felt the likes of Beggy, [Robbie] O'Malley and myself were picked on when the likes of Cassells, Lyons and O'Rourke were getting off with blue murder!'

One Saturday morning in training the pair of them even squared off. Gerry McEntee's brother, Andy, was marking Flynn, literally. 'Andy hit me and I said, "Andy, f*** off with that shit or I'll bust you." He did it again so I bust him. With that, Seán Boylan stopped the whole thing. "The pair of you, you're doing laps until we're finished!" We were only at the top of the corner flag when we started beating the shite out of each other again. What does Seán Boylan do? He stops the game again, runs over and hits Andy a belt into the stomach and gives me a belt into the stomach. I got a bloody fright. People don't realise how strong and tough Seán Boylan was. "The two of ye think ye're hard men!" he's roaring. "Alright, I'll take the two of ye on!" We didn't take him on. After that we were glad to do our laps.'

That was about the only time Flynn can recall Boylan advocating thumping and even then it was so McEntee and Flynn would stop thumping each other. 'In all my time in a Meath dressing-room,' says Flynn, 'Boylan never once told us to hit anyone.' He smiles. 'He never had to. He didn't have to tell Mick Lyons what to do, or Joe Cassells or Colm O'Rourke or Liam Harnan . . .'

Looking back, Flynn wishes Boylan had curbed that physicality somewhat. There were games when they seemed more interested in the man than the ball and it cost them All-Irelands. He's thinking especially of the '91 final against Down. They spent the first 40 minutes trying to soften Mickey Linden & Co. up before they started playing ball. By then they were playing catch-up.

Yet even in defeats like that there was an upside. There was something stoic, heroic about how they accepted it. They mourned together, healed together, stayed together.

'I look back on those Meath lads and you won't meet a more balanced, grounded bunch of lads in your life. You have to remember, we lost as much as we won – Leinster finals, All-Ireland finals, the lot – and it was a big thing for Seán Boylan how we conducted ourselves after we lost. Even after a league game we weren't allowed to moan. The only people we'd blame would be ourselves. That was coached into us. I see other managers now, crying and moaning at every turn, especially when they're beaten, detracting from their opponent's victory. That wasn't acceptable to Seán Boylan. We didn't moan, we got on with it, and that has definitely helped us in life. I know it has served me well when times have been hard these last few years.'

He first started taking cortisone shots for the hip around '87, '88. Before big games in Croke Park he'd skirt away from the rest of the team and head off to Malahide for his fix. Even then, before they were married, Madeline was telling him he was taking too many injections, too many tablets, for a man in his early 20s. But she didn't understand, he'd say to himself, and Seán Boylan didn't have to know. If Flynn didn't play, he'd miss out on winning. He'd miss out on playing the next day. Lining up to take his place were classy forwards like Mattie McCabe, Finian Murtagh and Liam Smyth; if fate had been a bit kinder to them, you'd never have heard of Flynn and Stafford.

'I look back on it now and I was probably too insecure, probably trying to prove myself too much. At that time we had some great leaders. Joe Cassells I think has eleven kids now, seven when he was playing, yet he wouldn't dream of missing a training session. Gerry McEntee was a surgeon, flying back from England and America without a word of complaint. Liam Harnan played in an All-Ireland final with a broken bone in his back. A broken bone in his back! So for me to get a jab to go out and play, I'd have kept it to myself. As it was some of the lads might say, "Ah, Flynn was moaning about a bit of pain." I actually suffered a lot more than I let on.'

His last game with Meath was in '94, the same year he helped them to a league, scoring two goals against Armagh in the final, but he was only 70 per cent of the player he was before the battle of Aughrim in '92. He now knows he came back too soon from too many injuries.

He can almost feel and hear Gerry McEntee on his shoulder:

'You feckin' eejit, Flynn! Why didn't you get the operation done years ago?!' It was McEntee who in '95 set up the appointment with Dr Pat O'Neill who told Flynn his career was over; if he played any longer he'd end up a cripple. It was McEntee who told him about insurance. He'd told him to get the hip replaced years ago too. Yet Flynn resisted.

He was a self-employed property investor. How could he take time off for the operation? In the boom years there was property to be snapped up, money to be made. After the crash he had the banks to talk to, a family to feed.

There was another kind of fear too. 'I just had a taboo about having a false limb in there at 44 years of age. It's grand at 74 going around with a false limb and being ready to hit the grave. My fear was, "Will I now need a second one at 54? A third at 64?" There was this weird, silly feeling inside me, "Jesus, if you go for that, you won't be a real man anymore." I'd think whether I'd be able to do certain things with the kids again. Could you fall and roll around the garden with them after playing football? Jump on the trampoline? Ski with them like we did before? But sure the way I was I couldn't do any of those things. I could barely put on my trousers.'

Looking back now it was a Faustian pact he had with football – play and win now, suffer later. Was it worth it? The question was put to him back in November 2009 as he lay up in his bed in Mount Carmel Hospital.

'First up, the way I am is my own fault. And umpteen county players have been here before me – the likes of Seánie Walsh, John O'Keeffe and so on. But I have to say when I think of the pain in the knee and the hip over the last few years, the fact I haven't been able to lift a golf club since May, that over the summer the kids had to put my socks and shoes on for me; I couldn't get up and down the stairs; if I'm being honest, the answer to your question is probably not. And I tell you, the pain I felt last Tuesday night my answer would have been definitely not. Christ, I thought I was going to die!'

That, though, was back in his darkest hour, when he was in the deepest pain. Six months later, after just completing his first round of golf in nearly a year, he felt differently. Yeah, it was all worth it. Sure, the pain was torture, but the winning was addictive and the craic and the memories were something else too. Rooming and partying with David Beggy. Enjoying the droll but sharp wit of men like O'Rourke and Harnan, the wisdom of Boylan. Where else would you want to be? What else would you want to do?

'I had a few complications after the operation but they've settled down now. My limp is gone and that severe arthritic pain is gone as well which is great. The only thing is my knee is exactly where my hip was two or three years ago. When the weather is cold the pain in the knee is dreadful but I'm not afraid to deal with it [that operation] when the time comes. I've learned a lot from this [hip] operation. You can't keep quenching fires, you can't keep running 100 miles per hour. I've learned to compartmentalise things. Leave your work and financial worries at the door before going home; leave it in a box. Maybe it takes until you're 43, 44 to really appreciate the simple things in life – wife, kids, friends.

'We're all going to be a bit more humble for this [property] crash. I know for myself, it's back to basics. My business probably needs a hip replacement. I made great money in the Celtic Tiger years and now every cent of it is gone. There's no doubt about it, this crash has put me back 15 years. We lost the plot as a country. I wasn't exactly extravagant – I'd have lunch here in the office – but I definitely took the eye off the ball. I overborrowed; took too much on. I'm not alone either. There are a lot of self-employed people in the GAA and in Middle Ireland that are now dangling outside the helicopter without any parachute.'

The operation and property crash underlined to him the need for a support network which is why he strongly applauded the negotiations and programmes that the GPA and Croke Park agreed to in the winter of 2009. After Tony Adams went public on his alcoholism, he would go around the dressing-rooms of England on behalf of the PFA, telling fellow pros his story and how there was help there for them if they needed. Flynn is convinced that the in-season no-drinking culture has created a binge-drinking culture and with it, at least one alcoholic in every inter-county dressing-room. There's probably a compulsive gambler there too. And very likely someone afraid of coping with their sexuality in such a macho environment, not having the courage and assuredness of a Donal Óg.

'Not all GAA lads are very confident or intelligent. I was lucky to have my insurance and know of a surgeon like Colm O'Rourke's brother. What about the average player who has no insurance? Who could he turn to in my situation? Players don't know everything about everything. A lot of lads have cried out for help from time to time and there hasn't been a helping hand there. There are very few Seán Boylans and Mickey Hartes out there, and then what happens if that manager is moved along?'

That is why Flynn accepted the invite to become a member of a GPA committee looking into welfare programmes for past and present players such as a proposed benevolence fund and counselling services. Even before the phone call came he'd observed that the players' body was dynamic, proactive, empathetic. By formally recognising them, Croke Park were embracing the same ethos.

'Christy Cooney I have to say has been a breath of fresh air. A few months into his presidency a few of us and our wives were invited to watch the Kerry–Meath All-Ireland semi-final in one of the corporate boxes. You had Seán Boylan, Graham Geraghty, Liam Hayes, a load of the Kerry lads. I was never in one of those boxes before. I got a shock going into it. Gerry McEntee said to me it was the first time that he felt really valued by the GAA. The wives really appreciated it. Just a little thing like a dinner and a good ticket.'

Flynn knows though that there are still too many County Boards that can be reactive, unwieldy, outdated, viewing the player as simply someone to help the county win, someone disposable. Who cares about you once you hand the jersey back? Or if you do hand it back? A whole change in mindset is required, Flynn believes. The 'lucky to wear the jersey' riposte no longer suffices. One of the jobs of a County Board and team management is to provide a life experience for young men that is worthy of time away from their loved ones and seeking or keeping down a job.

'In the GAA we have to look after our players and each other. Give business to each other. Give jobs to the players. The good young player coming out of college now; there's a real danger he's now going to head straight to Australia, America, London. It's going to be pretty poor to bad here for another while so County Boards will have to put a little structure in place to make sure these lads are looked after, in terms of jobs and the like, otherwise we're going to lose the best players we've never seen.

'A lot of GAA players were under pressure to go out and form their own business, cash in on their name. Inter-county players might be amateur but they're public property just like the pros. They're superstars one day, scapegoats the next and a lot of fellas struggle to deal with that. Who is there to help them? There has to be a facility in place that a player can turn to without having to spill his guts out to his manager and team-mates. People don't realise the pressure these lads are under. They should be afforded more respect, instead of being berated and knocked like they are. One thing a lot of players have to put up with is shite talk about them.'

Flynn is talking from experience. For years there was the rumour that he was run out of Laois after his and Mick Dempsey's business and personal relationship went sour. 'It was all bullshit. Mick and myself were running a bar and nightclub, we then agreed it was his patch, myself and Madeline got a few quid to buy a house, start our own business. That's all I wanted.' As recently as this past winter Dempsey, a vital member of Brian Cody's backroom team, was the guest speaker at a Meath GAA forum and refused to accept a cent because it was the county of one of his best friends.

'I played in two All-Ireland finals running a nightclub till five in the morning and then got a drive to come up from Meath, me with no sleep and these bags under my eyes. I couldn't open my mouth to the Meath lads, you suffered in silence a wee bit that way, but you took whatever work you could. I remember playing in the 1987 All-Ireland semi-final against Derry. I scored four points from play, went into work the next day and they got rid of me. I remember thinking, "Where do I go?" I probably regret not going to college, like a lot of GAA players of that time.'

Flynn recognises that in many ways the lot of the current player has improved since his day. They no longer are asked to flatten the hill of Tara. They have greater physio and medical backup. There'll be fewer and fewer players needing a hip replacement in years to come. But to make sure of it, he has this bit of advice for the kid thinking of taking that next injection to squeeze in that next game. 'Take responsibility for your own well-being because no one else will. If you're only half right, leave it and get it right. You'll play for longer.'

It's nearly time to leave. Before you go, you're struck by how chirpy his disposition and mood is. He talks enthusiastically about the 32 marathons in 32 days in 32 counties a couple of his friends are running for charity; the drapery business himself and Madeline set up in the summer of 2010; the chats himself and Seán Boylan had when they were both in hospital over the same winter; the primary school kids, including their own, that himself and Tommy Carr coach every week in Mullingar; the round of golf he got in last week, his first in nearly 12 months, and the GAA Legends All-Ireland charity golf tournament in Spain back in May that he organised. He loves that, time with old enemies that are now old friends.

To finish, he'll tell you about the Meath lads and the Cork lads. Twenty years ago they could barely stand the sight of each other. One January they both were staying in the same hotel complex in

Gran Canaria, and as Billy Morgan put it in his autobiography, 'there was a cold war' out there. Meath and Cork men would walk past each other without so much as a salute or how-do-you-do. About the only exceptions were when Liam Hayes and Larry Tompkins struck up a conversation one afternoon on a beach in Puerto Rico and then at night back in Playa del Ingles when Flynn and Madeline would break away from their own herd to have a few beers with Shea Fahy, Steven O'Brien and their partners. 'I tell you what, I was telling none of my teammates that I met with the Cork lads!' says Flynn. 'They'd walk by each other!'

Even at the time Mick Holden of Dublin would point out to them the childishness of their ways. 'Jaysus, lads,' he'd tell a few of them on that holiday, 'ye'll all be dead and there won't be a football in sight!' Flynn was actually back in the Canaries when Colman Corrigan phoned to tell him John Kerins had passed. Everything changed after that. In October 2009, Robbie O'Malley was the last of the Meath boys to walk up the aisle. There to witness him do it were all O'Malley's old team and his good friend, Anne Kerins, widow of John. The image of that night in the Mulranny Hotel in Westport will never leave Flynn. All of them laughing, all of them dancing, even Flynn with his dodgy hip, with not a football in sight.

He knew it then and he knows it now. He's one of the lucky ones.

Eamonn O'Donoghue

Diarmuid O'Flynn, *Irish Examiner*

INTRODUCTION

In your mind's eye, right now, picture the perfect hurler – what have you got? Silken touch, soft hands, absolute mastery of stick and ball; perfect athletic form, strong but mobile, an ability to move smoothly through the gears, accelerate sharply when necessary; artistry and the artiste.

From eras past we had the likes of Christy Ring, Eddie Keher, Jimmy Doyle, legends long established in GAA folklore; from today we think of King Henry, we think of the twin-named Eoin Kellys from Tipperary and Waterford, of the twin O'Connors from Cork, Ben and Jerry; before and after those, a galaxy of others – Nicky English, Jimmy Barry-Murphy, John Connolly, Jamesie O'Connor, and on and on, an almost endless list of gifted players, hurlers who didn't just make the ball talk, they made it sing like Ivan Rebroff, across nigh on five full scales.

We see those guys coming from a long way off, from the days when they were mere striplings at Under-12 but already making waves; men among boys, then giants among men, Joe Canning in Galway and Noel McGrath in Tipperary are the latest examples, starring on adult teams when they were still just raw teenagers. But what of all those others? What of all the hundreds and thousands of hurlers who have also won All-Ireland medals, who have played at the very top, and for a long time, but who never get that same recognition?

You know the *nostalagencia*, don't you, the lads for whom the only good days were the old days, when everyone and everything was incomparable – there will never be a hurler to even come near the incomparable Christy Ring, there will never be a GAA writer like the incomparable John D. Hickey, or Mick Mackey and Paddy Downey, or Lory Meagher and Carbery, or whoever you're having yourself from those truly incomparable days of the '30s, '40s and '50s. For those people, and alone among all sports, hurling reached its zenith back in those best of all days; they'll recall those golden times when men were men, when every hurler who ever wore the famous blood and bandage, or the black and amber, or the blue and gold, was a hurling genius, their likes never to be seen again.

Of course, they weren't all like that, not at all. Right through those decades, up to and including the present, there are also those hurlers who were more functional than fantastic, who did a job, albeit at the highest level, but who, almost as soon as they had left the stage, were forgotten, remembered for the most part only by their own.

Even among those, however, there were the guys no one thought would ever make it to the top. Again we notice them at an early age, but in this instance they stand out for all the wrong reasons. They are the long, gangly ones, so ungainly in their movement they seem to get in their own way, so awkward in their swing they're in danger of doing damage to themselves; or they're the small, pudgy ones, or the miserable skinny ones, or the ones all quiet and shy, or the ones all bombast and bravado. And yet from their ranks also can emerge a star, a top inter-county star. Such a one was Eamonn O'Donoghue from Blackrock and Cork, 'Ya-mon' as it's pronounced and as he's known in his native county.

At underage, he was barely noticed. 'Derry Cremin was the main man when I was growing up, a huge influence on me and on many a young hurler in Blackrock at that time,' he recalls. 'He suffered an injury himself at a relatively young age – playing soccer would you believe – which finished his career, but he became heavily involved with the Rockies. He was the chairman of the Juvenile section for years and under his guidance we won five minor county titles in the '60s, which became the foundation of all the success that followed at senior level through the 70s. A tremendous man, fantastic when it came to dealing with kids. There was never any kind of heavy criticism from Derek – if you played a bad match, he'd continue to encourage you, bring you along, and if we lost a match, it was no big deal, just back to the drawing-board. *Mol an óige agus tiocfaidh siad* – that was his philosophy, absolutely.

'Encouragement, that's how you improve kids, and long before there was any talk of sport psychology Derek had that ability, had it naturally – I owe him a lot. Four years in a row Blackrock won the Cork city and county minor championship, in 1966, '67, '68 and '69, and for the last year, 1969, I got on the Cork minor panel. I played in the Munster championship, but not in the All-Ireland (which Cork won, beating Kilkenny). I never played Under-21 for Cork, although in my last year, 1972, there was talk that I was going to be called up to the panel but nothing happened, and they were beaten by Clare in Munster.'

Later that year, however, there was consolation for Eamonn – 'I finished up as a sub for the senior team in the League, down in the Park.' And that's where it started, the inter-county career of an unlikely but much-loved hurling hero, a hero who, while he isn't one of its brightest stars, has fully earned his place in hurling's brightest galaxy. In his own words, this is Eamonn O'Donoghue's story.

THE CLUB-CRADLE

The club, of course, is where it all starts for every GAA player, and for those who eventually make the breakthrough to inter-county level – especially if you're not of those who are naturally most gifted – it helps if your club is doing well. Blackrock is the oldest club in Cork, actually predating the founding of the GAA

itself, formed in 1883 when it was known as Cork Nationals. Up
to 1931 and the emergence of Glen Rovers it was by far and
away the dominant club in Cork hurling, with 21 senior county
titles won at that stage. Then came 40 years of relative famine,
only two further titles (1956 and 1961), but just as Eamonn
O'Donoghue was entering the adult hurling arena, Blackrock
entered another golden era – the all-conquering '70s.

'That was a marvellous era for the club. We won five Cork
county senior titles in the '70s, five Munsters, and three All-
Irelands, in 1972, '74 and '79 – a real powerhouse. Even getting
on that Blackrock team was difficult – Cork also won four All-
Irelands in the '70s but we played them many times in challenge
matches during that era and ran them very close.

'My first year making the club team, 1973, we won the county,
went on to win the Munster, then the All-Ireland in 1974. That
was a tough one; we beat Rathnure in the final but only after a
replay. We drew in Croke Park, met them then in Fraher Park
in Dungarvan; we were five points down with eight minutes left
but won by four or five in the end. Danny Buckley was only
17 but he came on in that game and made a big difference. He
was very fast, and strong too, won a Munster Senior Cup medal
in rugby with UCC, on the wing. Played up till about '78, then
went to Dublin, working. But a marvellous talent.

'We had great players on that team, all over the field – Frank
Cummins, Ray Cummins, John Horgan, Frank Norberg, Paddy
Geary, Pat Moylan, Tom Cashman, Dermot McCurtain, John
O'Halloran, Donie Collins, Dave Prendergast and so on.'

Pause for a moment and look back through that list. Frank
Cummins won seven All-Ireland titles on the field at midfield for
Kilkenny, won another as sub, was still hurling so well towards the
end of his career that in the year of his final All-Ireland senior
success, 1983, he was named Hurler of the Year. Ray Cummins
(no relation of Frank) he man who revolutionised the full-
forward position, the man alongside whom Eamonn soldiered
for so many years with club and county – 'The best player ever

in that position, the most intelligent player I ever played with. So many qualities on the field, tremendous leadership, great reader of the game. He started off at half-back with the Rockies, at minor, and 'twas College (UCC) put him up to full-forward, and he transformed the position. From there, he controlled the game, brought everyone around him into play – a marvellous player. You played off him, always; if you were 40 yards from goal he'd call you – "Eamonn! You're not going to score goals from out there!"'

John Horgan, 'Blondie John', the long-striking corner-back, winner of five All-Irelands with Cork, Hurler of the Year in 1978; Tom Cashman, Dermot McCurtain, Pat Moylan, consummate hurlers all, multiple All-Ireland winners with Cork. They weren't all native to the famous Rockies, of course, but at the time it was customary in Cork for the better hurlers from smaller clubs to gravitate towards the 'big three' of Blackrock, the Glen or St Finbarrs. 'We had Jack Russell from Ballyhea, captained Cork in 1967, played midfield in the '73 county final – he gave us great service [Jack moved back to Ballyhea a year later, won county junior in 1976, county intermediate in 1980 and lost a senior county in 1984]; there was Eamon O'Sullivan from Mallow, and of course the three Kilkennymen in '73, Frank Cummins, Conor O'Brien and Dave Prendergast.

'I suppose with Frank already playing with us, any Kilkenny fella coming to Cork at the time would look to us, but you had a lot of different players coming to the three big city clubs that time. They were very dominant, and not just in Cork – they won every county senior title in the '70s, won every Munster title from 1971 to 1980, and won eight All-Irelands in a row, from '71 to '78. People used to come from all over the country to the Cork county final, and I can remember crowds of over 25,000 for a few of those games – a way bigger attendance than you see now. A lot of the focus today has moved on to the inter-county scene, which is unfortunate.'

At both club and county level it was a golden decade for

Cork, a period in which the city truly throbbed with hurling excitement, heated talk in the many pubs and clubs in the many little streets off 'Pana' – Patrick Street – of games just played or games just around the corner, a lot of slagging going on among supporters – and players – of the big three.

'There was fair rivalry alright, you'd always get the bit of banter, especially among the supporters. The club matches were very intense and if you were beaten, you were left to know all about it. I remember one year we lost to the Barrs, a game we should have won, to be honest – everything then went towards getting revenge the following year.'

Oddly enough, and though the Lee splits the city pretty much in half, with Blackrock and St Finbarrs on the south side, the Glen on the north, there was no real north–south fault-line. 'A bit maybe, with some fellas, but I never felt it, to be honest. The older fellas in the club alright, if the Rockies were beaten, well then they'd like to see the Barrs beating the Glen. I never felt that though. We didn't come into the city centre to socialise back then as much as they do nowadays – fellas from every part of the city are meeting in town now at the weekend, Blackrock fellas, Barrs fellas, the Glen, even Ballyhea fellas, from the country! They're all meeting up now around the city centre, a different scene altogether. Blackrock is no longer a small fishing village on the outskirts of Cork, that's for sure! We've broadened our base now, and the parish thing is almost completely gone in the city. Even with all the players who came from outside to play for us, it was still very much Blackrock parish when I was growing up, and if you were from the parish, you wanted to play with Blackrock. Now you have young fellas from different schools in the city playing with different clubs – that wouldn't happen back then. The parish rivalry was there, very strong, but it was a good rivalry too, healthy – we all had great respect for one another.'

THE COUNTY

On the inter-county stage, Cork too were thriving, five minor All-Ireland titles won in the '70s, four Under-21s, and eventually, four seniors, including the three-in-a-row of 1976, '77, '78. With things going so well for Eamonn with Blackrock it was only a matter of time before he came to the attention of the county senior selectors. As mentioned above, he first togged out for Cork seniors in 1972, in the League pre-Christmas, at a time when that competition was still played over two calendar seasons (winter/spring). Championship is where it's at, however, and here too, Eamonn made his mark. He was part of the famous three-in-a-row side, winning All-Ireland senior medals in '76 and '78, coming on as a sub in the final on both occasions. No caste lost there, of course; if the competition for places on the Blackrock team at the time was tough, for Cork it was cut-throat, and even an inside forward as effective as Eamonn O'Donoghue, as lethal on the goal-scoring front, was going to find it well-nigh impossible to disrupt the line of Charlie McCarthy, Ray Cummins and Seanie O'Leary.

As with the Kilkenny team of today, even being part of that side was a major achievement for any hurler, because they were a magnificently talented bunch. Unlike today's Kilkenny, however, they were almost a Hollywood cast, characters in every line, superb entertainers, dashingly cavalier in their play against the more pragmatic roundheads of today's all-conquering Cats. 'There was flamboyance in the team alright, and great camaraderie – Gerald McCarthy was a fierce character in the team, great man in the dressing-room, great man to rally a team, on and off the field. Gerald was a good man to have on your side, always there with a ready comment. Dermot McCurtain was another, when he came on the team, he was a fierce character as well, another Rockies man, as was John Horgan.

'Another man for the craic was Johnny Crowley, Mick Malone as well, Seanie O'Leary was another – looking back, they were all great fun, fierce characters. Everyone got on well, every fella had something to offer, in his own way, and there was a great dynamic in the group, always. Ah, we had great fun. A critical man in that era though wasn't a player at all – it was Kevin Kehilly. One of the most important men in any set-up is the trainer, and definitely, absolutely, Kevin was a marvellous addition. He had just graduated from Strawberry Hill, 1976, and was straight into the Cork set-up as trainer – that was a master move. He gelled very well with the players, but of course he was a fine hurler himself, and won a senior football All-Ireland with Cork in 1973.

'Cork were one of the first counties to have a qualified PE instructor in charge of the training – it wasn't just a case anymore of everyone doing the same training every evening, Kevin was able to pick out those who needed extra training in different areas, and go through that with them.'

Outside of the cauldron of the Munster championship Kilkenny, for any Cork hurling aficionado, are the one true rival. So it is with Eamonn O'Donoghue, and a measure of that rivalry was the attitude in Cork when it came to the All-Ireland final of 1978; completing the three-in-a-row wasn't what brought the pressure, he says – it was something else entirely.

'Beating Kilkenny in the final, that was the big carrot – Cork had beaten Wexford in the first two finals, but if you win an All-Ireland without beating Kilkenny, it's just not the same. Kilkenny are the team to beat, always, but beating them in an All-Ireland final to complete the three-in-a-row – that put the stamp on it.'

That put Cork in position to equal the feat of the legendary team of the early '40s, win four-in-a-row, but fate was to intervene. A selector for Cork for the three-in-a-row was the aforementioned Christy Ring, as much an influence off the field now as he had ever been on it for his beloved county. On 2 March 1979, however, the whole country was rocked with the news that Christy – still only 58, and a non-drinker, non-smoker all his life – had suffered a fatal heart-attack. A huge blow to his family and to hurling, and his funeral was a major national event, massive crowds bearing testimony to the legend of Christy Ring, a legend that will always endure.

Ring had been a central part of that original Cork four-in-a-row as a forward par excellence; now, however, as this new Cork side set out to equal that record, his absence was felt. 'I think it cost us, dearly. In 1979 there was a County Championship match between the Glen and the Barrs that was played only a couple of weeks before the All-Ireland semi-final against Galway, and that affected the training, had a very negative impact on preparations. I don't think it would have happened if Ring were alive, he wouldn't have allowed it to happen.

'The focus on Cork that year should have been directed towards winning the four-in-a-row – Christy would have made sure it was. He was central to Cork winning the three-in-a-row. He had tremendous hurling knowledge, a fantastic man in the dressing-room or on the sideline, very sharp. Just one illustration of his attention to detail: before the All-Ireland final of 1976, against Wexford, he went down to Kilkenny to see Paddy Johnson, the referee, in action. When he came back, he told us a few things, the most important of which was – "He doesn't mind a fella taking a few extra steps with the ball!" If you look at the video of that match you'll see that a few of our lads definitely took advantage of that bit of advice! A tremendous hurling man, great hurling brain; I only saw him play towards the very end of his career but I grew up on the legend – the hurley always in the cab of the truck, all of that. Then when I got to meet him – he became a neighbour of mine in Blackrock – I found him to be a very friendly man; a bit of a rogue at times though, loved a bit of fun.'

Four-in-a-row opportunity ended at the hands of Galway in the semi-final of 1979. That All-Ireland final of 1978 was to be the last time Eamonn would savour any such triumph, and in the All-Ireland finals of 1982 and '83, by which time he was a seasoned starter, Kilkenny got full revenge.

'It hurt, the first one especially – Cork were such hot favourites.

Maybe we got caught up in the whole thing, I don't know, but Christy Heffernan got those two goals in a minute before half-time and that was that – a lot of people say it wasn't a great game, and it probably wasn't. Nineteen eighty-three was a game we could have won, a lot of controversy over it. We were a bit unlucky, lost by only a couple of points, but we probably redeemed ourselves a bit after the previous year, when we were overwhelming favourites. Kilkenny have done that to Cork so many times over the years, pipped us by a few points – they seem to have some kind of hex over us. But I'd have an awful lot of time for Kilkenny hurling. They have a fierce pride in the county, that's a mark of them always, and you only have to read the first couple of paragraphs of Brian Cody's book to realise that.

'I met Brian many times on the field, at club [Brian Cody played with James Stephens] and county level – he was full-back for Kilkenny in '83. He was physically very strong, a good hurler too but very strong on the ball – hard, clean, very fair. There wouldn't be much conversation with him, but then the man in the corner made up for that – Fan Larkin! Fan had plenty to say, at all times. Fan is a tremendous character, but I believe his father before him was the same, and his son, Philly, is the same now.

'I remember one year in Nowlan Park, probably around the winter of '77, a League game, Cork were playing Kilkenny; the two teams were on the field, national anthem being played, no sign of Fan, who was named at corner-back for Kilkenny, marking me. Anthem over, we were getting ready to start the match, I was heading into the corner, when Fan comes running on to the field from the dressing-room – "Jaysus," he says, "I was sitting by the fire, wondering if I'd bother coming at all!" The first ball that came down our wing, BANG! He hit me a fierce wallop – I'll never forget it! "Did I hurt you, sonny?" he says. A fierce character, but a great man too. He was afraid of nobody, he told me, except maybe one – Gerald McCarthy. Maybe it was because Gerald wouldn't have had that much over him in size – Fan seemed to relish the challenge of marking big men [Eamonn is 6 feet 2 inches, around 14 stone]. He'd be in under you, his head under your arm looking up the field. But a great character, and a great man for the game.'

Begs the question, of course – which was the more difficult opponent for a big corner-forward, a big man like himself, an average-sized guy, or a small man, such as Fan? 'Probably the small fella – he'd be in under you, all around you, knocking the ball away from you. And he'd get all the breaks from the ref, because of his size – Fan wasn't slow to let the ref know if he thought he should have a free, there was an awful lot of guff out of him, always. But, as an opponent he was the most difficult I ever came across, very awkward. Pat Hartigan was also a marvellous player – at the opposite end of the scale to Fan, physically, a big man but a fine hurler. Very strong, a powerful man, but very clean, a ball player. A pity what happened to his eye that time, hit by a ball in training. At club level then, Denis Burns from the Barrs was a fine defender, very difficult to score against.'

THE END

Shortly after that All-Ireland final loss in 1983 Eamonn's inter-county career came to an end, but with no great fanfare. 'After we lost the All-Ireland final of '83 I played in the early League matches, before Christmas; my last match was below against Waterford, and after that, I heard no more. Justin McCarthy was there, Fr O'Brien [later Canon O'Brien, famed Cork manager], Tom Monaghan, not sure who else – doesn't matter. Brian Murphy [brilliant corner-back, the most honour-laden dual star in GAA history] also finished around that time. He was a Guard in Kilkenny, driving up and down to Cork a few times a week for years, over 90 miles each way on bad roads. You couldn't have asked for a more dedicated man, always there for training, very committed. A pity it ended like that, but that was the way; we both missed out then on 1984 and the centenary All-Ireland win in Thurles. Still, those were great days.'

Great days certainly, especially when you counted up the honours won, but surely also there had to be relief that the pressure of having to perform at that level was over? Or was he one of those lucky ice-cool cats who didn't feel such pressure? 'Ah you'd feel it alright, but I also enjoyed the day. A Munster final in Thurles, the atmosphere building up, the colour, the noise when you went on to the field – I enjoyed all that. You're out there in front of over 40,000 people, a great feeling. You'd be nervous enough before the match, but that was it.'

What about superstitions – did he have any? 'No, none I can think of anyway, but I did have a habit of going for a few pucks on the Saturday before championship games with Timmy Murphy, the Rockies goalkeeper – I was very friendly with Timmy. Training would finish on the Wednesday, you weren't supposed to touch a hurley then again till the game – that was the thinking of the time anyway. Throw away the hurley till Sunday so you'd really have an appetite for it on the day, but I liked to go for a few pucks on the Saturday. You had fellas who liked to sit in certain places in the dressing-room, beside certain others, or who liked to be the last to leave, or wear certain items of clothing, but I had nothing like that.'

TRIPS, FRIENDSHIPS, MEMORIES

It wasn't just the hurling itself of course, satisfying and all as that was. As an amateur sport, hurling offers much more than cups, medals, achievements on the field; it's also about friendship, making friends, building bonds that last lifetimes.

As a guy with a permanent twinkle in the eye, an extremely popular individual, so it was with Eamonn O'Donoghue. 'I went on three trips to America, a replacement All-Star one year and with Cork on two other occasions. And I played in Wembley, with Cork, in an annual hurling tournament that was played there at the time.' Did he score, become one of the few Irishmen to score a goal in Wembley in a Cup final? 'I can't remember, to be honest! But I do remember going into the dressing-rooms and the guy was telling us – "Bobby Charlton used to sit there, Bobby Moore over there . . ."

'That was '76 or '77 and we had our own hurling legend, Christy Ring, with us – he was a Cork selector at the time. We were in Ruislip too, opened the London GAA pitch there in '79, went off for a week to Jersey afterward – great craic. But the American trips were fantastic – New York, Boston, Chicago, San Francisco. We were very well looked after by the Irish in every location. It's different now, they stay in hotels, but we were with the locals. It was great to meet the fellas from the other counties, have a few drinks with them – the footballers travelled with the hurlers as well that time, a great mix, all the different fellas from the different counties. The year we won the three-in-a-row there was no trip, it was cancelled – the Americans were very upset, especially in San Francisco, where we were always very well looked after, huge Cork contingent there.' And has he maintained those contacts? 'No, not really, but you would meet every now and again, the odd match. A pity really.'

Of all those he played with and against over the years, who was the best? Who was the best he soldiered with, for example? 'That's very difficult to answer, so many great players to choose from. For pure hurling, nothing else, I'd say Tom Cashman – an artist, a marvellous, marvellous hurler. But as a key player, a team player, I thought Gerald McCarthy was as good as any I ever saw, a man you could always depend on, out around the middle of the field. Very strong wrists, great man for the big occasion, he's certainly a man I'd have on any team. Great hurling brain too.'

And among the opposition? 'Pat Hartigan and Eamon Cregan from Limerick were two great players from that era. In Kilkenny, you had so many great hurlers – Joe Hennessey was a superb hurler, the Tommy Walsh of his day. Even to this day, when I go to Kilkenny, I get a great welcome from Joe, couldn't do enough for you – one of the finest hurling men I ever met. Liam "Chunky" O'Brien was another, Billy Fitzpatrick – great man to take a score. You had the Clare half-back from that era, Loughnane, Stack and Hehir, a marvellous line, and of course Johnny Callanan up front, the Jamesie [O'Connor] of his day. Then you had the Connollys of Galway, John – a superb player for so many years for Galway – and Joe. Ah, so many, but no matter where you go, you'll meet great hurlers, and great hurling people.'

EARLY VERSION OF THE GPA

During his time with Cork there was an early effort by a few players to establish their own version of what is now known as the Gaelic Players Association, the GPA. Eamonn was one of those involved, the Cork organiser. 'I can't remember how it originated, but Johnny Callanan [famous Clare hurler of the time] was one of those who instigated it. I was good friends with Johnny, had played Railway Cup with him a few times. He spoke to me, I went to a few meetings – I remember going to a meeting in Portlaoise, Johnny was there, Robbie Kelleher [Dublin footballer], Colm O'Rourke [Meath footballer, current RTÉ pundit]; I can't remember what we were going to call the organisation, but we were going to take a pound off every player as membership. I think the lads went to Croke Park about getting official recognition for the players' body – that was around the early '80s, as far as I can remember. It didn't get anywhere anyway.'

Unlike the situation that pertained during the turmoil in Cork through the early part of the decade just past, player 'strikes' in three different seasons, there was no question of things not being right at the time, nor was there any question of the fledgling organisation being suppressed by the Cork County Board.

'I can't remember any meetings with the Cork County Board, never any talk at all about it at that level, never any problems with the players being involved in a player representative body. They knew it was going on, knew we were going to collect a pound off everyone. I couldn't say we were treated badly in Cork anyway; there were never any issues there, we always got what we wanted, plenty of tickets for everyone. In fairness to the Board they had everything in place, especially for the times that were in it. Dr Con [Murphy, team doctor even still] was there at every game, physios, everything – we never had any problem.

'There was a feeling I suppose that the top inter-county players should maybe be doing something for those who weren't being well treated in other counties – and that was happening. Improve their lot rather than our own. There was talk of looking after former players who had fallen on hard times, do something for them, if we could.

'The next step was to talk to Croke Park, and that's where it ended – I don't know who was to blame for that, but we heard no more about it anyway. It just faded away – fellas hadn't the stomach for it, I think, no one was really interested.'

Now that a players' representative body has been established, however, the GPA recognised by the GAA, Eamonn is pleased. 'I'm happy that they're now under the umbrella of the GAA. Some people think pay-for-play is still a hidden agenda with the GPA, but I don't. I wouldn't be in favour of it, and I know the GPA isn't talking about it. Thirty-two counties by thirty per panel – work it out, it's just not sustainable. You only have to look at what happened to club rugby in the AIL [All-Ireland League] after professionalism, look at the situation in Irish soccer, a lot of clubs going to the wall.

'I'd be very broad-minded on most issues anyway, but one thing I would NOT be in favour of is this thing about having thirty players on a panel, five or six fellas getting no game with either club or county – it's gone way over the top altogether. And no club games for three weeks before championship? That's not right either. In fairness to Cork there was a big improvement there last year. Denis Walsh seemed to be very amenable to taking care of the club needs, as was Conor Counihan. But there are too many players being tied up. I think that's something the GPA should take on board and sort out, working together with the GAA.'

EAMONN O'DONOGHUE TODAY

He has the air of a man who's more than happy with his lot, has Eamonn O'Donoghue, and why not? A long-time employee of Goldcrop (formerly IAWS), an agricultural supply company based in Springhill, Carrigtwohill, with whom he is a sales rep, married to Marian (née Waters, whose brother Fr Mick – if that makes any sense! – won an All-Ireland with Cork in 1966), with whom he has four kids, Shay (26), Eamon (24), Michael (23) and Niamh (18), he is enjoying life, still heavily involved with Blackrock at every level.

'I finished up playing with the club around 1990, and I enjoyed my hurling, every minute of it with club and county, and I'm still involved with the club, and still enjoy it.'

Long gone from the playing scene then, and yet, though he never reached the heady heights of contemporaries such as Ray Cummins and Jimmy Barry-Murphy, he is still being recognised. 'As a rep with Goldcrop I'm on the road, covering Cork, Kerry, Clare, meeting different people all the time. And they'd know you, which is flattering – you'd walk in to a place and people would know you immediately. A lot of them would be hurling people anyway. And you'd bump into people you'd know – I met Jim O'Brien from Bruree lately, played corner-back for Limerick in 1973 All-Ireland win; walked in to a place and there he was. A good player, marked him a couple of times – we had a good chat.

'On the family side, I have the four, three boys and a girl. Shay is in England at the moment, doing a post-grad in Liverpool; he got a degree in Food Science, went to Australia for a while but he's back now, hoping to get into teaching. He played intermediate with the Rockies last year, hoping to be back from Liverpool in time for this year's championship. The next fella, Eamon – I'd say he never saw a hurling match in his life, absolutely no interest in it, but none the worse for that – he's into swimming, reading. He's gone off to Australia now too, for a while, a great experience for a young fella – maybe the best thing he could ever do. The third lad,

Mikey, is still in college, doing Commerce; training mad, trying to make the senior team this year. He has buckets of hurling, a midfielder. Then there's Niamh, plays camogie for Douglas, mad into hurling, goes to all the matches. I'd be happy with them all, they all find their own way, eventually, don't they?'

What about hurling, is he happy with the way that's going, the direction it's taking? 'I think overall, yes, I would be. The people in Croke Park are doing as much as they can – you can keep throwing money at a problem but that doesn't mean you'll solve it. The Christy Ring, the Nicky Rackard, the Lory Meagher, I think those are all great new competitions, it means teams are competing at their own level.

'The McCarthy Cup is the most important of all, however, and I think it's critical that we should keep the strong strong, you wouldn't want to neglect the traditional counties. But you can go anywhere hurling is played – the Glens of Antrim, the Ards peninsula in Down – and you'll find a great passion for the game, a passion as strong as anything in Cork, Tipperary or Kilkenny. And that's why I'd say this – whatever the cost, they must keep the Féile going. I've been going for a few years now and it's there you meet the guys from all over the country, every corner, and it's there you see the love for the game, the people involved at underage, keeping it going – fantastic people. I know the GAA are talking about getting rid of some of the smaller competitions in hurling, but the Féile has to stay, no matter what. They're the people who are keeping the game alive.'

What about the compulsory wearing of helmets, does he agree with that? 'I always wore one myself, so, from a safety aspect, yes I do. Dental work is so expensive now, and this should prevent those injuries. I was very lucky injury-wise, broke a few bones in the hand, burst a blood vessel in the leg in 1982 in the first round of the championship, but other than that, nothing really. Hurling is actually a safe game, compared to a lot of team games.'

So, any other changes he'd like to see introduced? 'I wouldn't make any more really, I don't see any need – it's fine as it is.

The 2009 All-Ireland final between Kilkenny and Tipperary was proof of that, if any proof was needed – I think anyone would have to agree that it was a marvellous exhibition from two very talented sides, as was the League final between the same two teams. One issue that has to be addressed though is player unrest, all the strikes – that's not doing the GAA any good at all, Limerick the latest example. We don't know the full facts of that situation, everyone has their own story, but the big question is – how does it get to that crisis point in the first place? How do you prevent that from happening in the future?'

And what of the current Kilkenny team? In 2009 they did what his Cork team failed to do in 1979, completed an unbeaten four-in-a-row – are they the best that's ever been? 'I think so, yes. It's very hard to compare across the eras, and the Cork three-in-a-row team would have been competitive in any era, so many outstanding hurlers on it. But the game has changed, has moved on, and this Kilkenny team has raised the bar again. They have the structures in place down there to continue that dominance also.'

Finally, Eamonn, your best memory from all those years? 'Now that is a hard question! So many great years with Blackrock and with Cork, so many honours won – two All-Irelands with each, club and county, two Railway Cups with Munster – one as captain; several Munster titles, three National Leagues, an Oireachteas. Great years, great days. With the Rockies, I suppose the best memory is 1975, when I captained the team to win the county. As a small boy growing up in Blackrock, to make the senior team was the major ambition, to captain them to win the county was the dream – that was the high point. We won the Munster afterwards, but lost the All-Ireland to James Stephens on a wet day below in Thurles. With Cork, it's the first All-Ireland medal, in '76, that was a fantastic feeling. After those, so many others; I enjoyed it all, immensely.'

So did we, Eamonn, so did we – thanks for the memories.

Ciarán Whelan

Philip Lanigan, *Irish Mail on Sunday*

A trawl through the website of photographic agency Sportsfile offers a unique window on a 14-year career with Dublin. Type 'Ciarán Whelan' in the search engine and 818 results pop up. A life through a lens.

There he is in November 2009 wearing a fetching red swimming cap to promote the St Michael's House Santa Swim at DCU, an initiative to raise funds for educational and sporting equipment. Or at the All-Stars the previous month, all chiselled cheekbones and flashing teeth in the company of team-mates Alan Brogan and Barry Cahill.

And then there are the more exotic snapshots. In Galway, earlier in the year in the company of Seán Cavanagh, Henry Shefflin and Aidan O'Mahony, to celebrate the arrival of the Puma entry, *il Mostro*, in the Volvo Ocean Race.

Or the previous year with a ragbag of the great and the glamorous for the opening of Victor Chandler's new luxury betting lounge in the IFSC in Dublin – Cheltenham hopeful Andrew McNamara, model Felicia, Irish international scrum-half Eoin Reddan, not to mention snooker World Championship winner Ken Doherty.

He admits to logging on at times himself to look back on certain matches, certain moments which caught the mood perfectly, like that July Sunday in 2008 when he is in repose like one of the high kings of Leinster, the Delaney Cup in one hand, son Jamie cradled in the other.

Or all the way back to the first shots of him on the field where he carved out his reputation, against Meath in the 1996

Leinster final at Croke Park, when the Raheny player slipped in under the radar to make his first championship start.

After his retirement, Dublin County Board chief executive John Costello paid tribute to him in his annual report with a valediction that summed up his prized status in the capital. 'I wish to take this opportunity to acknowledge one of our best footballers of the modern era, Ciarán Whelan. His high-fielding, acceleration on the ball, power in possession and ability to kick the ball accurately off either foot when travelling at full pace were one of the finest sights of this or any era. The County Board thank him for the dedication, ambition and class in the Dublin jersey throughout the years until he finally hung up his inter-county boots a few months back.'

Sitting across the kitchen table from me in his home in Donabate, the player who made his debut as 'AN Other' in that Leinster final talks through his career and how he is adapting to life on the sidelines. What he misses? The buzz of playing for Dublin, the band of brothers mentality that is part of being on an inter-county squad.

Down through the years, Dublin have had players who were natural lightning rods for the opposition, who revelled in the role of Public Enemy Number One. Ciarán Duff. Joe McNally. Vinny Murphy. And when there was no larger-than-life persona to take down a peg with a handy insult or two, Whelan found himself cast sometimes in that bête noir role. Coming out of Croke Park last year after watching Kerry turn over Meath in the All-Ireland semi-final, he found himself showered with abuse by the latter's supporters as he walked down Clonliffe Road.

Clearly, Meath supporters will never forgive him – or referee John Bannon for that matter – for walloping Nigel Crawford at the throw-in of the 2005 Leinster quarter-final and escaping the censure of a red card. A different colour could arguably have changed the course of the season. No matter. He never claimed to be an angel and it was a rare lapse in a career that spanned 14 seasons.

Within the Pale, he was always highly regarded, and the chant of 'Whel-o, Whel-o' on a summer Sunday became his calling card. Perhaps the worst thrown at him is the lack of an All-Ireland to his name, or that he couldn't carry the team on his back for 70 minutes at a time.

So when the music stops, what happens then? Signing off after the ignominy of a 2009 All-Ireland quarter-final against Kerry was not exactly what he planned and less than a month later, he officially announced his retirement at the age of 33. He's still getting used to it.

'When I retired, it was pretty similar to every year for a while in that you're having a break anyway. Dublin hadn't played a game in a long time. It was on a break from training. So it didn't feel that different, the months up to Christmas. But there is always that feeling at the back of your mind that you're facing into a difficult year. I know how emotionally attached I am to the thing. It was a huge part of my life for 14 years.

'A lot of ex-players told me that it's the first year that is very, very difficult. The hardest part is trying to fill a void in your life regardless whether you have other things to do between work and family life. I suppose as a family, we were in a routine where my training took over from January. My wife Fiona revolved her routine around what I was doing. I had a set routine of Tuesday, Thursday, Saturday, Sunday. In my own head I'm struggling to fill that gap.'

There is a long list of players who stopped playing altogether after inter-county football and he imagined too that when the curtain came down on his time with Dublin, that would be it. Finished. Club and county. But Raheny has too much of a hold on his heartstrings.

When his eldest Jamie started nursery football training, it was on Saturday mornings in the club and Whelan too lent a hand coaching the next generation. With Jamie starting school, they'll both likely carry on the same process locally in Donabate.

'There is a big comedown. If you had have asked me five

years ago, when I finished, would I finish from everything, I would have said "yeah". That was always the plan. But I do feel I owe the club something, owe them that at least. From being an integral part of the club since I was 19 years of age, because I was so tied up with family commitments in the last four or five years, when we were knocked out of the championship I missed a lot of training and couldn't give the commitment that I should have.

'That's what's encouraging me to go back. I've missed the days of playing normal club football and just enjoying it. For 14 years you've targeted playing club football. There's a lot of pressure, a lot of expectation. I just want to go and play with no pressure and enjoy it. Go back to the way it was when I started off.'

He's reminded of a quote he gave to this interviewer on the eve of the 2002 championship, six years a Dublin senior and already fretting that his career might end without even a provincial title.

> If I finished after ten years and I didn't have anything to show
> for it I'd be just gutted. You're remembered for nothing then.
> You're remembered as a loser. That's what's driving me now
> – that hunger for success. I don't care what it takes. Winners are
> remembered; losers are forgotten. It doesn't matter how unlucky
> you are. Success is the bottom line.

Back then, all he had in terms of silverware to his name was an O'Byrne Cup medal. Or not as the case proves. There was never any presentation night and he certainly wasn't going looking for it.

And then, in the space of that same summer, the whole thing turned. A breakthrough Leinster title signalled the beginning of a new chapter for Dublin football and he remained the team's talisman during a remarkable run of five provincial titles in succession. A measure of that achievement? It was the 1970s, the heyday of Heffo's Army, when Dublin last dominated Leinster to the same extent. If there is an asterisk beside his name because he hasn't the All-Ireland to decorate his time in a Dublin jersey, he can live with it.

There have been no nights of maudlin introspection at home in Donabate. He's just not wired that way. A sense of regret or a lack of fulfilment is not something he is burdened with. 'Look at the facts. Dublin have won one All-Ireland in the past 25 years. There are many players that were lucky to be on that panel and many that missed the boat.

'You look back and think "six Leinster championships". There are guys in Wexford or Louth who would do anything for one of them. I've two All-Stars, four Railway Cups, got to represent Ireland in Australia a couple of times. I achieved a hell of a lot.

'There was just one thing missing. That's life. You just get on with it. It's not something I'll get bogged down with.

'As people say, "Would you like to have been a corner-back for one season and just happened to be in the right place at the right time and win a medal or would you like to have played for 14 years with Dublin and enjoyed all the ups and downs that went with it?" I think I'd plump for the joy of having played for 14 years. I'd be a very passionate Dub I suppose! That was my life. The Dublin jersey was something you strive to wear all throughout your career.'

Croke Park, 3 August 2009. All-Ireland quarter-final result: Kerry 1–24 Dublin 1–7.

It wasn't meant to end this way. The scriptwriter who wrote this final scene must have been a Hollywood cast-off. In the same way that *The Shawshank Redemption* invariably comes out on top in a vox pop of GAA players and their favourite movies, it's a given that the majority of inter-county careers end on a bum note. Only the lucky few get out at the top. But to endure Dublin's worst championship loss since the drubbing in the 1978 final – also, coincidentally, by 17 points to Kerry – and to be left out of the starting line-up for good measure?

Twelve months earlier, the abject nature of the 3–14 to 1–8 defeat by Tyrone at the same stage left him looking for the exit door. 'The previous year I did strongly consider whether that was it. I left Croke Park that day, did an interview with RTÉ. The stadium was empty and I just walked out onto the pitch for a few minutes and took it in because I had a sense that was it for me.

'For a while I kinda did feel it was over. Then I spoke to people, got a fair bit of support, saw that there was a new management team and thought, "What if?" The fact that Pat [Gilroy] didn't have management experience did concern me. If you look at all the other managers, a lot of them have won All-Irelands, a lot of them have come through the system or been involved with development squads right up along.

'I started with Dublin under Mickey Whelan and enjoyed the training. He was involved, had won a club All-Ireland with St Vincent's. You always had that "What if?" doubt. The team were so close. I would have had the height of respect for Pillar [Paul Caffrey] and the management team and I was sorry to see them go. That's why I said, if I'm going to go back, it's all or nothing.'

He didn't think it could get any lower than the feeling after the Tyrone game. He was wrong. Kerry put a final full stop to a career that deserved a more fitting footnote.

It was an emotional week all round in the Whelan household. On the Thursday before the game, his daughter Tiana was born. While others on the panel rounded the night off in the Dublin footballer's nightclub of choice, Whelan, not for the first time, went his own way that Bank Holiday Monday night. 'Particularly nights we lost; I was never one for Copper Face Jacks. It kinda did my head in a bit. I always went back to Raheny GAA club after any championship match. I was never one for going around town.

'Leinster final wins, I'd always end up back there. After a match, I just wanted to go back and find a quiet corner and have a few pints. I used to prefer meeting up with the team on the Monday when everything had died down and there wasn't as many people around. I used to enjoy that.

'The team left Croke Park and went back to the Clarion, which is where we always went back to. I had one drink with the lads and got a taxi across to Holles Street. Fiona was in there, in the Merrion Wing. The sister there who was looking after her was from Kerry! Really nice woman. I went over – Fiona was lying in the bed – and I was very emotional. There was a real sense of one chapter of your life coming to an end and, with a newborn baby, another one starting.

'It was the manner of the defeat and the fact that was it, that you weren't going to achieve your goal. I try not to get bogged down by that. That's one thing that annoys, people saying, "Oh I wish you got the All-Ireland medal." I know people are being kind, and great players haven't won medals but the philosophy I'd have is that it was a childhood dream to play for Dublin – that's what I wanted to do.

'I got 14 years playing in Croke Park in front of capacity crowds and was lucky in that regard. As much as being a Dublin player attracts a profile, you were nearly guaranteed six or seven spin-outs in Croke Park a year, in front of a great support. You can't beat that buzz of running out the tunnel to Hill 16, the rapport I would have built up with the fans over the years.'

A month later, he was officially an 'ex' Dublin footballer. 'I wanted to bring closure to it because everyone was asking.'

The letters, the goodwill messages from former team-mates and adversaries, the texts of support from guys like Declan Darcy and Paul Clarke who he had soldiered with in a different lifetime, all helped to make the decision easier to bear.

'I got a lot of nice letters,' he admits. 'From random supporters.'

All Dubs?

'No roses from Meath or anything like that! The only thing I would have got from Meath was a bunch of flowers saying "RIP", something like that!

'I kept them all. From six or seven year olds to Dubs who followed the team for 30 years. Just thanking you for the contribution to Dublin football. Saying sorry we didn't get over the line. Then from kids saying that they idolise you, that they followed you for years, want to play midfield. That's fantastic.'

He digs out a letter from a locker inside the front door by way of illustration (see facing page).

The image of him arriving in the church in full Dublin regalia is hard to shift.

'I only got one abusive letter when I did the Walkers crisps ad. Gary Lineker was over and it was myself and Darragh Ó Sé. The ref threw up the ball, blew the whistle.

'Gary Lineker shouted out something from the crowd. He interrupted us and we walked over to him and he was eating a packet of crisps in the Hogan Stand with another 100 bags or so scattered all around him. I got a letter from somebody saying that I'd sold my soul to the Queen! Promoting a British product, a disgrace to the nation.

'As if that wasn't enough, Pat McEnaney was the ref and we must have spent the whole day making it. I'd say the crew did 50 takes – and the one they used was of Darragh catching it. Of course the lads were on to me then: "You couldn't even catch that ball!"'

Only in the GAA!

Always held in high esteem by the Hill 16 faithful, the shock of being taunted on a street in the capital in the wake of the shock Leinster championship defeat by Westmeath in 2004 – 'Don't give up the f***in' day job' – was one isolated incident in all the years. And there was no sign that the quest for the Holy Grail would come unstuck in such dramatic fashion heading into his final season.

The year had started so promisingly in 2009. 'I knew that it was my last big push and I said I'd give it everything. I trained a

Ciaran Whelan
C/O Dublin County Board,
Parnell Park,
Donnycarney,
Dublin 5

Dear Ciaran,

I am twelve years of age. Besides being your biggest fan, I am also a distant relation of yours. I am a grandnephew of Tommy Daly of Brownstown Co Westmeath. Who I believe you will know because he is also granduncle to your wife.

We have met before when I travelled to Blanchardstown Shopping Centre to meet you with Jason Sherlock early last year. I was glad to meet you and get my Dublin jersey autographed and have my picture taken with you. I have seen you play many times. As well as many games in Parnell Park and Croke Park, I have travelled as far as Donegal, Cavan, Mayo and recently to Armagh, twice. I was sorry to see you injured and I hope you are better now. I am looking forward to seeing you play against Meath this coming Sunday, and win so we can play in the league final. I have not missed any of Dublin's games this year. I was glad to see you come on for the first time this year in Cavan, and thought you played very well. I also enjoyed watching you play against Antrim in the challenge match.

I would be greatly honoured if you would come to my holy confirmation and be my sponsor. It is on Friday 6th June 2008, at 11.30am in St. Jude's Templeoge, Dublin 6w. I hope you are not to busy too come.

Wishing you all the best in the rest of this year's matches.
Your friend
Luke Johnson.
Luke Johnson.

hell of a lot over last Christmas, trained nearly every day. Fiona was pregnant and I knew with a second baby that it was going to be tough as regards the time factor. I built all of that into the equation and knew coming back it was going to be one last push.

'I travelled with the squad to La Manga and felt good. Felt strong. We played the first League game against Tyrone in Croke Park and I had a good game under lights. That night really gave me the self-confidence that I could still do it in Croke Park. It gave me a huge lift for the year ahead. But the year didn't work out as I envisaged.'

From the outside, it was hard to fathom why the two-time All-Star as well as the team's current All-Star midfielder Shane Ryan were effectively frozen out. For someone who never felt in a comfort zone playing for Dublin, the treatment jarred.

'I was never one to throw the toys out my pram. I was always quite modest. One thing that maybe held me back over my career was that I didn't have the arrogance some other players would have. I can't stand arrogance.

'Now there's a level of confidence or self-belief that borders on arrogance, and maybe I didn't have that self-belief. I was always hardest on myself, first to knock myself. So I never felt that I had a right to be on the team. After the Tyrone game I felt that I would have shown the new management that I could still perform in Croke Park in that arena, that there was still another year left in me.

'Pat rested me for the Kerry League game which was a strange one. It was one of the bigger League games, Kerry in Parnell Park. That came out of the blue. I wasn't sure whether it was going to set the pattern for the year.'

Dublin played well that day, drew a game that was there for the taking and Whelan found himself watching it at home on television, omitted from the match-day 24. 'That was the first day the Kilmacud Crokes lads were back after the All-Ireland club championship. Darren Magee had a very good club championship and was back in. I think there was a message that day.'

Whelan was back in midfield when Dublin ran riot against Westmeath – 'a nothing game' – in the last round of the League. However, he didn't think a few missed challenge matches in the build-up to the first round of the Leinster championship against Meath due to a calf strain would leave him benched for the first summer in his career. 'I was back fit for the Meath game. When you don't make the first championship team, I'd know from over the years that there is very little alteration to a winning team.

'I was disappointed before the Meath game but I accepted that at some stage of my career I'd end up not playing. I'd seen it happen with all the players. There was a trend with new Dublin managers that senior players seemed to go by the wayside. When Mickey Whelan came in he fell out with John O'Leary, dropped Paul Clarke, Ciaran Walsh, Jayo [Jason Sherlock]. Tommy Carr came in and dropped Keith Barr. Tommy Lyons left off Dessie Farrell, Paul Curran. I'd seen the trend before and part of me thought this is part and parcel of life – get on with it.'

Indeed, he reveals how the management were planning to introduce him to an unsuspecting public as Dublin's answer to Kieran Donaghy. 'They had this idea of playing me full-forward. I spent a lot of time playing there in training. It was going well to a point but I had never played full-forward in my career. I had spent 13 or 14 years facing the goal. I was never 100 per cent comfortable that it would work in Croke Park.

'Pat's game plan was that they were going to spring me there at some stage. That was all very good but ultimately I was disappointed not to be considered at number eight or nine.

'I felt strongly that you get your sharpness in practice matches. There are several good midfielders in Dublin. Sometimes the fella you are going toe-to-toe with on Tuesday and Thursday is better than the guy you'll be facing on Sunday.

'I'm not bitter about it. Of course I was hugely disappointed, but for the sake of the team I didn't show it. When the team is in a championship run – we were Leinster champions after all – you have to buy into the system. So I didn't want to upset other players or I didn't want other players to be thinking, "There's Whelan throwing his toys out of the pram – who does he think he is?" I was willing to buy into it as much as I didn't necessarily agree with it.'

It felt particularly frustrating when, after having trained at full-forward for the whole summer, it was at midfield that he was thrown in to replace Darren Magee after barely 15 minutes of the Kerry quarter-final debacle. It was always going to be an uphill battle in such a situation.

So, did the background to the 2009 season play a part in his decision to retire?

'Not particularly. I met Pat soon after and I told him I was finished and I wasn't going back. And he seemed to accept that. He said to me that the door would still be open and that he would touch base with me again. I was never really comfortable with the full-forward role. It's not in my interests; it's not something that I would see working. I could go back and make a complete eejit of myself. I'm clear in my own mind that it's over.'

Gilroy has recast his team since that defeat, one which few saw coming after the high octane Leinster final performance, when Whelan's second-half introduction was instrumental to Dublin coming out on top against Kildare despite losing wing-back Ger Brennan after just 19 minutes. But Whelan provides his own personal insight into why it all fell apart so dramatically in the All-Ireland quarter-final.

'Although there was a mental side to it – the demons of the previous year came back to haunt the team and heads dropped and confidence went – there was a flatness there. The team was dead on its feet. Fellas had just given up, thrown in the towel. It was quite frightening – you could see that 25 minutes in. There was a huge element of mental weakness to it – I don't deny that – but I thought we arrived into it very flat. Maybe over-trained. I think of the Ireland rugby team at the World Cup. It had similar traits. That's my feeling on it anyway.

'I always feared that if Kerry got into Croke Park and we gave them a good start that they'd recover their mojo. They didn't become a bad team overnight, although they looked awful against Longford and Sligo and Antrim and they really looked like they had problems in the camp. I'd know some of the players well and would have been aware that things weren't great with Jack O'Connor. You have to hand it to them for being able to turn things around and win the All-Ireland.

'I did fear them getting a good start. And we handed it to them on a plate. Croke Park is as much Kerry's home ground as it is Dublin's and I feared all that bad form would go out the window.

'It was a disaster. Tactically, they got it spot on. I think I warmed up after three or four minutes. Alan Brogan had a chance; Diarmuid Connolly had a chance. Instead of being 1–6 to 0–3, they went down and got another two points and it was 1–8 to 0–1. If the gap had been closer even at half-time, the game wouldn't have been a dead duck.

'I hoped against hope that we could turn it around. If I was to be honest, I knew it was going to be a huge struggle. It was like seeing the previous year unfold again. The mental damage. It was quite frightening that after 20 minutes fellas had actually nearly thrown in the towel.

'I've never sat down and looked at it. I've no interest in doing that. There were mental scars there, no doubt. But it was a combination of both. There was definitely a deadness of feet, a flatness. There was no impetus, no one trying to go at pace. Nothing. The team looked flat from the start.'

From the moment he was thrown in at the deep end in the 1996 Leinster final against Meath, his career in a Dublin shirt was nothing if not colourful and incident-filled. Many things stand out from the 14 seasons of incident and accident, and his senior call-up under Mickey Whelan will always remain one of them.

'I played Under-21 against Louth in a Leinster championship match. We had two sent off early on – Keith Galvin and Darren Homan – and Louth beat us. I pity the guy at the end of Darren's punch though – Darren was a tough nut of a 20 year old who just happened to be wearing a sovereign ring at the time.

'I got the call that evening to go training with the seniors. Deep down I didn't think I was good enough. In my own head I thought I was a bit out of my depth. I shit myself that first night going to training. I'll never ever forget it. Dublin were All-Ireland champions at the time and here was I training with guys I idolised. I just couldn't get my head around it. Joe McNally was there at that stage. I was seven when Joe McNally won in '83! In fairness, he was one of the guys who was good to me that night. You always remember the guys who looked out for you.

'I remember being terrified – absolutely terrified. And it didn't get better on the Thursday or the Saturday after that. For the first couple of weeks, you were up the walls, going in to training every time with that sickening feeling in the pit of the stomach.

'That was the end of the League. Dublin didn't play till the first round of the championship. I made the panel for the Westmeath game, in Navan. We beat them easily. I was a sub. It felt like a huge achievement to get that Dublin jersey in a championship dressing-room. The second game, we played Louth and we were struggling. Charlie Redmond got injured. Mickey told me to warm up. Again, I nearly crapped myself. I remember running down the line that day and my legs wobbling. Navan was jammers. I remember thinking, "Oh f***, he's going to put me on! I'm not ready for this!" I think it was a blessing in disguise that I didn't go on. Then I started in the Leinster final.

'Niall Guiden was injured in the build-up to that final. I was replacing him in the A games so there was a hint I might start it. He was awaiting a late fitness test and when we got to the Tuesday and Thursday, I remember John O'Leary and Charlie Redmond talking to me, saying to get myself ready, offering words of encouragement. It was going to be a huge thing. I hadn't played a minute of championship football. Deep down, I'm sure they were a bit worried!

'Saturday morning, Mickey Whelan took me aside at training and told me I was going to start. It worked out because nobody had time to scrutinise me. Nobody knew who I was. I think some Dublin supporters thought I must be Mickey's son.

'The game went well from my perspective. Getting two points in the first half was always going to settle me down. I marked Paddy Reynolds and he was a bit of a rookie as well. Colm Coyle was on the other wing – I thought he might have a pop at me at some stage, put me in my box, but it never happened.

'To be two points down against Meath and score a goal in the last minute . . . if ever you were going to have a dream debut that would be it. To get the goal then only for Brian Stynes to be deemed in the square – the whole year turned on it. The goal was disallowed and Dublin were no longer All-Ireland champions.'

When Mickey Whelan's tenure was ended by the boo-boys in Parnell Park following a National League defeat to Tommy Lyons' Offaly, Tommy Carr stepped into the breach. Whelan takes up the story. 'Tommy Carr took over, again very inexperienced. I thought Tommy was a very good manager but if he had had three years management experience at some sort of level before he took us over, I think we would have been a different outfit. Because he was very organised, a very good motivator, he could get a team fit.

'I'll always remember Tommy taking over. At that time the National League took place before Christmas and we had three games played. We had a caretaker manager in for a while – Lorcan Redmond took over for a couple of matches and Liam Moggin took over the training of the team – and we finished up with a victory over Cavan before Christmas.

'We went to Jurys for a Christmas party. Keith Barr was captain at the time. Whatever way it worked out, we had no management team – and nobody from the County Board turned up. So the bar was our own for the night! Fellas really did a job

– I'd say the bill was something else. There were fellas booking rooms in Jurys and I've never seen more Irish coffees drunk after a meal!

'Tommy was appointed then. I'll always remember him taking over in January. He probably felt he needed to catch up. That month's training in January, I will never forget it for as long as I live. We went Monday, Wednesday, Friday, Saturday morning and played O'Byrne Cup on Sundays. It was just savagery.

'When Tommy took over, being the army man, he had us train in Cathal Brugha Barracks in Rathmines. We trained there for four years. It was like a Gaelic football version of Guantánamo Bay. Sheer torture. It still gives me the horrors thinking of driving through those gates. That and the Magazine Fort in the Phoenix Park, the runs up and down the hills on a Saturday morning often after a tough Friday session.

'We had three games left. Monaghan beat us in Parnell Park in the first game. We beat Tyrone up in Tyrone in the second. We finished up that National League beating Kerry in Parnell Park in our last game something like 1–18 to three points in 1998.' (He's not far wrong – it was 0–18 to 1–3.)

'Beat them out the gate. It was a super performance. Everybody thought, "This is it." Then Kildare beat us in the first round of the championship that year after a replay. And of course there was no back door. In hindsight that year we peaked in March. We probably went a bit flat come the summer. But you couldn't take any risks back then with no back door.'

He describes Tommy Lyons as 'very much his own man', and when Dublin ended a seven-year wait for a Leinster title in his first year in charge in 2002, it felt so sweet.

'Meath were the team we needed to beat. It goes in phases and we couldn't buy a win against them around then. So when we beat them in the first round, that gave us the confidence to go forward and win the Leinster title, beat Kildare in the final. Younger lads like Alan Brogan and Barry Cahill came in and gave the whole thing a freshness. At that stage I was pulling my hair out. Between 1996, '99, '00 and '01, I had lost four Leinster titles.

'We got two goals in the first half and took an early lead. Kildare came at us in the second half and it was tight enough in the end. It was certainly different from all the other Leinster finals because there was no pitch invasion. I don't know how they managed to keep people off but I remember the team doing a lap of honour that day. What I felt was just a sense of relief, of breaking down a barrier. I remember Trevor Giles recalling in his post-match interview after the Meath game that he had lost four Leinster finals to Dublin in the early 1990s before he got over the line. Timing is everything.'

It's funny. There were days when he paraded around Croke Park like a king in his own private fiefdom – nine clean catches, including four consecutive kick-outs, against Tyrone in the first half of the drawn 2005 All-Ireland quarter-final being one example – but the 2002 quarter-final against Donegal wasn't meant to be one of them. Laid low with viral pneumonia in the fortnight going into the game, the management started him in the hope that he would have 20 minutes to give. Instead, he turned in what he counts as his best display in a Dublin jersey, kicking four points – two off his left, two off his right – in between lording the skies.

Though it all ended in tears under Lyons following a Leinster championship exit courtesy of Westmeath two years later, there were plenty of light moments along the way. He recalls a challenge match against Kerry pre-championship. 'Pat Spillane brought us down to Templenoe for the opening of his local club pitch. He had to be nice to us for the day. Bertie [Ahern] was flown in, arrived by helicopter. We played Kerry and beat them. Tommy being Tommy decided he would get on the helicopter with Bertie after the match. Left us in Kenmare and told us to stay off the beer. Needless to say, Kenmare got it that night. There were items of Dublin gear being swopped for late pints at 2.30, 3 a.m.!'

He feels Paul Caffrey couldn't have done more when he stepped up from selector alongside Lyons, to be the main man in 2005, four successive Leinster titles following on his watch. 'I have a hell of a lot of time for Pillar. I think he was really unlucky not to achieve more. He took over the team at a low ebb in 2004 after losing to Westmeath, a time when I seriously considered quitting. That, unquestionably, was the lowest point of my career. I really doubted whether I wanted to return, went through some serious soul-searching. I was playing too at centre-forward where I was never fully comfortable.

'Paul Clarke was back in as part of the management team. He was living nearby in Swords and he did more than anyone to drag me out of that funk. I'd say we trained every day together that December in the gym. I was at a low ebb. I really doubted where the team was going – and where I was going. Finishing up was a real possibility.

'Pillar and the management team understood how I felt and helped me work through it. Pillar had been involved as a selector. When he took over, fellas were worried that he had been part of the old set-up. But he changed things totally, brought a whole new freshness to it. Lifted the team, brought a confidence back. Was very well organised.'

What about criticism of too many cooks? Of a backroom mentor to match every first team player?

'I think that was over-hyped. If you were to look at Dublin's backroom team now, it's not much different. If you were to line up the backroom personnel of every county, whether it's stats men or whatever, you'd nearly have the same. Very professional set-up. He was honest, straight up, knew how to deal with players. He knew how to get the balance right, when to tell players to take a break.'

He defends the *Blue Book*, a motivational guide for the players introduced by the management, that was leaked in the wake of the collapse against Tyrone in the All-Ireland quarter-final. 'It was an easy target. We'd been hammered by Tyrone and of course it was leaked. So we were going to be the laughing stock. If we had have won the All-Ireland, it would have been a genius idea. It was just someone being opportunistic in putting the boot in.

'I felt there was a lot of good stuff in it. Fellas were buying into it. I think he was trying to follow a concept that Clive Woodward had with the England rugby team – a black book. I remember reading Clive Woodward's book and when we did it, it was along similar lines – general team rules, principles. Unfortunately, it got out. It was meant to be a private thing among players.'

All through that time, he represented the touchstone for Dublin's All-Ireland ambitions.

His colourful potted history of Dublin under the various managers is matched by his account of some of the best players who conspired to thwart his own. Asked to name-check the best midfielders he rubbed shoulders with, he doesn't hesitate in selecting a shortlist of star quality. 'I suppose if you were to ask me the top three it would be John McDermott, Anthony Tohill and Darragh Ó Sé. They were probably the three best I came up against.

'John McDermott was probably in his peak while I was in the early stages of my career. He was a big, physical presence. Anchored the Meath team. He had that Meath attitude. You knew you were going to be up against it. He certainly knew how to dish it out – but that was all part of the learning curve.

'Probably the only time I really annoyed him was in Australia in '99 on the international rules tour. After the first test, I asked to swop jerseys with Nathan Buckley. The Australians weren't allowed to swop until the second test so he promised me after the second test. He was captain. So I got Nathan Buckley's jersey. John was captain of the Irish team so he wasn't too happy – he had a bit of a pop at me over that!

'I thought Anthony was one of the best all-round midfielders. A fantastic fielder, great going forward with the ball; had two great feet, could kick frees. He had everything. A solid guy as well. I got to know him when he captained the second trip to Australia. I spent a summer in 2001 marking him in the international rules training. That was one of the best experiences I could ever have gotten. Spending a summer marking him was of massive benefit to me.

'As my career went on, I was coming up against Darragh. We all know his strengths. Again, I shared a room with him in Australia. He's a good character, good auld craic.'

Ó Sé rarely gave much away in all the years of a gilded career, though the west Kerry roguery has never been in doubt. Whelan confirms as much, and knows him well enough not to need to speak in reverential tones about the midfielder who set the bar for everyone else.

'What's he like? A messer. An absolute messer. Ah, we'd good craic, good banter. I stayed in touch with him then after. We'd ring each other every now and then and have a good moan about bits and pieces!'

By way of example, he recalls the international rules series of 2001, the tale of the storied Ó Sé brother bringing a smile to his face as he goes. 'Brian McEniff was manager that time and Brian had an old-fashioned style of management. I pulled my hamstring in the first training session when we got to Adelaide – it was purely due to dehydration. I gave it an awful twang and missed the second test. I remember a lot of the Australian team were out that week – they weren't really taking it that seriously – and we won it handy.

'I'll always remember a time in the dressing-room, it was the first test in the MCG, with Australia leading at half-time, and Brian McEniff giving a team talk in the middle of the dressing-room with the tweed cap on. We're all in a huddle – Darragh being opposite me – and I can still see him trying to make faces to make me laugh. It was the only time I was in the middle of a team talk and there was still messing going on!

'On that tour, the running joke was "When the dust-up starts, who was going to be in the wrong place at the wrong time and get the first few slaps?"'

A personal highlight came on the '99 tour with a picture postcard goal after a trademark galloping run. The only difference was this was for Ireland. At the Melbourne Cricket Ground. In front of 60,000-plus supporters.

'It will always be a highlight, to be the first man to score a goal in the MCG. That was a great trip. High intensity. I always felt the GAA should do them every two years. I had opportunities to go back a third and fourth time but with the kids and that, it didn't work. The season was too long.'

He finished 1999 an All-Star. Back then, the rivalry with Meath was such that a county career was defined by whether a player could produce it in the championship against the old enemy. Whelan's Leinster final performance was one big reason why he finished the year, once more in the company of McDermott, this time in black-tie get-up.

'We got to the League final that year and I got 3–13, 3–14 from play in that campaign. That helped my chances, though I never considered it when Meath beat us in the Leinster final. It generally comes down to the last four teams.

'I know from going to the All-Stars in later years, when you're an older player and you get to know members of the media, you'll find out the team. When you're a young lad you're very much kept in the dark. I went that night not having a clue. Right up to the moment that the envelope was opened. It was a great surprise and a great honour.'

Whether through his columns in the *Irish Sun* or *Evening Herald* or the guest appearances as an analyst on radio or television, he has always had clear ideas about the game. Indeed, for someone who works in a management position with National League sponsors Allianz, he offers an unsentimental view from a players' perspective of how the competition needs to be re-energised and has a vision for the future that the GAA would do well to listen to.

'I would think that the way forward for the GAA is to play more mid-week games under lights. Sunday afternoon National League games were a pain in the backside. What used to gall me was that you could be playing Donegal away up in Ballybofey. You had the whole weekend preparing for it, you were back home half ten or eleven. Back in to work the next morning. It just wasn't good.

'As long-term sponsors of the National Leagues, Allianz deserve better, deserve a better product. I would replace the National Leagues with provincial leagues. If you're frank and honest about it or were to do a survey of the players, do Cork players want to be travelling to Derry in the middle of February? Do Donegal want to be travelling down to Kerry? Do Dublin want to be going up to Derry or down to Cork? The reality is "no". Because they want to be playing local. And I think you'd get better crowds. When Dublin played Meath on a Wednesday night under lights in Páirc Tailteann in this year's O'Byrne Cup, you had seven or eight thousand there. Meath would be lucky to get that at their League games.

'I fully agree with the Saturday night or Friday night principle of playing matches, but I think if you have provincial leagues you could have a bit of Wednesday night or mid-week football. People will go to matches more mid-week and on those nights than they will on a Sunday afternoon. The culture has changed a bit in that Sunday afternoon is not the best time for going out playing matches. People with family prefer Friday or Saturday nights.'

As if to make his point, the front of that day's *Irish Times* carries a photograph of die-hard Manchester United supporter – and former Taoiseach – Bertie Ahern wearing a pair of 3D glasses in Fagan's pub in Drumcondra at the launch of Sky's 3D sports service. Viewing habits, and thus supporters' habits, are changing.

What he's proposing is original and well conceived and comes with 14 years' experience of playing to back it up. But it comes at a price – the death of the provincial championships. Whelan's view is that you may as well be looking for a pulse as it is.

'I do think it's the way. And if you do provincial leagues, you have to abandon the provincial championships. I think they've gone stale. I really do.'

He holds Kerry–Cork up in Munster as the perfect example, how Kerry used the 2009 Munster semi-final replay defeat as a way to regroup and relaunch their All-Ireland bid.

'It didn't count,' he says of the provincial sparring between the old rivals. 'It doesn't count. In fact it can be totally counter-productive. If the GAA want to be serious, if they want to stop rugby swallowing it up and taking it over, they've got to be brave and go for a group-type Champions League format that would create novel ties in the middle of summer. Home-and-away format.

'I love the Heineken Cup model where the top team gets through but the second team, it comes down to points difference. I love the fact that you can get bonus points by winning by so much. What about bonus points for scoring so many goals? All these factors that would create that bit of excitement, that bit of interest come the summer. I understand that you're going to have teams that will be out of it but I think you could have a second level competition that follows on from it for these teams.

'You could have a provincial league where your finish dictates your seeding going into the championship. So if you don't perform well in the provincial league you end up third or fourth seed with Tyrone in your group and it has a serious impact on your year. That they are linked together.'

So the provincial model is outmoded?

'I think so. I firmly believe that the provincial model is there because we have four provincial councils. They run independently. In any company, if you were looking for synergies, you'd merge the four of them and put them under the control of Croke Park. Now I know that won't sit well with a lot of old fans but the GAA has to move on.

'It would spice it up. I'd love to see them create something where Croke Park would be utilised on a regular basis for games. Maybe a home-and-away system.'

The provincial straightjacket has been unbuttoned in so many ways already. The Ulster Council have already seen the commercial sense in abandoning Clones for Croke Park for their showpiece football final. Old boundaries no longer hold sway.

'Say Dublin draw Donegal. Think of the income to Donegal in June if you have 30,000 Dubs going up there. The other thing in relation to the Leagues and the Saturday night thing. It's well admitted in Croke Park that Saturday night games are great. How many games then have been played on a Saturday night in Croke Park?

'The one for the 125th anniversary between Dublin and Tyrone was an awesome night. For anyone involved or there, it was a night to be proud. It was just done so well. It was fantastic to be part of it. I played the match and we went in with the attitude of "let's go out and enjoy this for what it is". That was the approach. And it was a good one. Let's just get out and play football and enjoy the occasion. While the result went away from us, the night was about more than that. I went up to the stand after the match – Fiona was there with Jamie – for the after-match facilities. I thought it was the best night the GAA ever put on. Fantastic.

'They're not going to go and change the leagues just like that. But even through the current league system they should be having some sort of system in place where they can do double headers every Saturday night.

'They won't have rugby and soccer next year so why not give every county the opportunity to play there? Sex it up. Give free tickets. The 2010 Division Three and Four finals were a good example of rewarding players from the likes of Waterford, Limerick, Sligo and Antrim with an outing at Croke Park. There should be far more of that.'

If there is a compelling logic to his blueprint for the future, he knows it's not about to happen any time soon. Playing devil's advocate, it's put to him that maybe he's in a position to call for such radical change given Dublin's domination of the province in the latter half of the last decade. 'I know there are those who will say well you would say that – you have five Leinsters in a row and were caught nearly every time at the next match.

'I agree. Guys who haven't got provincial medals – you're taking away that opportunity. I fully recognise that. That is the big downside. That is the tough part. Unfortunately, with the current system, the big teams are only planning for the latter stages of the championship. Dublin haven't kicked on as the Kerrys, Tyrones and Galways have reinvented themselves to win All-Irelands through the back door.

'I've noticed the last few years that the championship takes off with a whimper. You'd hardly know it's up and running. What did we have this year? New York versus Galway as a stand-alone fixture.

'It's not until August that it really takes off. It just ticks away in the background. I've noticed a huge change compared to previous years. Four or five years ago, from the first round of the championship, it was high intensity stuff. Now, the whole bite has gone out of provincial championship games.

'Take last year's first round championship match between Dublin and Meath. It was a flat match. It was no more like a Dublin–Meath championship match. It was the worst I've seen. Lacking in intensity. That's why it's going downhill. Unless they're brave, unless they change things around, it's going to continue that way. They could do so much with it. It's such a brilliant brand.'

One of the GAA's concerns is that such a model could possibly generate the sort of finances and calendar of games that could push the game down the road to some form of semi-professionalism. 'And if it generates huge money, so what?' responds Whelan.

'Inter-county players are fairly easily pleased. I don't think there is a huge push to get paid. Yeah they look at some of their counterparts in other sports and say, "Wouldn't it be great." They are putting in a huge commitment. Once you look after players properly, give them generous expenses, that sort of stuff, you don't need to go down the route of any sort of professionalism because it is agreed at the moment that it is not sustainable.

'The interim greement with the GPA has recognised that too and worthwhile player welfare projects have been implemented which are not based around elite players, but players who need assistance. There is no appetite there among players at the moment. And I don't think it will happen because it will take huge moves within the GAA to change the whole format of the championship.'

Asked if he feels a provincial medal still carries the same lustre for players, he is unhesitating. 'I think it's gone past that. Maybe I'm saying that because I'm speaking having won five in a row. Other players mightn't agree with that. I'm sure if you're from Wexford or Limerick or Roscommon or Fermanagh it holds real currency. You have all these examples, and that is the downside to what I'm talking about – you are taking that away from guys.

'But the titles are being demeaned the way things are. In recognising that they are important to those counties, the general point is that the provincial championships have lost their intensity, lost that battle element, that win-at-all-costs mentality. If you were to compare games in the Ulster championship last year to games going back ten years ago you would see a massive difference. The GAA have got to find a format whereby every game you play in the championship is critical to your chances of winning it. And if you do lose once, unless results go for you, it really impacts on your chances.

'Home and away is critical to other sports. Look at the French rugby teams, they don't travel so well but Jesus, try beating them in France! All teams have got to a certain level. It would certainly be interesting to do on a trial basis.

'I think there would be an appetite from the players to move to provincial leagues. You're releasing players then for a weekend which would be a big help to the clubs. If you were to carry out a poll of players in relation to National League games, I'd say it would be very interesting. If you asked them honestly would they prefer to be playing under lights on a Friday night in a local derby in front of twice the crowd rather than on Sunday afternoons, I think I know where they want to be. With the amount of floodlit grounds out there now it's certainly doable.'

He's still getting used to the experience of going to games as a spectator, of being just another face in the crowd. Playing with the county, his reputation preceded him.

Before moving to Donabate, he lived with Fiona in Swords where he suddenly found himself on first name terms with the owner of the local Chinese takeaway. 'The lads used to slag me about getting the Chinese at home on the odd Friday night when we were in Swords. Someone who delivered obviously told him I played for Dublin so he'd answer the phone every Friday night, "Hello Mister Whelan," and have a full chat. He knew my house number when it came up. He used to send me free bottles of wine, things like that, but Fiona always drank them!'

Ah, the perks of playing for Dublin. He watched enough players go to know how quickly it all changes when you step – or are pushed – off the inter-county treadmill. 'A part of you is ready for it. Over 13, 14 years I would have seen a lot of fellas go ahead of me, fellas who were coming towards the end of their careers. And nobody gives a hoot once they're gone – nobody. That's the reality. OK, fans will say thanks – they can't do any more. But nobody cares. And that would be one of the reasons why, when I was approached to do this project for a players' hardship fund, I said yes.

'I was very lucky in that respect in that I had very good employers in Allianz. I joined Allianz in 2000, was two, three years into my career. Obviously, they were sponsors of the National League and were very supportive in terms of time off or if I had to do the odd bits here and there. A lot of GAA players need that support from employers. I used to see it with a lot of guys in trades who couldn't get the time off, got a lot of grief. I've seen a lot of guys in and out of work.

'I was lucky to be working for a financial institution that recognised the time and commitment that had to go into it. It was very good for me and certainly the profile helped me get to where I wanted in my job. Sometimes it can be a hindrance because people think that it's only because you're a footballer and that sort of stuff. But you are what you are. If people were to say does a football career help or hinder you, I'd say it helps you – as long as you keep your image clean.

'I think anyone in an office job or a standard nine to five is OK but certainly anybody in a trade or shift work, it has a massive impact on their life. Life is very difficult. They are chopping and changing all the time, they are losing money, there is no doubt about that. I was lucky in that I wasn't in that position but I saw enough guys moving shifts around, trying to catch up, losing out on overtime. And the demands have gone up every year. It's more and more time. Last year in particular we did a lot of weekend training. Challenge games during the week where fellas have to meet at 3.30 or 4 p.m. So there is a huge impact.'

As a leading light with the highest-profile county, he recognised how well looked after he was, laughing at how quickly things return to normal when the jersey is returned.

'I'm lucky in that I probably haven't bought a pair of runners or a tracksuit or any sports gear since I've been a teenager. Everything is supplied on a plate. You've the best of facilities, the best of food afterwards, you play on the best pitches – you're spoiled to a certain extent. So you have to drop your standards! I was ready for that. I was never one to get carried away with all that rubbish, all the trappings.'

Whether it was rubbing shoulders with Ken Doherty or any of the top Irish sport stars who enjoy a professional lifestyle, he says his own status as an amateur GAA player was one easy way of staying grounded, particularly when it came to the bottom line.

'I was with Puma for years. The guys in Horizon Sports were very good to deal with. All that so-called glam – the only thing you used to think at things like that was, "How much are they getting for this!"' he says, cracking up.

'That's what you always wondered! They were professional sports people in their own field. You reach the pitch of your own sport and you're meeting people in other sports who were set up for life.

'I've met a few of the Leinster rugby guys a few times and they're top guys. Very level-headed, down to earth, no arrogance about them. They work hard. I know they get paid well, but they've not gone beyond themselves, which is nice to see.'

As for what the future holds? He appreciates the time now with Fiona and the kids and enjoys coaching Jamie and the next generation.

Former Dublin team-mate Colin Moran has been appointed as a Juvenile Director in the County Board's coaching set-up and he has met him with a view to getting involved with one of the county underage squads.

As the road stretches out in front of him, he's happy with life on the other side of the fence.

Gerard McGrattan

Dermot Crowe, *Sunday Independent*

On 9 August 1992, those match-goers who entered Croke Park early enough witnessed a rare sight. Down senior hurlers emerged from the old tunnel located between the Canal End and Hogan Stand to boldly confront one of the game's masters, Cork, in an All-Ireland semi-final. It was a first. Down were Ulster hurling champions before, in 1941, but had chosen to play in the All-Ireland junior semi-final. Fifty-one years later the county was breaking new ground. No one gave them a prayer. They would be eyeballing a county with a record 27 All-Ireland senior wins. Most predicted a riot of Cork scores.

Those charged with the task of filling the match programme also faced a steep challenge. There was little to go on. The only past meeting between the two counties worthy of mention occurred in 1971 when the Down Under-21 hurlers made a daunting trip to the Cork Athletic Grounds to play an All-Ireland semi-final. It wasn't a life-enhancing experience for the visitors, soundly beaten 11–10 to 2–1. Starved of options, the programme thieved this mismatch from the vaults. In a memorable statement of the obvious, the programme informed readers that the Down Under-21 goalkeeper had had a 'most unhappy afternoon'. Cork's John Rothwell scored four goals, with the celebrated poacher Seanie O'Leary having to settle for one green flag. Soon Cork would complete an All-Ireland four-in-a-row at the grade. If it were of any consolation to Down, Cork scored seven goals in the final against Wexford.

And that was it, essentially: the counties had virtually no past. Twenty-one years later Down seniors arrived with little to suggest they could trouble Cork. The previous September, Croke Park had been a splash of red and black when Down footballers upheld a proud tradition of never having lost at Jones' Road in the championship. In the All-Ireland final they overcame that year's marathon men, Meath, and reawakened the spirit of their forefathers, the great Ulster pioneers of the 1960s. Hurling never enjoyed any of the same popular appeal, being a marginalised concern focused on a tight-knit community in the Ards Peninsula. The three Ards clubs of Ballycran, Ballygalget, and Portaferry created their own independent republic and pooled their scant resources to field a county team and fly the flag.

'A fella asked me to show him the back of my hand,' Belfast's Sean McGuinness, manager of the 1992 team explains, 'and said if it were the county of Down, my thumb was the Ards Peninsula and my thumbnail was where they hurled. It was that small.'

Down was another backstreet in the Ulster hurling ghetto. But that was about to change. In 1989 the province's senior hurling championship was revived after 40 years and Down contested three finals against Antrim before coming good in the fourth. Antrim had put Ulster on the map by reaching the All-Ireland final in '89, famously defeating Offaly in the semi-final, and in 1991 they went nail-bitingly close to shocking Kilkenny. They were hurling in Division One; they had acquired a respected status in the game. Then on 12 July 1992, Antrim were outplayed by Down in the Ulster final at Casement Park and the pendulum swung. Down opened a door to a different world entirely. To a Down hurler, playing Cork must have seemed scarcely believable. They were strangers beyond Ulster and it spoke volumes that perhaps their most recognised player, Greg Blaney, had earned notice primarily as an All-Ireland winning footballer and All-Star.

Blaney took up his position at centre-forward, marked by Denis Walsh, the current manager of Cork. Walsh played at centre-back in a late reshuffle in the Cork defence caused by injury to Jim Cashman. It would prove significant. Timmy Kelleher replaced Cashman and marked the young Down left half-forward Gerard McGrattan. He could have had no idea of what lay in store. McGrattan, a tall and athletic 20 year old from Portaferry in his first summer as a senior inter-county player, terrorised Cork's defence all afternoon. Later, with Kelleher struggling, Cathal Casey was moved across in an attempt to tame him. It mattered little. Cork eventually shook off a hardy Down challenge without playing well, while McGrattan took home the Man-of-the-Match award after scoring five points from play. Even with the main billing given to the meeting of Kilkenny and Galway in the second semi-final, the most talked about hurler that evening was McGrattan. Unknown to most people before the match, by the end of the year he would be voted an All-Star, the only hurler from Down to earn that honour.

His rise was meteoric. Before the Cork match, McGrattan had played only two senior championship games for Down, both in Ulster earlier that summer. He hadn't been part of their league campaign in the spring. Nothing about Cork or Croke Park stressed him. But for a fine save by Ger Cunningham, he would also have added a goal to his day's takings, and he won a free that resulted in a Down point and set up another. Down left the field with their heads held high. At one stage in the second half a goal reduced Cork's lead from eight to three points. The rank outsiders were growing in confidence, and the crowd that had mostly gathered for the second semi-final between Kilkenny and Galway cheered their gallantry. Cork's response was swift and lethal: a goal at the other end which the television cameras missed. It finished the Down challenge. The final whistle had them nine points adrift.

Immediately afterwards McGrattan found himself abducted by a team from RTÉ and spirited up to the crow's nest with the rest of the day's commentary team for the second semi-final. Eighteen years later, seated in the kitchen of his home in

Portaferry, he recounts how that was his most nerve-wracking moment of the day: having to go on television and give his analysis of the match. This was infinitely more terrifying than playing Cork. Even now, watching himself being interviewed by a youthful Michael Lyster, he cringes. He is back there, reliving the horror.

> It was not what he came to Croke Park to do. Beside him Ciaran Barr, who had been on the Antrim team beaten by Down that year, strikes an altogether different pose: he is a veritable machine of smooth talking and carefully polished syntax, a fearless and confident font of opinion. McGrattan looks a fish out of water, willing the end so he can rejoin his mates. You can tell he isn't comfortable. The replies are clipped and don't have legs. If he plays a great game, he doesn't talk one. By the time he gets out of the RTÉ gantry and makes his escape, the rest of the squad and manager Sean McGuinness are waiting for him on the bus, ready to head back up to the North of Ireland and to some version of reality.

Portaferry, April, 2010. The crossing from Strangford takes around five minutes, a route familiar with many hurling teams down the years who have travelled over the Lough to play a League match against Down in Portaferry or maybe Ballycran or Ballygalget. Gerard McGrattan meets you at the other side and you follow his car up a hill to where he now resides with his wife, Kathy, and their three children. He has the same job he had when he started working almost 20 years ago, in Belfast. He is treasurer of the GAA club, juvenile secretary and looks after the Under-14 hurling team. He hasn't changed very much although he is a different man from the callow youth let free in Croke Park in 1992. A serious knee injury the following year meant he could never reach the same performance levels. After four major knee operations he finished hurling in 2006.

'After my last operation my consultant told me the joints

were eroded and I'd need a knee replacement if I kept hurling. The same guy did all four operations, Joe McClelland in the Ulster Clinic in Belfast, and he was very black and white. I had to make a decision at that point. "I don't want to see you back here again," he said to me, "your knee is in a terrible state." It took me a while to come to terms with it.'

Injuries plagued him. In the Down hurling final that year he was captain when Portaferry won but was unfit to play in the Ulster championship that followed. The county final would be his final appearance on a hurling field and he left feeling there were a few years still in him. Instead, he flung himself into the club's administrative affairs and into coaching, gaining a qualification and insisting later when he became juvenile secretary that all coaches obtain similar badges. Two years ago Portaferry won the minor championship after a long stretch, and moments like those help compensate for his playing disappointments.

His first season with Down seems a long time ago now. In 1992 the GAA was beginning to embrace change and try new experiences. That summer Clare footballers shocked Kerry in the Munster final, winning the provincial title for the first time since 1917. Donegal won the county's first-ever All-Ireland senior title, Anthony Molloy returning gloriously across the hills to beautiful Ardara, and Down had set the standard for Ulster football's upwardly mobile claims the year before. The Meath and Dublin four-match saga in 1991 opened the GAA's eyes to two empirical truths: the limitations of the knock-out system; and the scope for increasing the game's appeal if it were to be reformed. In 1993 Derry would win a first All-Ireland and Ulster would lead sweeping revolutions and the overthrow of the old oligarchies. Leitrim footballers awoke in Connacht. It was from this period of popular revolt and regime change that Down hurlers emerged.

In 1989 Down represented Ulster in the All-Ireland minor semi-final at Croke Park against eventual winners, Offaly, with McGrattan lining out and scoring the first point of the day. Exam commitments meant he didn't make his senior championship bow until the summer of 1992, in the provincial semi-final against Derry, a 9–18 to 0–10 cakewalk. Antrim started as warm favourites in the final but Down had their measure and won 2–16 to 0–11. It was a noted date in the north, 12 July, and reflecting those troubled times the referee for the day's minor match, Meath's Martin McCormack, missed the opening half of the curtain-raiser after being held up at a police checkpoint. McGrattan caught the eye in Down's breakthrough victory with four points from play.

Sean McGuinness couldn't conceal his admiration. 'They played their shirts off,' the proud Down manager said afterwards. Antrim manager Jim Nelson also paid tribute to McGrattan. 'We were at a loss as to who would be best to mark him. We switched different players on him but to no avail.' He added that McGrattan had 'the speed of an Olympian athlete'. The stage was set for Down's trip to Croke Park but McGrattan was still a well-kept secret to most of the hurling world.

In the McGrattan home a recording of the Cork–Down match in 1992 is among the family possessions. Six-year-old Tom McGrattan, the youngest of the children, includes it on his favourite playlist. 'He would take it to bed with him,' says his father, 'when he was very young.' Gerard McGrattan slides the video into the player and we are transported back in time. Jim Carney is commentating and Ciaran Barr offers analysis. Down run onto the field wearing unfamiliar amber shirts. In the studio Michael Lyster is sporting an outrageously ornate tie. McGrattan is the youngest hurler, 20 since the previous March, on a Down team that's ageing. His brother-in-law Kevin Coulter is playing at right corner-back and gives a fine performance, driving out lengthy clearances. The midfielder Gary Savage is McGrattan's first cousin. Noel Sands, captain of the Down team, is the current chairman of Portaferry and manages the Under-12s. The right half-back, Marty Mallon, coaches the Portaferry seniors and the Down centre-back Paul McMullan is in charge of the Portaferry minors. Three clubs feed the Down team: evenly distributed between Ballycran, Portaferry and Ballygalget.

Despite the mammoth challenge they headed south in high spirits. In the lead-up to the game the Down football captain Paddy O'Rourke attended one of their training sessions to give a powerful motivational speech. Sean McGuinness also had a reputation for good mental preparation. Later it was disclosed that facing Cork had so unnerved one player that he got sick on the morning of the game. But McGrattan felt no nerves at all. Nothing. The players are warming up as we hear Ciaran Barr announce that McGrattan is entering the match with a reputation after the Ulster final and that if he can do it against Cork he can do it against anybody.

'I had watched Gerard McGrattan playing for the Down Under-21s,' says McGuinness, 'and he was what we needed: a big, strong lad who could field a ball and run like a greyhound. People don't realise how important Greg Blaney was. As soon as [Noel] Keith was pucking the ball out, Greg went in one direction and everyone followed; it left McGrattan with space.'

Down show no inhibitions and open brightly, taking the game to Cork. Sands puts them in front briefly but Cork, while not hurling fluently, pose a constant threat. In the sixth minute a high ball is contested by two Down defenders and Kevin Hennessy, a natural goal poacher, steals in behind. In spite of a poor first touch he fires the ball past Noel Keith into the goal. Yet they can't shake off Down and the first of McGrattan's five scores is served up, reducing the Cork lead to four points. He breaks through and strikes off his left side, right-handed – his signature stroke. Soon after he gets into a good position about 25 yards from goal to the right-hand side and shoots diagonally across Ger Cunningham. The sliotar whizzes and hops before the goalkeeper but he makes an excellent save, conceding a 65 in the process. Kevin Coulter steps up and drives it straight between the posts. The crowd rise to acclaim the score. Halfway through the first period of play Cork are discovering that Down will not be rolling over. They cannot push out the lead. McGrattan finishes the half with four from play. Cork lead by four at the interval.

After McGrattan's goal chance there is increased urgency in Cork. Gerald McCarthy, the team coach, is on the line with Canon O'Brien, the manager of the team. O'Brien is reputed to have once held up the red-and-white shirt of his county before playing Tipperary to extol its virtues then referring less kindly to the Tipperary shirt and the 'yellow streak' running through it. It is doubtful that the Canon had spent much time denigrating the Down colours – they meant nothing to Cork. But Down are riling them. And as we watch it is evident that they are striving to move up a gear.

'I remember Canon O'Brien going frantic with his wing halves for not stopping him,' McGuinness remarks. 'These weren't from the Glens or the Ards, but Cork hurlers who were expecting to win an All-Ireland, the cream of the crop. After the match I said to him, "Well done, big lad." And he just said, "I did my best, Sean," like he was half-apologising. He was a nice kid. He trained hard. No nonsense, lovely to manage.'

Last year the Down comedian and television personality Patrick Kielty had his knowledge of local GAA affairs tested in an ambush quiz conducted by a Sunday newspaper. Of the ten questions posed, he answered eight correctly, an impressive return, but of the two he didn't know, one was the identity of Down's sole hurling All-Star. McGrattan isn't insulted by this. And he doesn't appear surprised. Even winning an All-Star won't guarantee the level of recognition and popular appeal that's a given for a Down footballer. Certain things conspired against him: serious injury; Down only managing to win two more Ulster titles and none after 1997. In 1998 Derry reached the Ulster final against Antrim, leaving Down out in the cold, and Down didn't reach an Ulster final again until 2001. By then McGrattan had started a family, having married Kathy in 1997. Erin was born in 1999, Gerra arrived in 2001 and Tom followed in 2003. He finished playing for Down in 2004, his career, like March, arriving like a lion and going out like a lamb. 'I was 32. I didn't want to be someone put on the team for his name,' he says of the finish. 'Younger guys were coming through. You have to go at some point.' Retiring afforded him more room to enjoy the twilight of his club career, giving him three campaigns free of inter-county distraction. In 2006 he won a seventh county medal.

Injuries meant he could never relive the dashing play of his maiden season. 'I had my cruciate operated on in December, 1993. I hurt my knee the following March after the Cork game. We were down in Galway with the county team for a training weekend when it happened.' McGuinness remembers him leaping to catch a ball in trademark fashion and turning to dash clear when the knee snapped. Nobody near him. One of those things.

This was the start of constant interruptions and it took him two years to get himself back. He thinks his decision to stay playing that summer may have aggravated the injury. 'I believe I did the damage by not getting the proper [medical] attention at the time. I felt I would be OK after few weeks' rest. It wasn't properly diagnosed until December. You were being told you would be out for a year. That was 1994 gone.'

McGuinness's final day as manager of Down coincided with McGrattan's last appearance at Croke Park, the 1995 All-Ireland semi-final against Offaly. He watched him struggle to become the same player again, aware of the long lonely hours in physio, the cycling and weights in a slow process of rebuilding his knee. 'The training he had done was unbelievable to try to get back. I always remember Joe Connolly doing a coaching course at Queen's [University] and him and Pat Spillane got their knee operation done the same day. He never played again and Spillane won four more All-Irelands. It either goes for you or it doesn't with those injuries. Gerard was never the same player again.'

McGrattan isn't tormented by those lost years. The last time McGuinness was in Portaferry he spotted him umpiring at an

Under-10 hurling match. An ex-All-Star umpiring at an Under-10 match – where did it all go wrong? He would not see it that way himself. 'In fairness I never really had the opportunity to do it,' he says, when asked if he ever felt he came close to hurling like he had in 1992. 'The following year I was injured and I missed two years of training. I did my cruciate and had another three operations. There was constant rehab and I'd be up in the morning before work training and with physios before and sometimes after work. I was well looked after, we had some of the best physios around. But I had three operations in those three years and the last was in 2006. All on my left knee. After the fourth I was finished.'

Despite the first serious knee injury, he lined out against Antrim in the 1993 Ulster final. The Glensmen were plotting revenge and McGrattan had been earmarked as an obvious threat. In the League the previous winter the sides had had a tempestuous clash at Casement Park from which McGrattan departed early with a rib injury after taking a dig off the ball. He spent the night in the Belfast Royal Hospital and his manager talked of him being targeted. Afterwards he received a letter from the Antrim manager Jim Nelson explaining that no player had been given instructions to injure an opponent.

The Down clubs play in the Antrim League and the level of familiarity between hurlers from both counties is unusually high. Resentful of Down's new status as the province's hurling champions, Antrim were eager to regain their title. They won emphatically, 0–21 to 0–11. McGrattan scored one point and Down's bubble had burst. After undergoing an operation at the end of the year he didn't hurl again until the spring of 1995. As a spectator he watched Down lose again in the Ulster final to Antrim in 1994, this time by six points. A year later they regained the Ulster title after defeating Antrim in a replayed final. McGrattan came on after an hour as he worked his way back to fitness. He took no part in the replay. In August they were back in Croke Park against Offaly, rampant victors over

Kilkenny in the Leinster final. McGrattan wasn't named in the team but a late injury to one of the players selected earned him a call-up. It was his first full game back after a long injury stretch and he went in at right corner-forward on Martin Hanamy, later passing some time on the wing on Kevin Martin.

In the previous two years Antrim had been routed in Croke Park by Limerick and Kilkenny and doubts were growing about the province's ability to maintain a worthwhile challenge. Yet Down had an experienced outfit and might have hoped to profit from Offaly complacency. Offaly won comfortably, however, and never allowed Down to gather momentum. An early goal from Michael Duignan set the pattern and they were nine points in front after 26 minutes. McGrattan, who had illuminated the Croke Park audience three years earlier, was largely anonymous and failed to score. The margin of victory of 11 points didn't flatter the winners. In 1996 Antrim won back the Ulster title, the last year the Ulster champions would have automatic entry to the All-Ireland semi-finals.

Injuries forced his early departure from three county finals. In 2001 he was hit in the eye with a ball in the county final and lost his eyesight for 48 hours, spending the night in hospital while Portaferry celebrated a title win. In the 2004 final he went off with a dislocated shoulder and in his last match, the 2006 county final, he tore cartilage and knee ligaments in the defeat of Ballycran. The nearest he got to recovering his best form and fitness was in 1997. 'I was playing well then,' he says. 'I was getting there. [But] I probably never [fully] got there to be honest.'

In the 1997 Ulster final they overturned Antrim with a much-changed team, McGrattan scoring 1–3 as part of a two-man inside attacking line. Tipperary were much too strong in the All-Ireland quarter-final in Clones, though he scored one of their three goals. Then Down hurling regressed and has never recovered the lost ground since. Nine years after losing 10–18 to 0–10 to Down, the day of McGrattan's senior inter-county debut, Derry beat the Mournemen in the 2001 Ulster final. In the following season Down reached the Ulster final, beaten by Antrim, and then lost out heavily in the qualifiers to Galway: a 7–15 to 0–13 hammering at Casement Park on 16 June 2002, ten years after his All-Star beginnings. McGrattan scored three of Down's points but they could not live with teams like they used to.

Down failed to reach the Ulster final in 2003 and were back there in 2004 after winning the Division Two League final, playing an exciting brand of hurling. By then he was being upstaged by a wonderful young hurler, Paul Braniff, who has since been plagued by knee injuries like his predecessor. McGrattan played in the 2004 Ulster final draw and replay against Antrim, which Down lost by five points. His last match came at Ballycran in the qualifiers in late June. Galway again showed no mercy, winning 5–19 to 1–14. McGrattan signed off with one point. Of the team that played Cork in 1992, only McGrattan and his cousin Gary Savage were left.

It was time.

Cork and Down hurlers have historically been poles apart, aristocrat and peasant, but for that one day in 1992 the exploits of McGrattan helped close the margins. It is his enduring legacy. His All-Star award is currently residing in an exhibition of Down GAA memorabilia in a museum at Downpatrick. His county's performance at Croke Park 18 years ago excited genuine hopes of further sallies south in the years ahead but it wasn't long before both the career of McGrattan and the fate of the county's hurlers had fallen into decline. After winning Ulster again in 1995 they regained the provincial title two years later, the first season of the 'backdoor' experiment which meant winning Ulster earned a ticket into the All-Ireland quarter-finals, not the last four. Down's reward for winning the 1997 Ulster title was a meeting with defeated Munster finalists Tipperary at Clones.

McGrattan played in a two-man full forward line and believes he was closest then to rediscovering his old form. But they were well beaten and that is more or less the last most of us have seen of them and of him.

In his book *Last Night's Fun*, the Belfast writer Ciarán Carson recalls travelling to Cork for an All-Ireland minor hurling semi-final in 1965, and the realisation that he and his Antrim team-mates operated to a different time and rhythm. Cork hurled faster and infinitely harder; they wiped Antrim off the field. That segregation still exists to a great extent and it is a constant struggle for Ulster counties to compete and feel they belong. The trouble is that hurling will always be Cork's game whereas the young hurler in Down and Antrim is faced with innumerable distractions and conflicts and a history with harsh lessons in failure.

The same day Gerard McGrattan was mincing the Cork defence, Brian Corcoran guarded Ger Cunningham's goal, the youngest member of the Rebels' backline. In many respects he was McGrattan's mirror prodigy. Playing in the right corner-back position, a year younger, he had been creating major headlines in his maiden season. Corcoran would have the disappointment of losing the All-Ireland final the following month but he was voted Hurler of the Year in his first season, an extraordinary achievement. Like McGrattan he had an explosive career start. For several years after that Corcoran carried a reputation of the player whose talents deserved greater reward. He hurled through a lean spell for Cork hurling, the absolute nadir being their 1996 hammering from Limerick in the Munster championship. Not until 1999 did he finally win an All-Ireland senior medal and for some time before there was the very real possibility that he might have to go without. For a Cork hurler, especially one of Corcoran's talents, that would have deemed something of a sporting tragedy.

Eventually, Corcoran's fortunes changed and he ended up with the considerable compensation of three All-Ireland medals, winning again in 2003 and 2004. McGrattan would never recreate the magic of that day against Cork. But he had other memories worth recounting. Before suffering his first serious injury, he enjoyed a season in Division One of the National League in 1992–93. Down proved a match for most teams, good enough to reach the quarter-finals where they lost to Cork. In their final regulation game at Nowlan Park a win over Kilkenny sent the home team into Division Two. McGrattan played in the middle of the field. At one point John Power moved out on him. He rates Power as the hardest hurler he ever encountered.

'He hit me really hard,' says McGrattan, as if reliving the shuddering impact of the wiry Kilkenny farmer. 'We travelled down in cars, stayed in the Montague Hotel [in Portlaoise]. There was a great crowd at that match, and I think Kilkenny were shocked they were beaten. Myself and my brother-in-law Kevin Coulter had our photograph taken afterwards with the McCarthy Cup.'

He was now an All-Star hurler, chosen at right half-forward in an attack also featuring John Power, Tony O'Sullivan, Michael Cleary, Liam Fennelly and DJ Carey. It didn't massively alter his life although that winter he was much in demand at various events around Ulster.

'At the time I was at a lot of functions and I was only really out of minor and was still learning myself really so I was a bit overawed, I wasn't that comfortable with all that. Every weekend you were off somewhere. I remember being at a function in Tyrone and the following day we were playing Wexford in Dublin and I had to get down to that. After a while it does become a weight on your shoulders because you are only as good as the last game, and that is what I would say to the juveniles I train. You only do your best; you can't rise to that standard in every game.'

For a while everyone wanted a piece of him. McGuinness remembers coming off the field after the Cork match in 1992 and a Kilkenny man approached him and said he would guarantee

McGrattan a job if he'd move to the county and play there. 'I nearly fell over. This guy was prepared to give him a job if he came down and played. "Excuse me," I said, "he's a Down player," and I walked off. I was astounded. He was a young lad; he had everything in front of him. I thought there was so much there for him after that and it just didn't happen. He was a terrible loss to Down.'

The second half of the 1992 All-Ireland semi-final between Cork and Down gets underway. Watching it again now, he remembers the day being so warm that he felt his body over-heating in the dressing-room at half-time – he recalls having a 'wild sore head'. But he couldn't complain – he had four points scored against Cork. For one of those Timmy Kelleher had won a ball and it popped out of his hand to McGrattan who raised a flag. The breaks were going his way. After his second point Casey moved over on him. He responded by scoring a third, over the shoulder on the turn. For the next he robbed Casey and finished. Four between them and everything to play for. 'We realised we were in the game. When we scored the second goal I never considered that we would have been in an All-Ireland final. We started off just trying to compete.'

The second half of the 1992 All-Ireland semi-final gets underway and McGrattan wins a free that Sands should score but he strikes it too low. Then he fires over his fifth to reduce the lead to four again. Cork stride out to six points twelve minutes after the interval. Three minutes later the gap is eight. 'Ger McGrattan has been isolated really,' says Jim Carney. 'He's not getting enough of the ball.'

The truth is that he is still lively and involved. He provides an assist for a score by Danny Hughes. They knuckle down and cut the lead down to six with a great score from Sands. Then Sands pounces for a goal. Only three points in it once more. A great roar goes up. But it is short-lived. Cork's retaliatory goal is an immediate killjoy, scored by Ger Fitzgerald, after a quick puck-out by Cunningham. It finally breaks Down's resolve. Cork add on two points and the final ten minutes is played on Cork's terms, the match safe.

There follows the terrifying ordeal of having to analyse the Galway–Kilkenny match as he is taken away by RTÉ. In a way it captures the innocence of the day – Cork didn't frighten him, being live on television did. 'I was a bag of nerves.'

He isn't soured that the rest of his career could never reach the same levels. When he looks at how Down have struggled in the last 13 years the miracle may be that he made it there at all. For the foreseeable future a second Down hurler winning an All-Star is long odds.

McGuinness remembers getting calls from all over Ireland after the Cork match from clubs hoping to get McGrattan's shirt to raise money in raffles. After the All-Star there was a night of celebration in Portaferry where one man spoke of having spotted McGrattan's talent from afar, despite telling McGuinness some time before that he would never cut it as an inter-county player. 'His brother-in-law, Kevin Coulter, was drinking a pint and nearly spilled it over himself.'

Is his old manager sorry he didn't achieve more? 'Very much so. See that day; I could not have imagined he would do that [to Cork]. I could have seen him playing rightly, but never seen him playing like that. This was Roy of the Rovers stuff you know. It was only his third senior match.'

They still meet from time to time and McGuinness's son works for the same company as McGrattan in Belfast, Bombardier. Before last year's All-Ireland final they met in a Dublin hotel and had a lot of fun, reliving moments from their best days and some of the worst. 'We gate-crashed a 25th wedding anniversary,' McGuinness smiles. 'Oh what a night we had.'

Gerard McGrattan is grateful for what he has: seven county medals he cherishes and a club that's an anchor for life. Portaferry's playing fields are less than a mile from his home. Serving as an umpire in an Under-10 match is not seen by him as beneath his station, but a way of reciprocating the umpires who stood there when he was ten playing on the same fields, dreaming of being a great player.

The previous Sunday he was at an Under-10 camogie blitz which featured his younger daughter, Gerra, then he had to drive an hour to Warrenpoint to see Erin, his eldest, play and score two goals for Portaferry Under-12s. His young son is playing for the Under-8s the following weekend and two nights mid-week will be devoted to training the Under-14s boys. He also has to keep a handle on the club's purse strings as Portaferry treasurer. Does it match playing? No. But it has its rewards. Watching his kids deriving such simple pleasure from playing matches – he can't put a value on that. 'I never put any pressure on them,' he says. 'I would have always encouraged them but there is no pressure.'

At 38, he's not sure what the future will bring. He may seek more advanced coaching qualifications. Perhaps at some stage he will be part of a Down management team. He will always be Down's All-Star hurler and the man who astonished those privileged enough to see him play against Cork in summer, 1992. He feels that winning an Ulster medal in 1997, and a county title the year before, were noble achievements considering the injuries he had to contend with. He also cites captaining Down in 2001 as a highlight and leading them out in Gaelic Park to play New York. It wasn't an All-Ireland semi-final but he captained his county and regarded it as an honour. He will always be remembered for the Cork game, though, and the All-Star who probably inspired some of the Down hurlers who followed. That, one suspects, is what might please him most of all.

Anthony Molloy

In an interview with Karl O'Kane, *Irish Daily Star*

DESTINY

'I always believed from the time I was a young fella I was destined to walk up those famous steps and, there I was, leading the way up the Hogan Stand.

'Without a doubt it's the greatest moment of your life. You will never do anything better, no matter what you do. There is so much adrenalin and power running through your veins. You are the most powerful man in Ireland for them five minutes.

'You could say what you like and it would be accepted.

'I remember watching All-Irelands as a young lad, and you'd have modelled yourself on the likes of Jack O'Shea and Brian Mullins, those boys who had done it.

'You'd say, "Jesus, I could do that myself some day and it would be great."

'I knew we were going to win that day and I'd a speech prepared but I left the house without it, but you are taken up those steps and it's not hard to talk. If anybody seen where I came from it would be fairly remote, rural, one of the most scenic places in Donegal. That's where Sam was going back to. It just came out, it wasn't pre-planned, "Sam's for the Hills".'

THE HILLS

'Our hill was high above Glengesh on Leamagowra Mountain. There were only four houses in my townland and for a long time there was nobody at all living there as people died off and others moved closer to towns. There is one family living on Leamagowra now.

'Emigration was rife in the late '70s and early '80s. Four of my family are still in America, and in 1986 there were seven or eight of the family there. I had what they would have called a pensionable job with the ESB [Electricity Supply Board] that kept me at home at the time.

'America was a great place to go to then, no problems, off the plane and you had a job in the morning, but it's different now with all the regulations, green cards, and the work isn't there anyway.

'I came from a family of 12. There was nothing else to be done, no pastime other than football. I think we didn't get electricity until 1975. We were using gaslight in them days, no washing machines and no mod cons. It was tough going for my father and mother, Lanty and Nora.

'Neighbours would come round and you'd have games with other townlands. There was one black-and-white TV, at John Gallagher's, a few miles from us. On the big match days you'd have to be there early or you wouldn't get into the house, and then afterwards there'd be a full blown 15- or 20-a-side game. Any spare time you had you played football. When the farm work was done you had the ball in your hand.'

THE PRICE
'The new left knee's not too bad. It bends 100 degrees. It should bend more. It had always troubled me and it had come to the stage I had to get it replaced. October two years ago I got the job done. By that stage I'd had about seven or eight different operations down the years on the knees and I would have funded all that on my own insurance, and everything else.

'I was given a choice of the Mater Private or wait for a year, and the cost was something like €22,000 for the week. The way I saw it I had no option. I was left on the scrap heap, the knee riddled with arthritis.

'I'd bought a bar a few years earlier, the Hills. It had reached the point where I'd be limping behind the bar on a very busy night. Nights I had to leave the leg hanging over the side of the bed to get some sleep. The knee had stopped swelling up and it was total pain all the time.

'There was no joint left and when I saw the scans it was bone on bone. Dr Austin Kennedy, our team doctor with Donegal, said it was one of the worst knees he ever seen. He couldn't understand how I was playing at all towards the end. I was taking them "all in one hundred" anti-inflammatory tablets, but they were sore on the system and are banned now. I never took injections. I thought I had top cover with my own insurance but it turned out it only covered me for something like €13,500, €14,000.

'I went ahead anyway and the date came up. It took a long time for the GAA to row in behind me and pay the outstanding amount and I even received solicitor's letters from the Mater Private regarding payment. I knew the GAA would pay at some stage. The way I saw it at least they owed me that much.

'My own County Board weren't too interested in my welfare. They never bothered their ass to ask how I was or what I was doing. There was no word from anybody. I made a few phone calls, one to Brian McEniff, and he got on to the GAA Director General, Paraic Duffy. Fair play to Paraic, he sorted it out eventually for me and Croke Park did pay, but I shouldn't have had to go through all that.

'I had one full-time bar staff and I had to go and get two part-timers. The first month I was on the sofa with the leg up. I'd to go back behind the bar within six weeks after I'd been told to do nothing for the six months I was on sticks. In that game you have to be there to keep an eye on things. It cost me a lot of money, but do you think the GAA would even think about you? I feel strongly that there should be something there for past players falling on hardship, injuries, businesses going wrong and other things so I joined the GPA late last year.

'The GAA have definitely fallen down in this area. Once you

hang your boots up you are finished barring you go into reporting or something like the media game, but that's for some and it's not for others. People say it's your own choice, but if a man hadn't have won the All-Ireland . . . here I am, 48, can't run any more, have a knee replacement. I didn't choose that.'

DARKEST HOUR BEFORE THE DAWN
'The trouble started when I was playing in an inter-firms final for John Sisk and Sons Limited back in 1981. I was living in Dublin at the time working as a site clerk on £45 a week. It was a Monday night, a day after we had played Gweedore in the championship.

'It was mainly cartilage problems then but later I broke the kneecap in the same knee. I got an operation done in Jervis Street at the time and I don't think it was a great job. It probably was the real start of my troubles.

'Plenty of times I was told I was finished, six operations on the left knee, two on the right. It was tough enough going in them days coming back. You didn't have the same level of back-up, physiotherapists, doctors, compared to what they have now.

'In 1991 there were certain journalists in Donegal felt I should have hung up the boots. Down hammered us in the Ulster Final and I felt I should have played.

'I was captain and I'd got my latest knee operation done in January. I felt I had recovered, and I was back playing again. I'd played five or ten minutes in the earlier games but I never made the final and I felt hard done by. I remember myself and Martin Shovlin were on the bench that day. We togged back out with ten minutes to go and we were gone out of the dressing-room. I think if things were managed better in 1991 we would probably have overcome Down in that Ulster final.

'Who knows what would have happened then because we were there in 1990, in the All-Ireland semi-final, played very well against Meath, had about 70 per cent of the play but they got two goals, one a fluky oul goal that came off the post and in off Gary Walsh's head. I retired then shortly after that '91 defeat by Down and I had a major falling-out with our manager at the time, Brian McEniff. I went to the States that summer and won a New York championship medal with Donegal.

'Then, at some point in January of 1992 I bumped into Brian McEniff, or maybe he bumped into me, I don't know but we buried the hatchet anyway and I came back on a few conditions; that I was captain again, and we'd forget about what happened in '91. I was captain from 1988 at that stage and I was going back on my own terms. The captaincy wouldn't have been an issue with Brian anyway. I was only coming up on 30. I was missing the game and the boys. I was always coming back as, deep down, I still thought I had a bit to offer.

'There was nothing different about 1992, nothing that would have made you sit up and take notice or show what was going to happen later that year. Training was as it always was, even starting out in the championship. You could still come and go and do what you wanted at the beginning of the year.

'Brian McEniff, to be fair to him, would be a good tactician and a good man to motivate a team in the dressing-room but on the discipline side of things I don't think he was great. If we had the proper discipline and training, and if we'd done what we done at the latter end of 1992 we'd have won a heap of stuff, for the footballers were there.

'We struggled past Cavan in the Ulster championship and were lucky to come out of Breffni Park, and it was only the last 15 minutes we pulled clear against a Fermanagh side that wasn't very good. It was just like any other championship game, but that evening, that's when things changed. Myself and Martin McHugh reckoned we better start doing something fast. Derry were starting to show on the other side of the draw. We had a meeting that evening in the dressing-room. We demanded that training be upped and discipline tightened.

'The following Tuesday there were no footballs. The ball was thrown away and we trained for an hour without the ball. That was the start of hard training . . . the 200 metres, 400s, 800s, all that. We did that once a week for that whole summer; then followed it with ball work. As a result of that Donegal were fit to play the ball they wanted to play, which they were good at, the short ball, and play it as well as they ever did.

'That Ulster Final against Derry was one of the best displays from a Donegal team against the odds. We were terrible in the first half – we lost John Cunningham to a red card, Tony Boyle to injury and only went in a point up at half-time after having a nice wee wind behind us.

'It was gone from us. We had half an hour. It was the end of my career and it would have been the end of the road for the likes of McHugh, Donal Reid and Martin Shovlin. We might have played on but I don't know if we'd have come back after that.

'We turned it around and that second-half performance won the All-Ireland for us. It was even better than the All-Ireland final. Our reaction to that win was right too. We were training that Monday night, harder than we ever trained before. Normally if you won an Ulster title you would be on for a few pints, Jesus Christ, maybe to Wednesday. Training would be called off Tuesday night, or you might be given a week off. This time, though, funny enough, everybody was on the same wavelength. It proved that you won't win anything until you have 25 or 30 lads on the same wavelength, with the same aim.

'You won't win anything either when there are wee cliques here and there in the squad. There were no cliques now and everybody went everywhere together.

'After winning Ulster, the biggest thing for us then was to get over that mental thing of winning an All-Ireland senior semi-final, which Donegal had never done before. There was a thing in Donegal that it was all right going to Croke Park, putting up a performance, and going down the road getting beat.

'There was a Croke Park issue. I remember 1972, Donegal went up with a good team and should have beaten Offaly but didn't, and Galway beat them in 1974, another good Donegal team. They didn't have this oul belief. We had that belief in ourselves and it carried us through that semi-final.

'We played terribly against Mayo. They didn't let us play properly. We only played in the last ten minutes and won by four points. The Dublin team already in the final who were watching it must have thought, "We are going to have no bother with these boys in the final." I think we caught them, but I also believe no matter what they had done, we were going to beat them anyway.

'Going to Dublin every game was going to be a last chance saloon for me and I knew I had to do the business. There were going to be no second chances and everybody thought like that at the time. It was shocking the way we played against Mayo, and Dublin, I still think to this day, had no homework done on us.

'For example, I can still never understand how the Dublin manager Paddy Cullen left Mick Deegan on Manus Boyle for the whole game, and Manus scored nine points. We had played Dublin in the quarter-final of the National League in Omagh. We were beating them by five points with two minutes to go but they threw in two goals and beat us. We played well that day and we knew in our hearts that we could match that Dublin team. They had the same personnel as that day.

'To be fair McEniff would have covered every angle and he was good at that. I think the massive training we had done though and the togetherness in the squad instilled a belief in us, because everybody did that training. I can go back to other years. You could pull out of a training session any time you wanted, tog off; no big deal.

'I was involved from the National League of 1982 and here, ten years later, we were finally doing this training and had the discipline we needed. We should have been doing it ten years before and that's why the Kerrys and Dublins had so much success. They were doing that training a decade before teams like us started it. If somebody with the ideas of a Mick O'Dwyer or Kevin Heffernan was about, I think we might have won more because we had the footballers. There's no doubt about that.

'It's hard to believe, looking back, how somebody didn't take us under their wing. To be fair Tom Conaghan did start it. He was in charge of us in 1982 when we won Donegal's first All-Ireland Under-21 title, and he was big on discipline.

'I get on great with Brian McEniff now and I call regularly to him because I have great respect for him, but Brian, in my opinion, was involved with Donegal for far too long. Brian was involved as a manager from around 1966–67. I don't believe he was great on discipline. When Tom Conaghan came along then you were on the field, togged at 7 p.m., and if you weren't you were sent home.

'We lost one or two players. Leslie McGettigan was a great player and I recall Tom sending him home and he stayed at home and went to the States the following week. He wouldn't have been too far from the '92 team if he had been at home. But that was Tom, discipline, and that's what we had now.

'They call Brian Mr Donegal and he probably is Mr Donegal. I've still the utmost respect for Brian McEniff. I'd be very friendly with him at the minute. If you are going to be involved with somebody for 20-odd years then you're going to have your fall-outs. It is not natural, or else you are not your own man.

'By nature I never held anything against anybody and it was the same on the field. I wouldn't change that. I got some hard old hokes, but once the game was over I would be the same way. Big Brian McGilligan would have been one of the toughest I came across and we'd some great oul tussles, some hard oul shots hit and taken on the chin, and we'd be good friends now. He won some, and I won some.

'Of course there were fallouts in the squad, but we had in-house meetings in '92, which wouldn't have been done before, and if you had a grievance with a man, or a problem with the management, felt someone wasn't pulling their weight, it was aired in there, not in the pub. It was sorted out behind closed doors and there was no more us and them with the players and the management.

'There were never any fights or rows in the pub anyway. We'd have been a happy enough bunch, closely knit, and had plenty of sing-songs. I would never have been far from the back of the bus. 'My Lovely Old Finn Town', about a wee townland outside Glenties, was our favourite.

'Naturally enough there would have been a fair drinking culture and still is around GAA, and around any sport. It always ends up in the bar. I would have got caught up drinking. There is no doubt about that, but there is plenty of men would have drunk as much as me. Probably one of my biggest faults would be I never said "no" to anyone and if there were 50 people in the bar I always gave my time to them 50. That's the kind of person I was. And I would probably try and have 50 pints with them 50 boys if that was the way it was.

'Anywhere a man went there was a pint bought for you, drink coming from all angles. I hate to see, and I've heard about it, that lads won't sign an autograph for people. There are other boys, they'd say "hello" and that would be it. I would give my five or ten minutes to that boy if he'd be good enough to come up and want to speak to me. That's the way I'd carry on and I'd never have changed that.

'I don't drink any more. I had a problem with drink, no doubt about that. The drink would have been overdone by times. In 1992 I didn't take a drink from January until we won nearly, in September. I was going to give it one good shot anyway.

'I'd a fair following in Donegal in them days, probably because I talked to people, and I still think that's important. We had a massive support for that '92 team, a lot more than Donegal have now, simply because we were around in the pubs. There were other boys there as well, but I can't mention any names. We were very close to our supporters, more than boys are now.

'All right there was maybe an odd Monday spent drinking

but that's the way it was prior to '92. There was no better way to get to know a fella than have a pint with him. The way it was in them days, you played your National League match, championship match, 3.30 p.m. whatever, you were finished at 5 p.m. and went straight to the pub.

'Then it was all night and possibly on Monday. From what I'm led to believe every county was doing the same thing. I'd know the story well about Kerry and players would have said it to me. Them boys drank as much as any Donegal man ever drank. But when it came to knuckling down to serious business, when championship kicked in, that's it cut, no nothing from St Patrick's Day or maybe April, to the end of the League.

'That never happened in Donegal. Things were too loose regarding discipline. We were never told not to drink and we never thought not to. The drink is something you can look back on and regret, maybe with my own club Ardara more than anything. I would have gone out under the influence of drink and thought I played well and if I hadn't drank I would have been ten times better. Sure I never thought about them things at the time.

'Often I'd be on the pitch, worse for the wear. I'd never have thought I'd have as much influence on club games as I did, but when I think about it now we might have won more than one championship if I'd played a bit better. I only played ten minutes of the final we won, 1981, and we lost three other finals.

'I finished football totally in 1995, having done my shoulder in my last club game. We were leading by eight or nine points in the championship when I hurt myself and we got beat. I regretted quitting as I could probably have struggled on a bit, played for another year.

'I found golf a great substitute later on. I'm hitting it fairly well now, playing off 18 and minding my handicap for the summer. But after I quit football initially I had loads of time on my hands. I was used to doing something all my life, training Tuesday and Thursday, and playing on Saturday or Sunday.

'There was a big vacuum there and all of a sudden you found you had nothing to go to, no club or county training, and I wasn't playing that much golf at the time. I was drinking excessively around 1997 and 1998.

'The pub was easy, but there comes a time there isn't much enjoyment left because of the excessiveness of it, pleasing everybody and not pleasing yourself, not saying no when you should. It was not in my nature at all to say no and I usually didn't.'

FALLOUT

'I don't remember much about the 1992 All-Ireland final, just what happened afterwards. I wouldn't have a great memory and if you asked me to start naming the 1992 team now I would struggle but at the time we were inseparable. Going up the steps is an unbelievable trip, the fulfilment, and believing that we have done it. I always remember John Leonard, he'd be married to a lady that lives not far from me, trying to get me up the steps. I'd still meet him the odd time.

'I remember Donegal took us down to Cork in 1990 for what they call a bonding weekend now. They had won the double that year. I was looking at these boys in awe at the time. They had the Sam Maguire and the National League in the room. I had never seen the Sam Maguire in my life. Here, just two years later, I was picking it up. It's something that will always live with me. Every year that goes by you get more appreciative because they are hard to win. I have made a lot of friends through the GAA. Every county you could call on a fella. Some players put in the same effort I did and played the same amount of football and never achieved it.

'We had a fantastic group of players too, the amount of talent. When you can put the likes of Noel Hegarty and Barry McGowan in at corner-back, more ability than was believable and still with some to spare, and so comfortable on the ball, you have something going for you.

'What happened after the All-Ireland final was hard to believe. I don't know when it sunk in, maybe only later on when I finished playing. I was one of them sort of fellas who never dwelled much on what I won. I would have taken that achievement the same way but the celebrations were unbelievable and people wanting you here and there and all over the country and out of the country.

'I'd sooner go back to my own bar, down in the corner with a lock of oul boys. I would be happier like. It was OK for a while, but six months later I was never as glad to see any Cup going back. We could have won another All-Ireland, but I was on the road night and day, and so were the other lads.

'August 1991 I had got married to Briege McGowan, a sister of Barry from the '92 team. Looking back at it the All-Ireland came along and it put a massive strain on both of us. We were newly married, I was away a lot and the rumour mongers were out there as well about different stuff. It definitely didn't help our marriage at the time. The ESB had given me six months off and I was away night and day, two or three functions a day. I was in every single school in Donegal and I travelled to plenty outside the county. It was a stressful enough time. I enjoyed it but you were looking into cameras every day.

'It was a difficult year or two and my marriage broke up in 1995. People were thinking you were having a great time and you were known everywhere but that's not the way it works. It wasn't great at all. It depends on how you handle success and it can work both ways.

'There was a bit of fallout with the team after winning in 1992. I was asked to everything and McHugh was asked a fair bit too. Money started coming into it and some of the lads would have thought these boys are getting it all. That crept in and I could see wee changes happening then. By 1993 it was back into cliques again.

'I didn't make any wild fortune. One particular evening I went up to a do in Faughanvale for the Derry player, Enda

Gormley, and landed back down in Meath at 1 a.m. that same night. Whatever few bob you got you earned it but it changed the closeness within the squad.

'As well as that there was one awful thing that happened and it will stay with me. The County Board decided our reward for winning the All-Ireland would be a trip to Playa de Ingles, Gran Canaria, on 1 January. The money was rolling in big time at that stage. There were boys handing in Ir£5000, Ir£10,000 cheques. There was plenty of money in the kitty. Me and McHugh met the County Executive and we'd agreed Ir£800 per squad member for expenses.

'I was at the Dungloe dinner dance the night before we were due to travel out, so me and Tony Boyle, who was from Dungloe, went up the road to Belfast happy. Tony was only working part-time and I was waiting on the £800 myself. Everybody was, for the two weeks away. We landed up fairly early, got a few pints, everybody waiting for Danny McNamee the treasurer to come along with these bundle of envelopes.

'There was no sign of Danny at all. Along came Noreen Doherty, the secretary, and I got my envelope and Tony got his. We were sitting at the bar, a lock of us. I opened my envelope, Ir£800 no problem, Tony opened up his, Ir£400. I'll never forget, Tony turns around to me and says, "Jesus, Molloy, you must be twice the man I am."

'I have a bad memory but I'll never forget the look Tony gave me. He was serious. Tony was heading out the door home. We got all pacified anyway, but then Rambo [Martin Gavigan] opened his envelope, Ir£400. You don't do things like that to Rambo. Another man opened his, Ir£800, another, Ir£400, and so it went on. It was a frigging mess. That was a good start to the holiday, total disharmony in Belfast airport.

'The County Board could do nothing right. I was taking the wife at the time so they gave the married men Ir£800, the single men Ir£400, and then the likes of Rambo that were teachers and were only going for a week, Ir£400. I got Tony Boyle's other

Ir£400 sorted out three or four days into the holiday. I think Rambo got his money about four or five months later, but he had to keep fighting for it.

'The Kilkenny team were out in the exact same place, a great bunch of lads. We'd a great holiday, played indoor five-a-sides, Donegal and Kilkenny.

'Kilkenny got their Ir£2000 a man. That's the difference. That caused an awful split in the ranks in Donegal among the players. It was never the same after that. Could the County Executive not do it right and them with bundles of money? It was a big let-down for me as captain because myself and McHugh promised the boys Ir£800, and here the boys threw it back in my face. I had words with Danny McNamee when he landed out on holidays later that week.

'That's why the likes of me would never get nowhere with the County Executive in Donegal. There is personal stuff there. How was I ever going to get a job in Donegal if I went for it and him [Danny McNamee] sitting across from me?

'I went for a minor job in 1995 and I sat in front of this interview committee. There were a lot of oul questions thrown at me. You'd think I'd never kicked a ball. The last question I was asked was would I be a manager with a suit or a tracksuit on me. I asked him what planet he was living on. I had a suit on for the interview as I was in the oul financial services game at the time. Was I going to be walking around the field with a suit on me? That's what you were up against.

'Team manager selections in Donegal are crazy. They took the power off the clubs. At one time the clubs would have had three delegates and they picked the team manager. Over the last few years they have officials, some of whom wouldn't know if the ball was blown up or stuffed, with two from outside the County Board, doing the interviews.

'There were interviews done for the senior job a year and a half ago and not much had changed. Jim McGuinness was going for the job and I was going to be his assistant. He showed me what he had on his laptop. Now, it was mind boggling stuff. It was a three-year plan. Fair play to Jim, and I know right well these people that were interviewing him wouldn't even know what he was on about. When you were involved and played with the county for a long time you'd have brushed up against these people and maybe, if they didn't like you, you hadn't a hope anyway. Within all these County Boards I see all these people have wee agendas in their golden circles, like Fianna Fáil, and if they have something against you, where do you go?'

THE GAME

'In 1982, after winning Donegal's first Under-21 All-Ireland, there were eight of us drafted into the senior team for the championship. Jesus, we ran though and won Ulster, were narrowly beaten by Galway in an All-Ireland semi-final. I thought it was going to happen for us every year. I think one of the best teams I would have played on was the 1983 side. Galway beat us with a fluky goal. Everybody knows Val Daly in Donegal. It was a harmless 50 that ended up in the back of the net. We were leading by two points. That was the final where Dublin went on to beat them with 12 men. It was six years later before we got back into an Ulster final. If there had been a backdoor system then we could have won two or three All-Irelands. We were getting beat by a point in Newcastle against Down, a point in Armagh, never progressed, never had a chance. The backdoor has opened it up for good teams, teams like Kerry and Tyrone.

'They can say whatever they like, say that it has given the weaker counties a chance, but it hasn't – it has given Kerry a bigger chance to win the All-Ireland. You'll beat Kerry one day but you won't beat them the second time round. They don't have to put in the same effort as any other team. They have to start training around now. Our men, remember, are in heavy training since probably January, and before the backdoor days you had to be or you were gone in the first round of the Ulster championship and it was all over for another year. That's the difference. You are burnt out. It's hard to keep that going until September. You ask any Kerryman. Normally come Easter, Kerry start getting serious about their football and they know right well that if they do anything they are in an All-Ireland semi-final. They almost got caught in 2009 by Longford, Sligo and Antrim, but they were still fresh when it came to September.

'I think there should be an open draw but the boys up in the crow's nest know there is going to be too much revenue lost if that was the case.'

MOVING ON

'We have only got together once as a team since we won the All-Ireland in 1992. Some winning teams get together every year. Once you are finished you are finished as far as I can see. You are just totally forgotten about in Donegal anyway. I am not looking for red-carpet treatment. Maybe it might be up to the players themselves but the County Board could do different functions. They'd have to take a certain amount of the blame.

'We had a massive chance to build on 1992 but we never built on it whatsoever. Every young lad in Donegal at the time was wearing a green and gold jersey. Every single youngster, but our County Board lost the run of themselves and starting going around with briefcases instead of looking at the football end of it. There was a massive falling out from that and that's why we've won absolutely nothing since.

'There would have been a lot of cash rolling in and they got hung up on money and different stuff. In Donegal now they are talking about spending millions on 3G pitches. It would suit them more to put their millions into primary-level and secondary-level education and get proper coaches in there. I think that's where we are falling down compared to the Tyrones, Armaghs and Downs of this world.

'I think we have one full-time coach, Paddy Hegarty, but Donegal is a big county. He hasn't much time to spend. It is only touching on the ground. If we are to start we have to look at the coaching. It doesn't happen by chance you have Peter Canavan in a certain school in Tyrone, another county player in another school and so on. We are playing catch-up and we better get moving fast.'

FOOTBALL

'Football now is like a cross between basketball and soccer and the hierarchy has a lot to do with that. There was nothing wrong with the game 20 or 30 years ago. I don't know what they are trying to do, copying the soccer men with yellow and red cards, and they have tried to nearly make it a non-contact sport.

'Ciaran McDonald, the young Tipperary full-back, his first yellow card against Donegal in the All-Ireland Under-21 semi-final a few months ago. God almighty you'd never have got that in my day. The second one and he's sent off on one of his biggest days of his life. They've tried to make it a mammy and daddies game to watch on an armchair at home. It's still a man's game and I always felt you were there to take the shots. They've taken a lot of the skills out of it. The shoulder has gone completely, high fielding is nearly gone, long-range scoring too. When did you last see a corner-forward throw a couple of dummies, skin a boy and score? It's all run, run, run now. I put that down to all these rule changes. All they have done is confuse referees and players.

'Watching the game sometimes you'd say it's just as well a man isn't playing now. You wouldn't be around too long.'

LAST DAYS

'We still reached the National League final in '93 even though things were crazy at the time. Brian McEniff could have rested about eight of us. I remember doing a photo shoot down in the Limelight, a big place in Glenties, not far from me, and I didn't get out of there until 6 a.m.

'I jumped in a car and was way down the road to play against Carlow. We could have put out a second team no bother and survived in the league. It all took its toll. We lost Rambo to injury that year. I'd another auto-scope on my knee to clean up a bit of cartilage. I played three and a half weeks after it and came on for the last ten minutes of that Ulster final against Derry, that bad oul day at Clones. It was pure madness.

'We had chances, Tommy Ryan and McHugh, the wee man, chances to put them away, and you see what they went on to do, win the All-Ireland. We were still close enough though.

'But the next year, 1994 against Tyrone at Breffni Park, we knew it was all over. I'll always remember that day. The wee man was carted off and I was taken off with 20 minutes to go and I knew that was it. That's not how I'd hoped it would end for us.

'There were plenty of lows and regrets along the way too, on the journey, and that was one of them, but sure at the end of the day one massive high erases those lows, and it was a fair high.'

Jimmy Barry-Murphy

Denis Walsh, *Sunday Times*

The careers of even the greatest players are reduced to fragments in our memory. Images, moments: the stuff of television highlights reels and nostalgia packages. In that process, however, there is an element of vandalism. Satisfied with the bits we will never forget we become blasé about the bits that are hidden in the attic of our memories. We lose sight of the details of greatness.

When TG4 compiled a list of hurling's greatest goals to celebrate the GAA's 125th anniversary it was no surprise that Jimmy Barry-Murphy came in at number one. His doubled goal against Galway in the 1983 All-Ireland semi-final was an incomprehensible piece of timing. In terms of reaction speed it was comparable with the start of an Olympic sprint where, waiting for the starter's gun, every one of the athletes is primed to break on the B of Bang. John Fenton's delivery was a rocket and if Barry-Murphy's swing had been out of synch by a millisecond the goal couldn't have happened. In a career punctuated by brilliance that contact between ball and hurley was a moment of exclamatory perfection.

There was another moment in that match that is never quoted but, in an important sense, it captured the essence of Barry-Murphy more eloquently than the goal. It wasn't a score and he didn't even touch the ball but it was a window into his mind. Conor Hayes, his marker on that day and many others, spoke about it years later. A ball came down the wing that wasn't intended for him and didn't appear to carry any threat. It looked to Hayes as if Tomás Mulcahy, the Cork corner-forward, wasn't going to reach it but Barry-Murphy had made an instant calculation and come to a different conclusion. Barry-Murphy darted right out to the corner, gambling that Hayes would follow him. He did. Mulcahy gathered the ball and headed straight for the Galway goal along the path that JBM had cleared in advance.

'You couldn't predict what he was going to do,' said Hayes. 'He wasn't waiting around on the edge of the square, he was always looking to make things happen. He'd move out the wing or out to the corner. He might go 30 or 40 yards from goal. He was always on the go and he always had you thinking, "What's happening here now?" You couldn't out-think him.'

More than his class and his pace and his predatory instincts the heart of JBM's brilliance was his mind. He was cute and cool and deadly. All the sophistication that Cork people like to ascribe to Cork hurling at its best resided in him. Very few could have carried it.

We remember him as one of the great dual players even though that phase in his career represented less than half of his time in the Cork jersey. The footballers picked him first in 1973 – a couple of years before his debut in the senior hurling championship – and he quit inter-county football in 1980, six years before he laid down his hurley. It was terrorism that forced him out of football rather than exhaustion or the burden of his schedule. The mark he made with the footballers, though, was the first entry in his legacy.

He was only a teenager in his rookie season: long and lean with a crew-cut and a swagger. Billy Morgan was the Cork captain and the strongest personality in a stellar dressing-room. He made it his business to take JBM under his wing, picking him up on the way to training and dropping him home again. For Barry-Murphy it was a formative relationship.

'I was totally overawed by him. I was totally under Billy's

influence really. It was a very healthy influence because of his impact on me as a competitor and his will to win for Cork football. The one thing that struck me going down to the Park with him was that he lived for it. What it meant to him. I learned from Billy that Cork was something special and to appreciate it. I never lost that to this day.

'He taught me an awful lot. I remember we [St Finbarr's] were playing Nemo [Rangers] in the County Championship – 1972 or '73. I was marking Eddie Brophy, who was a tough player. Myself and Eddie had a bit of a punching match and a bit later I went through and put the ball over the bar. I went to mock Eddie or say something sarcastic and Billy came out to me, "Jimmy – don't do that." That had a big effect on me. You do things when you're young and cocky but when Billy came out to me I stopped immediately. I always thought of that – "Don't ridicule opponents."'

In his breakthrough season Cork won the All-Ireland for the first time since 1945. To many other players on that Cork team that triumph had come at the end of a long and draining climb; to JBM, it was a breeze: 'Going into the All-Ireland in '73, I'll never forget it, I didn't have a care in the world. I didn't care. I'd no doubt we were going to win. I'd no doubt I was going to play well. I was cocky going into it. I'd played in the minor final the previous year against Tyrone and scored 2–1. Came out against Galway in the senior final and got the exact same score. Pressure? What was pressure? It meant nothing to me. I was surrounded by great players – Billy Morgan, Frank Cogan, Ray Cummins, Kevin Ger O'Sullivan, our coach Donie O'Donovan. I didn't see the impact of it all.'

With the hurlers things moved more slowly. He played championship under Justin McCarthy in 1975 but Galway turned them over in an All-Ireland semi-final and at the beginning of 1976 the footballers seemed to want Barry-Murphy more than the hurlers. Christy Ring, though, was part of the new hurling selection committee and, without making it sound like a profound intervention, Ring told Barry-Murphy that he was good enough. He invited him to a challenge match against Limerick and he made it into the championship fifteen.

A few months later, with the All-Ireland final against Wexford in the balance, Cork shifted JBM to centre-forward for the last ten minutes. Mick Jacob had played the game of his life for Wexford at centre-back and JBM had hardly pucked a ball on the wing. The story goes that the move was devised by Ring, independently of the other selectors. Jacob was tiring and he simply couldn't cope with JBM's pace. He rattled off four points in quick succession, tearing through the heart of the Wexford defence. At the final whistle JBM's tally was precisely the difference between the teams. Ring went straight for JBM and wrapped him up in a bear hug in the middle of Croke Park. 'I knew you'd do it, boy,' he said. 'I knew you'd do it.'

There is a famous picture of them at Cork training before a Munster final a year or two later. Against the back drop of the Open Stand in Páirc Uí Chaoimh JBM is in a Barr's jersey, looking at the ground, while Ring is in a suit and tie, looking straight ahead. When you know the story you can see the tension.

'I've been asked a million times about that and the truth is he's giving me a dressing-down. He said that I was doing OK but there was far more in me. I was going through the motions in certain games and that. It wasn't in a nice way because he wasn't that kind of man for light conversation. He was saying you'd want to get your act together and start playing to your potential, in very short words. I was there and you can see from the photograph I wasn't overly impressed [laughs]. I thought I was doing grand but not in his eyes though. He was raising the bar for me I would say.

'I'd be a great hurling follower and over the last couple of years I've read a load of articles and stories about Ring and most of them were lies and rubbish. All these half made-up stories about one-liners and quips. I never heard him at that kind of stuff. He wasn't that kind of man at all. The reality is that anything he said to you, you took on board because he rarely spoke.

'And when he did speak to the team or to individuals he cut to the bone straight away. As the three-in—a-row team developed [1976–78] he had a huge part to play – his presence on the line and in the dressing-room. We were in big trouble in the 1978 Munster final and I read somewhere recently that Ring didn't say much at half-time. That's rubbish. He went ape at half-time. I never heard a speech like it before and he did lift the Cork team that day. No question about that. He went ballistic.

'And before the final against Kilkenny [1978] he spoke in the Victoria Hotel and spoke about the goal he got against Kilkenny in 1946 when the rain fell off the net. It was inspiring – but there were very few occasions when he was like that. This thing about Ring being a raconteur and cracking jokes around the dressing-room is rubbish. We were all in awe of him really. We were scared of our lives of him. He was a huge figure to us in the '70s.'

After 1978 it was six years before Cork won the hurling All-Ireland again. In 1982 and '83 they reached the final with JBM as captain; both days they crashed and he had to be cut from the wreckage. In a playing career defined by glory those were the darkest days. At this remove, nearly 30 years later, his friends use it as material for slagging. Back then, the sensitivities were such that slagging was inconceivable. In so many ways his playing career had been the realisation of every boy's fantasy but on those two days his greatest dream was shattered.

'I think at the time I made too much of it – being captain. I definitely played my best hurling with Cork in 1982 and '83 – no question about it whatsoever. I was never playing better but I didn't play well in the finals and looking back I can see why. The whole captaincy thing got to me. The pressure of being captain of Cork got to me. I was talking to Conor Counihan [Cork football manager] about the All-Ireland last year. I gave my opinion about why certain players don't play well on the big day and I said, "I can talk because I flopped on two big days." I'm not ashamed to say it. I bombed out on the two days I wanted most to win.

'I'm convinced now that I wanted it so badly – captaining Cork to an All-Ireland – that I waited for other people to do it for me. I was hoping that it would happen. I'd made the mistake too of going public about my desire to captain Cork to an All-Ireland and I should never have said that. You should be careful about leaving hostages to fortune and it did come back to haunt me.

'I think it got to me again in '83, even though Johnny Clifford was coach and we got on great. The best hurling I played was in Munster in '82 and '83 – no question in the world about that. I was on fire. Going into '83 I didn't analyse it deeply why I had played so badly in '82. I was only hoping it would happen I think rather than going and making it happen. The pressure got to me way more as I got older and I felt the pressure of having to do well. The disappointment of losing in '82 and '83 was shattering. I suppose if I was playing now there'd be a sports psychologist involved with the team to help out. I'd be the first to admit that I would have scoffed at all this stuff years ago. If I'd had a sports psychologist after '82 to break it down . . . I would have laughed at that years ago. I wouldn't now. Even though Johnny Clifford was great with me and boosted my confidence I needed to unscramble certain things in my head going into that game and I didn't do it. But the pressure got to me again and I flopped on both days.

'Looking back on it, does it haunt me now? Not in the slightest. I'd a great career, thank God. I see players from other counties, great players who never won anything. I was privileged to be born where I was with the opportunities that gave me.'

Cork won the National League double in 1980 and Barry-Murphy played on both teams. At the end of that season, though, he pulled out of inter-county football. He continued to play football for his club St Finbarr's until 1985 when he broke his ribs in a club championship match eight days before an All-Ireland hurling semi-final against Galway. The Cork hurling management requested a postponement of the club football match but the County Board refused. Cork were beaten and in a moment of desperation they brought on Barry-Murphy for the last few minutes even though he was basically unable to swing the hurley. By the end of his inter-county football career he was sour with the game.

'I found it very depressing in the end. I'd love to be playing now with yellow cards and things for persistent fouling. I really hated my football career in the end – it was a depressing game for me with the amount of fouling going on off the ball. It wasn't an enjoyable game at all and I really opted out because of that. It broke my heart in '83 when Tadhgie Murphy got the [last-minute] goal in the Park [to beat Kerry in the Munster final]. I'd have given my right arm to be out there. I was over in the Open Stand and I was jumping around with joy when Cork won but I'd have given anything to be out there that day.

'Football was very cynical back then. There's a great myth about Kerry – Billy Morgan often said that. I've no grudge to bear, I'm long gone beyond all that, but they were a very cynical team when they needed to be. You don't win 35 All-Irelands by being nice guys as we learned to our cost in Cork. I felt guilty to a certain extent about the football because you always feel you're letting the other side down – but you move on. Let's be honest about it, hurling in Cork city was always going to be my number one choice. I still had a great affection for Cork football but hurling was my number one and I loved it. I lived for hurling.'

His exit from hurling wasn't contaminated by any of that bitterness. He left on his terms, in good time. In his *Irish Times* preview of the 1986 All-Ireland final, Paddy Downey speculated that it might be his last game in red but Barry-Murphy hadn't given any clues about his plans in public. Cork delayed their arrival in Croke Park that afternoon and watching the first half of the minor match in his hotel room he told his old friend

Johnny Crowley that he was finishing up. Crowley was stunned. In the Cork set-up the only other person he told was Dr Con Murphy.

'If I was asked to pin down why I quit then I suppose I couldn't take the disappointment any more if I'd played badly. Like, in '86 if we'd lost and I hadn't scored I wouldn't have been able to handle it, in a sporting sense. Let's not over-dramatise it either, it's only sport. I was always proud of my scoring record in big matches but I hadn't scored in the previous three All-Ireland finals which was a deplorable record for a full-forward, let's be honest. It was a big thing, not scoring. The real pressure of not performing in Croke Park was getting to me.

'There was instant relief for me when I scored in the second half. Ger Fitzgerald crossed the ball from the Cusack Stand side and I doubled on it in the air. It could have gone into the net just as easily but it flew over the bar. When I got that point it was like a weight lifted off my shoulders. I caught a ball then and won a penalty and it contributed quite a lot on the day. I felt I played well. My last score was the last score of the game and it put us four points clear. It was a great feeling. I gave my hurley to Con [Murphy] in the dressing-room after the game and I've never held a hurley since in public.

'I must say I didn't find it easy watching the Munster final in Killarney in 1987. I regretted then, I did. I told lies over the years that I didn't miss it – I did miss it. I didn't so much miss it in Thurles when they drew [Cork and Tipperary] but I missed it in Killarney when Tipp were coming back and getting on top. I was raging then that I was gone.'

On the Monday night after Limerick slaughtered Cork in the 1996 Munster championship a local television channel showed the match again with a couple of extra interviews. Cork hadn't lost a championship match at home since the 1920s but, in the middle of a bullish period, Limerick were indifferent to that sequence and smashed their hosts to pieces: 3–18 to 1–8. High on the adrenalin of the moment their goalie Joe Quaid gave a post-match interview in which he referred to Cork's tradition being washed 'down the Lee'. Jimmy Barry-Murphy didn't need any further clarification of what had happened in Páirc Uí Chaoimh the day before but, sitting at home in Bishopstown, Quaid's remarks turned the knife again.

It was his first championship match as Cork manager. Along with Tom Cashman and Tony O'Sullivan he had accepted the job to a great fanfare of optimism nine months earlier. Eschewing any leap of imagination, they were dubbed 'The Dream Team'. It stuck. On one level, Cork had some momentum. In 1995 JBM had guided the Cork minors to their first All-Ireland title in ten years having brought another Cork minor team to the final in 1994. Cork still had a core of older players with All-Ireland medals from 1990 and in the early rounds of the League before Christmas, Cork carried all before them. In a newspaper survey of inter-county managers in January of 1996 Cork emerged as favourites to win the All-Ireland. At that point the hype reached a ludicrous peak.

Cork's form collapsed in the second half of the League and in their final game against Clare in Páirc Uí Chaoimh they could only manage five points. Does that mean they were written off against Limerick? In those days, that's not how it worked. Cork were at home, JBM was in charge: something was bound to happen. That was the thinking.

'I didn't realise when I took over. I thought, "Big deal – I'd take over." We were after winning the minor All-Ireland and I was naïve enough to think that my presence alone would be a big factor. Clare had come through [as All-Ireland champions] and I didn't realise how far behind Cork had fallen in terms of preparation and the level of talent throughout the county. I didn't realise how poor it was. When Limerick wiped us out it was a culture shock. I was so naïve going down the Páirc that day. I thought, "Look, down the Páirc, Cork will come good." I couldn't believe it.

'After the match I was in a state of shock. Literally. I was shell-shocked at how bad we were and in retrospect my part in it because I was the coach. It's your hand on it. When I heard Joe Quaid's interview I said, "Fucking hell, have I presided over this?" I swore that night that I'd do everything to put that right. He [Joe] didn't say it to get at me but I said to myself, "I'll do everything I can to ram that down his throat again." Because I'm a very proud Cork man and here I was, having presided over this shambles. Which is all it was. We were a shambles of an outfit and it was a shambles of a preparation, looking back on it now. I was a disgrace as a coach and naïve in our preparation.

'One thing I will say is that Frank Murphy and the board were very loyal to me as a coach. I'll never forget it. I sat down with Frank Murphy the following week and he spoke to me. He went through what we had done and he went through the players and he went through the young players coming through and we had a long chat for about two hours. He convinced me there was a way forward for me – and I was doubtful myself about staying on at that stage. I met Tom Cashman and Fred Sheedy, who came in as a selector with us [instead of Tony O'Sullivan] and we decided then there was only one way forward. Come hell or high water – whether we were going to be gone in a year or two years – we had to try to leave a legacy for the people coming in after us. Winning an All-Ireland was a million miles from my thoughts. I couldn't see it happening.'

In many ways this was the greatest challenge of Barry-Murphy's sporting life. Winning All-Irelands with Cork and with St Finbarr's was something he started doing as a teenager. It was a normal expectation. For all the defeats he suffered as a player his career was overwhelmingly defined by success. He knew what failure was and he knew how traumatic it could be but in his playing days it had always been a temporary condition. Treatable, controllable.

This was serious. During his first year in charge Cork had probably reached their lowest ebb since the early 1960s. From where they stood, at the foot of the mountain, the peak was shrouded in clouds. Being JBM with great deposits of affection from the Cork GAA public in his personal account was no protection against a recession such as this. Hostile letters were printed in the local press – some without full names or addresses. Some of the local commentary was savage too and he kept one article in his desk at work for years afterwards. He had been criticised before but never on this scale.

The climb was slow. Clare beat them by just four points in 1997 but by twice that amount in 1998 after Cork had won the League. At the time, though, they were grateful for small mercies: 'We went up to play Clare in '97 and we rattled them. Played with great spirit. We could have won it at one stage. I'll always remember leaving the Páirc the previous year and Cork supporters slagging me in the tunnel – one guy said a horrible thing. Just shows – short memories. I remember saying this to the team before the game in '97.

'I remember getting off the bus at the Opera House in Cork that night after the Clare game and Brian Corcoran came over to me: "There'll be no one slagging you tonight anyway." I felt relieved about that. Here I was, after being beaten by Clare, and I felt relieved that we had put up a spirited performance. We stopped in Charleville on the way home for a drink and people were coming over to us, thanking us for putting a bit of pride back in the jersey. Here we were, having lost by four points, and people were actually happy with that. We were too – I'm not going to tell lies. I was happy with it as well because we'd got such a hammering the year before I felt there was no future for Cork hurling. But that day I felt there was a future.'

The darkest hour was just before the dawn. A few weeks before Cork met Waterford in the 1999 Munster championship they played Tipperary in two challenge matches, home and away. The second performance was worse than the first. In despair, Barry-Murphy told a few senior players that he felt a change might do them good. Brian Corcoran and Fergal Ryan pleaded with him to stay and he gave in to their petition.

As a management team they sat down and reviewed everything. They decided to pick the best 15 hurlers in Cork – even if that meant playing some of them out of position, even if that meant leaving out players with more aggression or experience. In the end it meant picking six championship debutants. They gambled. It clicked.

'I remember the relief beating Waterford that day. Here was my dream. At least we were back in Croke Park [as provincial finalists]. What a defeatist attitude, in a way. I didn't give a damn about the All-Ireland. That was the last thing on my mind. We'd brought Cork back to Croke Park. It was a big relief. Gerald [McCarthy] was training Waterford – who I'd played under with Cork and the Barrs. That was a big factor for me. I didn't want to be beaten by a Cork man training Waterford really. That was the harsh reality of it. We asked the players before the match to go out and do it for us and for Cork. They were phenomenal that day.'

Like an accumulator, the gamble rolled on. In September, they collected the pot. That year the presentation was on the pitch and in the lap of honour afterwards JBM could hardly contain himself. He climbed on the railings at the bottom of Hill 16 and waved the Liam McCarthy Cup at the drenched Cork fans standing on the terrace. When they returned to the dressing-room the Cork trainer Teddy Owens stood on a bench and held up a photograph taken of the Cork management during the 1996 mauling by Limerick. Devastation and bewilderment was grafted on to their faces.

'Take a look at that,' roared Owens, 'and take a look at Jimmy now.'

'That was the greatest day of my sporting career – I would have to say that. Going into Croke Park with the youngest Cork team ever, to bring Cork back to the top after being so low since 1990 – a long time for Cork. Having been part of some of our worst years as well. Having been part of the debacle against Limerick and being part of Cork hurling being ridiculed. Not having a player on the Munster team, not having a player nominated for an All-Star. It was playing on my mind that I was presiding over a horrible time for Cork hurling. I wanted to be part of a new era.

'The young players – I was so proud of them. What they gave me was phenomenal. And then Brian Corcoran – for him to win his first All-Ireland. When I took over in '96 I foolishly said, "Can you imagine being coach for the next couple of years and Brian Corcoran not winning an All-Ireland? I said that couldn't happen." The way things went it could have happened. Mark Landers was our captain – a great captain – but Brian was our leader really. He was the man we looked to. In the final he caught the first ball over John Power's head. I'll never forget it. I knew we were on our way then.'

Barry-Murphy quit after Cork lost the All-Ireland semi-final to Offaly 11 months later. Gone before the first of the strikes and a decade of tension between the Cork players and the County Board. Along with Dr Con Murphy and Tomás Mulcahy he volunteered as a mediator early in the third strike but they soon realised that they had no solutions to offer. John Gardiner asked him and Mulcahy if they were prepared to get involved with the team and for different reasons they said no. Barry-Murphy had done his time.

Some of the players who were at the heart of that conflict he had known since they were minors: Dónal Óg Cusack, Seán Óg Ó hAilpín, Joe Deane. The GPA was only a fledgling organisation when Barry-Murphy was the Cork manager but Cusack was involved then and so was Corcoran. He knew it was there in the background but it wasn't an issue at the time.

'To be honest, I was very sceptical. I was a conservative in the GAA and I was very doubtful about it. And I've told Dónal Óg in conversation since that I didn't like the idea of it. Charlie McCarthy said to me one day, "You were reared in the GAA of the 1960s and '70s." He was right. You hardly spoke to the selectors in those days. They were fellas up on a pedestal, way above you. You didn't speak to them – they didn't speak to you either, by the way. That doesn't make it right. But things have moved on completely from when I started playing. Life has changed, business has changed, work practices have changed. These guys see that they're giving a huge part of their lives to this. Of course they should have a say in who the manager is.

'I would be honest now and say there are times when I cringe at what I put up with as coach for the players. Not that they ever wanted for anything major but there were things happened that people wouldn't know about that I should not have allowed happen. We should have supported the players better and made things better for them and seen the bigger picture. The only excuse I'd make for myself is that it was different times. It was just starting to develop in relation to the players' needs and requirements and I was at the very early stages of that with Ted Owens and with dieticians and with Seánie McGrath [trainer] getting involved. I would feel embarrassed now about certain things that happened. I should have seen the trouble that was coming down the line. It's when I look back now I do see it.'

It was no stain on him. A lot of the players who won their first All-Ireland under JBM in 1999 would have been very young when he was in his prime. They loved him as an idol first; then they worked with him and loved him all over again as a mentor and a friend. More than once during that summer JBM told the Cork players that their success meant more to him than anything he had achieved as a player. It was the greatest compliment they could have imagined. The former Cork player Fergal McCormack tells a story from the Cork dressing-room on the day of the 1999 All-Ireland final that captures their affection for him.

'We were presented with our jerseys by Jimmy and it was a very emotional thing. There was a handshake and a hug. It was fierce spontaneous. Everyone was brought up with JBM as a hero and a legend and here you were up in Croke Park receiving your All-Ireland jersey from him. It was something else. You know, you'd like to win a match for yourself first but you'd like to win it for Jimmy next.'

Generations of Cork people know where that feeling comes from.